WILLIAM MORRIS

Born at Walthamstow in 1834. Educated at Marl-
borough and Exeter College, Oxford, where he met
Edward Burne-Jones, the painter and his lifelong
friend. At first wanted to become an architect, then,
under the influence of Dante Gabriel Rossetti, a
painter. First important work was in fact in poetry.
Founded in 1860 a firm of craftsman-decorators,
whose products had a great effect on Victorian design
and helped to inspire the Arts and Crafts Movement
later in the century. Grew increasingly critical of the
ugliness and squalor of Victorian England, giving
many lectures on art and society and becoming a
declared Socialist in 1883. In *News from Nowhere*
(1891) gave his picture of a Utopian England. In
1890 founded the Kelmscott Press to produce books
of a high quality. Later works, apart from the lec-
tures, were imaginative prose romances. Died in 1896,
having established a high reputation for these diverse
activities.

WILLIAM MORRIS

Early Romances
in Prose
and Verse

Edited, with an introduction, by
PETER FAULKNER
Senior Lecturer in English, University of Exeter

J. M. Dent & Sons Ltd, London

CONTENTS

Contents

NOTE ON THE TEXT

The text of *The Defence of Guenevere* printed here follows the first edition of 1858, including some awkwardnesses of punctuation. When Morris was persuaded to reissue the poems in 1875, he made some corrections, especially to 'The Chapel in Lyoness', but these were not used. (They may be seen in *Collected Works*, ed. May Morris, I, xxii–iv.) For the Kelmscott Press edition of 1892 Morris made some minor revisions, which are pointed out here in the Notes.

The text of the contributions to the *Oxford and Cambridge Magazine* is a corrected version of the original Everyman edition of 1907, which is based on the contributions as they appear in the *Magazine*. The posthumous 1903 reprint entitled *The Hollow Land and Other Contributions to the Oxford and Cambridge Magazine*, done at the Chiswick Press in Morris's Golden Type, tidies up the punctuation and paragraphing, and is followed by May Morris in the *Collected Works*, I.

INTRODUCTION

This volume contains the early creative works of William Morris in prose and verse, all written by the time he was twenty-four. They are of interest and value both in themselves and as exhibiting in its first stages a sensibility which was to become one of the most authoritative of the later Victorian period. Morris is now respected as a richly inventive designer and a deeply committed social critic; in these writings can be seen the stirrings of that imaginative power, though in forms which seem remote from the practicality of his later achievements. Yet the Yeatsian aphorism, 'In dreams begins responsibility',[1] suggests a possible continuity, which reveals itself on closer reading of these youthful works.

EARLY LIFE

The two aspects of Morris's early life which find expression in these writings are the physical environment and his feeling for the English past. Morris was born in 1834 into a family successful in business. In 1840 his father bought the Georgian Woodford Hall, which had its own park, adjoining the beech glades and hornbeams of Epping Forest. Here Morris played as a boy, the eldest of a family of seven, with a Shetland pony and a miniature suit of armour. His early reading concerned the ages of chivalry, and he is said to have read all Scott's Waverley novels by the time he was seven. In 1848, the family moved to Water House, Walthamstow, which had its own moat. Morris went to Marlborough in 1848, but learnt little at school. His free time was spent mainly alone, enjoying the Wiltshire countryside and taking brass rubbings of medieval tombs. He also gained a reputation for making up interesting stories. After leaving school in 1851, he studied for a year with a private tutor.

Morris went up to Oxford in January 1853 intending to take

Holy Orders. At Oxford, however, new influences affected him. He made a number of friends, including the young Birmingham man Edward Burne-Jones, who was to become his lifelong friend and a celebrated painter. In his long vacation of 1854 he visited Belgium and France with Burne-Jones, and was immensely impressed by the architecture of Amiens, Beauvais and Rouen;[2] 1855 also included a visit to France, and on this tour Morris and Burne-Jones made the important decision not to enter the Church, but to try to fulfil their sense of social responsibility by devoting their energies to art. Fortunately for Morris, he had inherited £900 per annum on coming of age, so that there was no financial barrier to this plan, although his mother was disappointed by it.

Thus in 1856 Morris became articled to G. E. Street, then in Oxford, a well-known architect whose work continued the tradition of the Gothic revival. In the same year Morris used his money to carry through an idea formed with his friends while still an undergraduate, of publishing a literary magazine to carry on the work of the Pre-Raphaelite publication *The Germ*. The journal became known as *The Oxford and Cambridge Magazine*, and in it appeared Morris's early work, most of which is included in this volume. In the same year Street moved to London, and so did Morris. He and Burne-Jones shared rooms in Red Lion Square. He met Dante Gabriel Rossetti, then twenty-eight and a delightful and charismatic figure in artistic society. Rossetti, who had been associated with J. E. Millais and Holman Hunt in the Pre-Raphaelite Brotherhood which had challenged conventional artistic taste in the years following 1848, encouraged Morris's interest in painting. Morris not only bought a number of Pre-Raphaelite works, but decided to become a painter himself. In 1857 he was one of the group of enthusiastic young artists led by Rossetti who decorated the walls of the Oxford Union with frescoes on Arthurian subjects.

In Oxford, too, Morris first saw the beautiful Jane Burden; he persuaded her to sit for him and his friends, and found in her the epitome of Pre-Raphaelite beauty. Her face is now well known as the subject of many of Rossetti's later paintings. Morris painted her once, quite successfully, as Iseult, and gave a verbal portrait of her in 'Praise of My Lady' (pp. 134–6). He married her in 1859, thus beginning an enigmatic and only partially happy relationship. Before this, in 1858, he had published a volume of his early poems under the title *The Defence of Guenevere and Other Poems,* thus completing the literary activity of his early period. But he was still only twenty-four.

THE PROSE ROMANCES [3]

Morris was the most substantial contributor to *The Oxford and Cambridge Magazine,* which ran for twelve monthly numbers in 1856. In addition to the romances and poems included in this volume, he wrote an article on Amiens cathedral, a review of Browning's *Men and Women,* an article on two wood-engravings by the German Alfred Rethel, and a story of unhappy love with a modern setting entitled 'Frank's Sealed Letter'.[4] But the seven other prose stories, whose archaic settings and air of mystery make the descriptive title 'romances' appropriate, constitute Morris's main early achievement.

Morris had been known as a story-teller from his boyhood days, and here he continued his habit of telling himself stories about the past as he knew it through architecture and books. His comment in a letter to Cormell Price in July 1856 may be related to his stories and poems as well as to the painting which he was then doing under Rossetti's influence:

I can't enter into politico-social subjects with any interest, for on the whole I see that things are in a muddle, and I have no power or vocation to set them right in ever so little a degree. My work is the embodiment of dreams in one form or another.[5]

The a-political sentiments were to be repudiated later, but the emphasis on dreams is most important for these early works.

The idea of the dream may serve to recall an important aspect of the Romantic movement, and it was that movement which had reintroduced the romance as a literary form. The stories must be seen against the background of a number of literary works with which Morris and his friends at Oxford were familiar. Interest in folk traditions, particularly those of the North, is shown by the success of such works as Edgar Taylor's translation in 1823 of the *German Popular Stories* of Jacob and Wilhelm Grimm, Carlyle's two volumes of *German Romance* (including Fouqué, Hoffman and Richter) in 1827, versions of Meinhold's *Amber Witch* in 1844 and *Sidonia the Sorceress* in 1849,[6] and Benjamin Thorpe's three volumes of *Northern Mythologies* in 1851. As a parallel development may be considered

the new edition for Bohn's Antiquarian Library of George
Ellis's *Specimens of the Early English Metrical Romances* in
1848. And at the same time, there was the growing cult of
Malory, whose *Morte D'Arthur* was to be an almost sacred
book for Burne-Jones and, to a lesser extent, Morris.

But if the romances are to be seen as 'the embodiment of
dreams', it is the methods and success of their embodiment
that matter. The prose style Morris adopted was a simple one,
though with a vocabulary and syntax appropriate to the roman-
tic subjects. It is far more direct and effective than the archaic
style Morris adopted in his later romances like *The Wood Beyond
the World* (1895), so much enjoyed by Yeats and now receiving
a fashionable revival in American paperbacks of Adult Fantasy.
The reader is taken into a world of the romancer's own creating,
but it turns out to be a very concrete one. Whereas in Fouqué,
as Carlyle put it, the past 'comes imaged back to us faint and
ineffectual like the crescent of the setting moon',[7] in Morris the
dreamland is solidly realized, generally in the vivid pictorial
details which show his affinity with the Pre-Raphaelite painters.
This is particularly true of 'The Story of the Unknown Church'.

It is this combination of imaginative freshness—the invita-
tion to expand our horizons suggested by an opening like 'Long
ago there was a land, never mind where or when'—with a
realistic sense of detail which gives these tales their particular
atmosphere.[8] This atmosphere is not a markedly happy one;
the dreams which underlie Morris's early writings are by no
means escapist fantasies. Most of the stories celebrate human
love, but the lovers find themselves in worlds of ignorance,
confusion and evil. The evil is most marked in 'Lindenborg
Pool', while 'The Story of the Unknown Church' has a much
gentler tone. These two are probably the most successful of the
romances because of their comparative brevity.

Finally, what of the meaning of these stories? Can we discern
in them elements of allegory or symbolism? Mr Edward
Thompson discerns in all Morris's early writings radical dis-
satisfaction with contemporary England; he refers in particular
to 'Lindenborg Pool' as an expression of anger at the debase-
ment of values, and to King Valdemar in 'Svend and his Breth-
ren' as the embodiment of a rejected Utilitarianism. Such
social implications may be present, but they are not the main
features of the stories in which they occur. If the question of
allegory is raised, it is relevant to recall Morris's denial when a

critic attempted an allegorical interpretation of one of his later
prose romances, *The Wood Beyond the World*.[9] The romances
cannot usefully be interpreted into political or psychological
commentary; they are works of imaginative literature. The
themes with which they are concerned—love, fidelity, the
search for permanence—are the great themes of romantic
literature. The characteristic notes in the rendering of these
themes at this stage of Morris's development are bewilderment
and anxiety—as D. M. Hoare puts it: 'It is almost as though
one were in a troubled sleep disturbed by images of disaster
and dissolution, and could not throw off the nightmare'.[10] These
characteristics should be seen as part of Morris's youthful sensi-
tivity, evidence of his openness to experiences which he did not
attempt to regulate or rationalize.

THE POEMS

  Morris seems to have begun writing poetry soon after his
arrival in Oxford: May Morris included some of the earliest
poems in the first of her two supplementary volumes, *William
Morris: Artist, Writer, Socialist*, in 1936. When he published
The Defence of Guenevere and other Poems in 1858, Morris des-
troyed what he excluded. The volume itself was not well re-
ceived. Critics dismissed it as a work of 'Pre-Raphaelite min-
strelsy', remote from the world of current concerns and often
hard to understand. Yet it had its admirers, both among
Morris's Oxford friends and beyond; and modern critics have
generally shared this assessment—if they have taken any
interest in Morris's poetry at all. Jack Lindsay in particular
has written with keen appreciation,[11] and Geoffrey Grigson's
Faber anthology has drawn heavily on this volume. In fact
there are clumsy and unnecessarily obscure features in the
poems, but these are by no means prominent in the general
impression, which is one of vitality and imaginative power.
  In 1868 Walter Pater reviewed Morris's poems in an article
which he later reprinted in *Appreciations*, with the significant
title 'Aesthetic Poetry'; he saw Morris as exhibiting a 'pro-
founder medievalism', expressive of the soul separated from the
body, poetry of 'dreamlight.'[12] The link with the prose
romances is clear. A later critic, Dixon Scott, elaborated
Pater's account in a penetrating though sometimes cryptic
essay on 'The First Morris' in 1912. He argued that the

emphasis on solidity and visual detail may be so marked as to produce an effect of hallucination.

The more muscularly young Morris pressed upon his medium, delighting in its growing distinctness, the more fiercely did it start up from the page and accost us with the brittle colours of delirium.[13]

Dixon Scott compared this with the effect of some Pre-Raphaelite paintings, instancing Millais's 'Autumn Leaves' in which the details are so vivid as to become quite unrealistic. This vividness which is closer to dream than to normal experience is characteristic of many of the poems, but distinctions need to be made. The poetry of the volume is usually divided into three groups, the Arthurian, the Froissartian, and the 'fantastic'. Discussion can profitably proceed with these groupings, although they will not be totally satisfactory. But first something must be said of Morris's immediate predecessors and their influence.

Morris, like the other Victorian poets, inherited the Romantic tradition of Coleridge and Wordsworth, Keats and Shelley. But a young poet is generally influenced more by his older contemporaries, and in Morris's case this meant Tennyson, Browning and Rossetti. By the time Morris went to Oxford Tennyson was already an established figure, having followed his 1832 volume with *English Idylls* in 1842, *The Princess* in 1847, *In Memoriam* in 1850 and *Maud* in 1855. Browning had published *Dramatic Lyrics* in 1842, *Dramatic Romances and Lyrics* in 1845 and *Men and Women* in two volumes in 1855. This last book Morris reviewed in *The Oxford and Cambridge Magazine* in March 1856. The review is youthful and in some ways naïve, but it shows Morris's respect and enthusiasm for the two older poets. Tennyson's feeling for the past and his eloquence no doubt appealed to Morris, while in Browning he responded to the vitality and sense of drama. On the obscurity for which Browning was often criticized, Morris argued that if poetry was to be more than 'light literature', the reader must be prepared to make an effort of comprehension. It may also be suggested that Morris admired the variety of forms used by Browning, as Morris's volume shows a similar freedom. Finally, Rossetti must have influenced Morris. We know from the letters how impressed Morris was by Rossetti's personality, and al-

Introduction

though few of Rossetti's poems were yet known, the 'Blessed Damozel' had appeared in *The Oxford and Cambridge Magazine*, exhibiting a unique combination of sensuous and spiritual feeling. Morris's volume is dedicated, however, to 'Dante Gabriel Rossetti, Painter', and this suggests that Morris thought of Rossetti principally in that light. The pictorial element is significant in the poems, as it had been in the prose romances, and was encouraged by Rossetti's friendship.

ARTHURIAN POEMS

The first four poems in the volume are concerned with Arthurian subject matter. The development of interest in the stories of King Arthur during the Victorian period is a large subject; [14] here it is sufficient to recall some of Tennyson's poems, and Rossetti's enthusiasm for subjects derived from Malory. Morris was by no means singular in his interest; what is significant is how he embodied it in poetry. Jack Lindsay, in a lecture called 'William Morris, Writer', gave a perceptive account of this:

The romantic vision is merged with sharp emotional realism. The diction is often archaic, yet its effect is of a casual direct speech wrung-out at the height of an experience that reaches to the depths. The words have almost a stammering slow force as if each word is being searched for, all but lost, then brought doggedly out. [15]

The opening poem justifies Morris's placing of it by its dramatic intensity, the strict verse form of the *terza rima* serving to embody Guenevere's great effort of self-control, combined with her refusal to deny the value of the ill-fated love. A similar intensity marks 'King Arthur's Tomb'. Here the decasyllabic quatrains give more impulse of movement to the narrative of Lancelot's journey to see Guenevere after the death of Arthur. She is now a nun in Almesbury, struggling to kill her previous feelings. The lovers meet, by dramatic coincidence, at King Arthur's Tomb. (Rossetti had painted a watercolour of the scene in 1854.) In her last speech Guenevere upbraids and taunts Lancelot until he faints at her feet; the triumph of the poem is that one feels Guenevere destroying something of herself at the same time. 'Sir Galahad, a Christmas Mystery', also in decasyllabic quatrains, dramatizes the discouragement and doubt, and finally the encouragement through a vision, of the celibate Galahad. Because the reader is made to share his initial discouragement as he contrasts himself with his father Lancelot and Palomydes who are sustained by human love, the vision too comes convincingly. 'The Chapel in Lyoness' is a more strangely imaginative poem, not derived from Malory. The triple rhyme with the emphasized final shorter line gives a more stylized effect. Sir Ozana's death is related to an unhappy love, and at the end Galahad is able to see the lovers finally united beyond the grave.

FROISSARTIAN POEMS

The next and larger group of poems begins with the dramatic piece, 'Sir Peter Harpdon's End' (pp. 35–59). These poems derive from Morris's reading of Jean Froissart, the French chronicler of the wars of the fourteenth century. The Tudor translation by Lord Berners (1525) is best known and Morris's most likely source, though he may also have known the 1805 translation by Thomas Johnes. As Robert Steele put it, 'No writer ever realised so completely as William Morris in this volume the ideal of chivalry which lay unconsciously in Froissart's mind when writing. The courage, the fidelity, the courtesy, all are there.' [16] But the other aspects of the time, the brutality and coarseness which made the courage and courtesy so necessary, are there too. Morris recreates this world vividly through the vigorous language and the dramatic incidents. He uses medieval terms, particularly those associated with warfare, with unforced naturalness. We are taken directly into the world of Sir Peter Harpdon, with no sense of the backward complacent look.

Many of the best poems in the volume belong to this category; they include 'Concerning Geffray Teste Noire', 'The Eve of Crecy', 'The Judgment of God', the slighter war-songs of Father John and Sir Giles, and most effective of all, 'The Haystack in the Floods' (pp. 118–22). This poem uses the octosyllabic couplet, but without the briskness which that form often produces. There is movement, but it is a movement of sombre resignation to unalterable fact. The scene is effectively realized in the depressing wetness, with the small band of figures, at first anonymous, trying to get away. Then Godmar appears with his thirty men to take Jehane from Robert. This is accomplished without heroics, just as Robert is killed without any chivalric generosity. Finally attention is focused on Jehane, stunned by the events, and the poem ends as it had begun with a couplet about the parting. Here scene and deed are blended into a dramatic unity by the inevitable movement of the poem to the flatness of its final mood.

A number of other poems may be related to the Froissartian group. 'A Good Knight in Prison' and 'Riding Together' both refer to the battles against the Pagans, perhaps at the time of Charlemagne; the latter is a very effective expression of comradeship-in-arms. 'In Prison' is a successful evocation of the sense of abandonment and desolation. 'Old Love' refers to the probable fall of Constantinople and is presumably set in the fifteenth century, but its main emphasis is, as the title suggests, romantic and psychological. 'Shameful Death', regarded by Geoffrey Grigson as typical of Morris in its directness and manliness,[17] suggests the tough world of the border ballads, while 'Welland River' is a convincing ballad of the more romantic kind. 'The Little Tower' recalls the prose romance 'Golden Wings' in its resolute assertion of love against the 'grim King' and his demands, while 'The Gilliflower of Gold' suggests the more romantic side of medieval chivalry. The longer narrative poem 'Golden Wings', one of the best-known poems in the volume, belongs also to this romantic world. The opening evocation of happiness has been much admired, but the poem moves inexorably through the disappointment of love to final disaster.

THE POEMS OF FANTASY

This group of poems, which excited the greatest contempt among conventional critics and the greatest enthusiasm among youthful admirers, includes 'The Wind', 'The Blue Closet' and 'The Tune of the Seven Towers', with which may be associated 'Rapunzel', 'The Sailing of the Sword', 'Spell-Bound' and 'Two Red Roses across the Moon' (although these have a stronger narrative element), and 'Near Avalon' (with its Arthurian associations). The strange, remote atmosphere of these poems is remarkable, and sets them apart from the sense of human reality which is so marked in the Froissartian poems. The strong emphasis on pattern rather than feeling led Gordon Bottomley in 1930 to argue perceptively that, though these lyrics may suggest a relationship to Coleridge, Keats, or Poe,

they are 'more notable for their kinship to things that came
after them—to the early, valuable works of Maeterlinck, and the
designs of Khnopf and Carloz Schwabe, and some poems of
Mr de la Mare's.'[18] They point forward in time, that is to say,
to the aesthetic movement and *art nouveau*.

'Rapunzel' belongs to the world of the fairy story, but differs
from the other poems in its stronger narrative and its happy
ending. Morris uses a variety of verse-forms within the poem,
to suit the characters in it. He succeeds in conveying both the
perplexity of the prince when he is waiting for the chance to
rescue the maiden, and his exultation when he is able to set
her free. Indeed, the lines in celebration of their love, beginning
with the Prince's words 'I, Sebald, also, pluck from off the
staff/The crimson banner' and continued in his song 'Twixt
the sunlight and the shade' (pp. 68–9), stand out in the volume
for their untrammelled happiness and lyrical beauty.

The two poems not discussed, 'Praise of My Lady' and
'Summer Dawn', are love poems of very different kinds. In
the first, rhyming triplets and the Latin refrain give a sense of
ritual which suggests the Provençal idea of romantic love or,
more directly, Rossetti's 'Blessed Damozel'. Although Morris's
lady is on earth and Rossetti's in heaven, both are equally
remote from normal humanity. 'Summer Dawn' is the only
directly subjective poem in the volume without historical
associations. A. Clutton-Brock made the point that in this very
early poem Morris 'seems to dream without energy', while in the
'medieval poems he is still dreaming, but with an energy too
fierce for a pure dreamer such as he still took himself to be.'[19]
In these poems, Clutton-Brock concluded, Morris played 'the
romantic game . . . in deadly earnest.' It is this earnestness, this
intensity of many of the poems, which gives *The Defence of
Guenevere* its quality as an original and exciting volume.

MORRIS'S LATER CAREER

The poor reception of *The Defence of Guenevere* in 1858 no
doubt discouraged Morris from writing poetry for a time. He
seems to have abandoned a cycle of poems on the fall of Troy,
and any intention he may have had of adding to his Arthurian
poems, especially after the great success of Tennyson's first
group of *Idylls of the King* in 1859. Moreover, after his marriage

in 1859, his interest shifted to domestic matters. Finding no suitable house available, he commissioned Philip Webb to build him one, and the Red House at Upton in Kent was then built. It is now considered an important building in architectural history for its red-brick simplicity and irregularity. Morris soon found that it was impossible to furnish the house fittingly because of the poor quality of contemporary workmanship and design, and from his attempts to correct this developed the firm of Morris, Marshall, Faulkner and Co., which did much to improve the quality of English decorative work in the later part of the last century. This also meant that much of Morris's remarkable energy had to go into the running of the firm.

Nevertheless he returned to poetry, and with great popular success. *The Life and Death of Jason* (1867) and *The Earthly Paradise* (1868–70) were widely read and enjoyed. But the poetry in them is of a quite different kind from the earlier work. These are slow-moving narrative poems, picturesque rather than dramatic and now little read. Morris's description of himself in the 'Apology' to the *Earthly Paradise* as 'The idle singer of an empty day' suggests the limitation of the role he saw for himself as a poet at that time. Morris became increasingly interested in Iceland and its literature in the 1870s, and this inspired his last major poem, *Sigurd the Volsung* (1876). Although the poem has vigour, it lacks the compression and intensity of the early poems. Discouraged by lack of interest in *Sigurd*, which he had hoped would recall the English to their Nordic roots, Morris wrote less poetry thereafter, though there are good short poems in his last volume, *Poems by the Way* (1893).

However, he now began a new activity as a social critic. His outrage at the effects of industrialism on the worker, in particular its denial to him of all chance of self-expression in his work, led him to make fundamental criticisms of society. He articulated these in lectures, some of which were published in *Hopes and Fears for Art* (1882) and *Signs of Change* (1888). He joined the earliest English Marxist group, the Democratic Federation, in 1883, but resigned at the end of 1884 to help found the Socialist League. In *News from Nowhere* (1891) he expressed his hopes for a just society based on pleasurable work and social equality. He also helped to found the Society for the Preservation of Ancient Buildings (1877), the Art Workers Guild (1884) and the Arts and Crafts Exhibition Society (1887). He set up the Kelmscott Press in 1890 to improve the

quality of printing, and there published some of his own full-
length prose romances such as *The Wood Beyond the World* in
1894 and *The Well at the World's End* in 1896, the year in which
he died. Thus his enthusiasm for romance and for story-telling
persisted to the end.

   In the twentieth century Morris's many-sided creativeness,
his concern for a humane environment and his determination
to put ideals into practice have gained widespread respect. In
the influential book *Culture and Society* in 1958, Raymond
Williams placed Morris as a central figure in the tradition of
English social criticism, carrying forward the insights of the
nineteenth century into our own time. This may suggest a very
different sort of writer from the Romantic represented in the
present volume, to whom dreams and the past meant so much.
But there is an essential continuity, suggested by A. Clutton-
Brock's remark about Morris's early disinclination to write
about the present: 'This feeling was not the result of a vague
dislike of reality, but of a very clear liking for a reality different
from that in which he found himself.' He was not to be satisfied
with dreams: he was an idealist, not an escapist. The intensity
which marks the best of these early works by William Morris,
especially the Arthurian and Froissartian poems, is the quality
that was to drive him to accomplish so much in the remaining
thirty-eight years of his life.

1. W. B. Yeats: one of the epigraphs to the volume *Responsi-
   bilities* (1916).
2. See his essay on 'The Churches of North France: Shadows
   of Amiens' in the *Oxford and Cambridge Magazine* for Feb-
   ruary 1856.
3. The term 'romance' is particularly suitable for Morris's
   stories, and is frequently used now in reference to his later
   and longer stories such as *The Well at the World's End* (1896).
   The title of the present volume is that of the 1907 Everyman,
   edited by Alfred Noyes: the poems may be considered as
   romances because of their subject-matter; Browning des-
   cribed some of his 1845 poems as 'Dramatic Romances'.
4. See Note to 'In Prison' (p. 297).
5. Philip Henderson (ed.), *The Letters of William Morris* (1950),
   17.
6. See J. W. Mackail's Introduction to the World's Classics
   edition of W. Meinhold, *Mary Schweidler. The Amber Witch*

(1928); Morris printed *Sidonia the Sorceress* at the Kelmscott Press in 1893.

7. T. Carlyle, *German Romance*, 2 vols (1827); in *Works*, ed. H. D. Traill, vol. xxi (1898), 213.

8. See May Morris (ed.), *William Morris: Artist, Writer, Socialist* (1936, 2 vols), I, 383–8; see also J. W. Mackail, *The Life of William Morris* (1899 and 1950), 99–102, and D. M. Hoare, *The Works of Morris and Yeats in relation to Early Saga Literature* (Cambridge, 1937), 35–6.

9. Morris, letter to the editor of *The Spectator*, 20 July 1895; in *Letters*, ed. Henderson, 371.

10. Hoare, *Works of Morris and Yeats*, 35.

11. Jack Lindsay, 'William Morris, Writer' (1961), esp. 7–9.

12. Walter Pater, 'Poems by William Morris', in *Westminster Review*, vol. xxxiv (1868), 303.

13. Dixon Scott, 'The First Morris', in *Primitiae. Essays in English Literature* (1912), 218.

14. See H. Maynadier, *The Arthur of the English Poets* (1907); M. J. C. Reid, *The Arthurian Legend* (1938); R. Barber, *Arthur of Albion* (New York, 1961).

15. Lindsay, 'William Morris, Writer', 7.

16. R. Steele (ed.), *The Defence of Guenevere* (1904), xvii.

17. See the Introduction to *A Book of William Morris's Verse*, ed. Geoffrey Grigson (1969), v.

18. G. Bottomley, Foreword to *Guenevere. Two Poems by William Morris* (1930), pages unnumbered.

19. A. Clutton-Brock, *William Morris: His Work and Influence* (1914), 85.

BIBLIOGRAPHY

PRIMARY SOURCES

The Collected Works of William Morris, ed. May Morris, 24 vols (1910–15); two supplementary vols, *William Morris: Artist, Writer, Socialist* (Oxford, 1936).

The Letters of William Morris to his Family and Friends, ed. Philip Henderson (1950).

SELECTIONS AND EDITIONS

G. D. H. Cole (ed.): *William Morris: Selected Writings* (1934 and 1948).

Asa Briggs (ed.): *William Morris: Selected Writings and Designs* (1962).

A. L. Morton (ed.): *Three Works by William Morris* (1968).

Geoffrey Grigson (ed.): *A Choice of William Morris's Verse* (1969).

James Redmond (ed.): *News from Nowhere* (1970).

Lin Carter (ed.): *The Wood Beyond the World* and *The Well at the World's End* (New York, 1969 and 1970; London, 1971).

GENERAL BOOKS ON MORRIS

J. W. Mackail. *The Life of William Morris* (1899 and 1950).

E. P. Thompson. *William Morris: Romantic to Revolutionary* (1965).

Philip Henderson. *William Morris: his Life, Work and Friends* (1967).

Paul Thompson. *The Work of William Morris* (1967).

OTHER CRITICISM

Stopford Brooke. *Four Victorian Poets* (1908; reissue, 1964).

B. Ifor Evans. *English Poetry in the Later Nineteenth Century* (1933; 2nd edition, 1966).

C. S. Lewis, in *Rehabilitations* (Oxford, 1939).

Graham Hough, in *The Last Romantics* (1947).

Raymond Williams, in *Culture and Society* (1958).

Jack Lindsay. 'William Morris, Writer' (a lecture to the William Morris Society; 1961).

JOURNAL

The Journal of the William Morris Society covers all aspects of his work.

SUPPORTING READING

Sir Thomas Malory. *Le Morte D'Arthur*, ed. Janet Cowan, 2 vols (1969).

Jean Froissart. *Chronicles*, ed. G. Brereton (1968).

THE DEFENCE OF GUENEVERE

AND OTHER POEMS

EARLY ROMANCES

THE DEFENCE OF GUENEVERE

But, knowing now that they would have her speak,
She threw her wet hair backward from her brow,
Her hand close to her mouth touching her cheek,

As though she had had there a shameful blow,
And feeling it shameful to feel ought but shame
All through her heart, yet felt her cheek burned so,

She must a little touch it; like one lame
She walked away from Gauwaine, with her head
Still lifted up; and on her cheek of flame

The tears dried quick; she stopped at last and said:
"O knights and lords, it seems but little skill
To talk of well-known things past now and dead.

"God wot I ought to say, I have done ill,
And pray you all forgiveness heartily!
Because you must be right such great lords—still

"Listen, suppose your time were come to die,
And you were quite alone and very weak;
Yea, laid a dying while very mightily

"The wind was ruffling up the narrow streak
Of river through your broad lands running well:
Suppose a hush should come, then some one speak:

"'One of these cloths is heaven, and one is hell,
Now choose one cloth for ever, which they be,
I will not tell you, you must somehow tell

" ' Of your own strength and mightiness ; here, see ! '
Yea, yea, my lord, and you to ope your eyes,
At foot of your familiar bed to see

" A great God's angel standing, with such dyes,
Not known on earth, on his great wings, and hands,
Held out two ways, light from the inner skies

" Showing him well, and making his commands
Seem to be God's commands, moreover, too,
Holding within his hands the cloths on wands ;

" And one of these strange choosing cloths was blue,
Wavy and long, and one cut short and red ;
No man could tell the better of the two.

" After a shivering half-hour you said,
' God help ! heaven's colour, the blue ; ' and he said, ' hell.'
Perhaps you then would roll upon your bed,

" And cry to all good men that loved you well,
' Ah Christ ! if only I had known, known, known ; '
Launcelot went away, then I could tell,

" Like wisest man how all things would be, moan,
And roll and hurt myself, and long to die,
And yet fear much to die for what was sown.

" Nevertheless you, O Sir Gauwaine, lie,
Whatever may have happened through these years,
God knows I speak truth, saying that you lie."

Her voice was low at first, being full of tears,
But as it cleared, it grew full loud and shrill,
Growing a windy shriek in all men's ears,

A ringing in their startled brains, until
She said that Gauwaine lied, then her voice sunk,
And her great eyes began again to fill,

Though still she stood right up, and never shrunk,
But spoke on bravely, glorious lady fair !
Whatever tears her full lips may have drunk,

She stood, and seemed to think, and wrung her hair,
Spoke out at last with no more trace of shame,
With passionate twisting of her body there :

"It chanced upon a day that Launcelot came
To dwell at Arthur's court : at Christmas-time
This happened; when the heralds sung his name,

" 'Son of King Ban of Benwick,' seemed to chime
Along with all the bells that rang that day,
O'er the white roofs, with little change of rhyme.

"Christmas and whitened winter passed away,
And over me the April sunshine came,
Made very awful with black hail-clouds, yea

"And in the Summer I grew white with flame,
And bowed my head down—Autumn, and the sick
Sure knowledge things would never be the same,

"However often Spring might be most thick
Of blossoms and buds, smote on me, and I grew
Careless of most things, let the clock tick, tick,

"To my unhappy pulse, that beat right through
My eager body; while I laughed out loud,
And let my lips curl up at false or true,

"Seemed cold and shallow without any cloud.
Behold my judges, then the cloths were brought :
While I was dizzied thus, old thoughts would crowd,

"Belonging to the time ere I was bought
By Arthur's great name and his little love,
Must I give up for ever then, I thought,

"That which I deemed would ever round me move
Glorifying all things ; for a little word,
Scarce ever meant at all, must I now prove

"Stone-cold for ever?   Pray you, does the Lord
Will that all folks should be quite happy and good?
I love God now a little, if this cord

"Were broken, once for all what striving could
Make me love anything in earth or heaven.
So day by day it grew, as if one should

"Slip slowly down some path worn smooth and even,
Down to a cool sea on a summer day ;
Yet still in slipping was there some small leaven

"Of stretched hands catching small stones by the way,
Until one surely reached the sea at last,
And felt strange new joy as the worn head lay

" Back, with the hair like sea-weed; yea all past
Sweat of the forehead, dryness of the lips,
Washed utterly out by the dear waves o'ercast

" In the lone sea, far off from any ships !
Do I not know now of a day in Spring?
No minute of that wild day ever slips

" From out my memory; I hear thrushes sing,
And wheresoever I may be, straightway
Thoughts of it all come up with most fresh sting;

" I was half mad with beauty on that day,
And went without my ladies all alone,
In a quiet garden walled round every way;

" I was right joyful of that wall of stone,
That shut the flowers and trees up with the sky,
And trebled all the beauty: to the bone,

" Yea right through to my heart, grown very shy
With weary thoughts, it pierced, and made me glad;
Exceedingly glad, and I knew verily,

" A little thing just then had made me mad;
I dared not think, as I was wont to do,
Sometimes, upon my beauty; if I had

" Held out my long hand up against the blue,
And, looking on the tenderly darken'd fingers,
Thought that by rights one ought to see quite through,

" There, see you, where the soft still light yet lingers,
Round by the edges; what should I have done,
If this had joined with yellow spotted singers,

" And startling green drawn upward by the sun?
But shouting, loosed out, see now! all my hair,
And trancedly stood watching the west wind run

" With faintest half-heard breathing sound—why there
I lose my head e'en now in doing this;
But shortly listen—In that garden fair

" Came Launcelot walking ; this is true, the kiss
Wherewith we kissed in meeting that spring day,
I scarce dare talk of the remember'd bliss,

" When both our mouths went wandering in one way,
And aching sorely, met among the leaves ;
Our hands being left behind strained far away.

" Never within a yard of my bright sleeves
Had Launcelot come before—and now, so nigh !
After that day why is it Guenevere grieves ?

" Nevertheless you, O Sir Gauwaine, lie,
Whatever happened on through all those years,
God knows I speak truth, saying that you lie.

" Being such a lady could I weep these tears
If this were true ?　A great queen such as I
Having sinn'd this way, straight her conscience sears ;

" And afterwards she liveth hatefully,
Slaying and poisoning, certes never weeps,—
Gauwaine be friends now, speak me lovingly.

" Do I not see how God's dear pity creeps
All through your frame, and trembles in your mouth ?
Remember in what grave your mother sleeps,

" Buried in some place far down in the south,
Men are forgetting as I speak to you ;
By her head sever'd in that awful drouth

" Of pity that drew Agravaine's fell blow,
I pray your pity ! let me not scream out
For ever after, when the shrill winds blow

" Through half your castle-locks ! let me not shout
For ever after in the winter night
When you ride out alone ! in battle-rout

" Let not my rusting tears make your sword light !
Ah ! God of mercy how he turns away !
So, ever must I dress me to the fight,

" So—let God's justice work ! Gauwaine, I say,
See me hew down your proofs : yea all men know
Even as you said how Mellyagraunce one day,

"One bitter day in *la Fausse Garde*, for so
All good knights held it after, saw—
Yea, sirs, by cursed unknightly outrage; though

"You, Gauwaine, held his word without a flaw,
This Mellyagraunce saw blood upon my bed—
Whose blood then pray you? is there any law

"To make a queen say why some spots of red
Lie on her coverlet? or will you say,
'Your hands are white, lady, as when you wed,

"'Where did you bleed?' and must I stammer out—'Nay,
I blush indeed, fair lord, only to rend
My sleeve up to my shoulder, where there lay

"'A knife-point last night:' so must I defend
The honour of the Lady Guenevere?
Not so, fair lords, even if the world should end

"This very day, and you were judges here
Instead of God.   Did you see Mellyagraunce
When Launcelot stood by him? what white fear

"Curdled his blood, and how his teeth did dance,
His side sink in? as my knight cried and said,
'Slayer of unarm'd men, here is a chance!

"'Setter of traps, I pray you guard your head,
By God I am so glad to fight with you,
Stripper of ladies, that my hand feels lead

"'For driving weight; hurrah now! draw and do,
For all my wounds are moving in my breast,
And I am getting mad with waiting so.'

"He struck his hands together o'er the beast,
Who fell down flat, and grovell'd at his feet,
And groan'd at being slain so young—'at least.'

"My knight said, 'Rise you, sir, who are so fleet
At catching ladies, half-arm'd will I fight,
My left side all uncovered!' then I weet.

"Up sprang Sir Mellyagraunce with great delight
Upon his knave's face; not until just then
Did I quite hate him, as I saw my knight

" Along the lists look to my stake and pen
With such a joyous smile, it made me sigh
From agony beneath my waist-chain, when

" The fight began, and to me they drew nigh;
Ever Sir Launcelot kept him on the right,
And traversed warily, and ever high

" And fast leapt caitiff's sword, until my knight
Sudden threw up his sword to his left hand,
Caught it, and swung it; that was all the fight.

" Except a spout of blood on the hot land;
For it was hottest summer; and I know
I wonder'd how the fire, while I should stand,

" And burn, against the heat, would quiver so,
Yards above my head; thus these matters went;
Which things were only warnings of the woe

" That fell on me. Yet Mellyagraunce was shent,
For Mellyagraunce had fought against the Lord;
Therefore, my lords, take heed lest you be blent

" With all this wickedness; say no rash word
Against me, being so beautiful; my eyes,
Wept all away to grey, may bring some sword

" To drown you in your blood; see my breast rise,
Like waves of purple sea, as here I stand;
And how my arms are moved in wonderful wise,

" Yea also at my full heart's strong command,
See through my long throat how the words go up
In ripples to my mouth; how in my hand

" The shadow lies like wine within a cup
Of marvellously colour'd gold; yea now
This little wind is rising, look you up,

" And wonder how the light is falling so
Within my moving tresses: will you dare,
When you have looked a little on my brow,

" To say this thing is vile? or will you care
For any plausible lies of cunning woof,
When you can see my face with no lie there

" For ever? am I not a gracious proof—
' But in your chamber Launcelot was found '—
Is there a good knight then would stand aloof,

" When a queen says with gentle queenly sound:
' O true as steel come now and talk with me,
I love to see your step upon the ground

" ' Unwavering, also well I love to see
That gracious smile light up your face, and hear
Your wonderful words, that all mean verily

" ' The thing they seem to mean: good friend, so dear
To me in everything, come here to-night,
Or else the hours will pass most dull and drear;

" ' If you come not, I fear this time I might
Get thinking over much of times gone by,
When I was young, and green hope was in sight;

" ' For no man cares now to know why I sigh;
And no man comes to sing me pleasant songs,
Nor any brings me the sweet flowers that lie

" ' So thick in the gardens; therefore one so longs
To see you, Launcelot; that we may be
Like children once again, free from all wrongs

" ' Just for one night.'   Did he not come to me?
What thing could keep true Launcelot away
If I said ' come '? there was one less than three

" In my quiet room that night, and we were gay;
Till sudden I rose up, weak, pale, and sick,
Because a bawling broke our dream up, yea

" I looked at Launcelot's face and could not speak,
For he looked helpless too, for a little while;
Then I remember how I tried to shriek,

" And could not, but fell down; from tile to tile
The stones they threw up rattled o'er my head,
And made me dizzier; till within a while

" My maids were all about me, and my head
On Launcelot's breast was being soothed away
From its white chattering, until Launcelot said—

"By God! I will not tell you more to-day,
Judge any way you will—what matters it?
You know quite well the story of that fray,

"How Launcelot still'd their bawling the mad fit
That caught up Gauwaine—all, all, verily,
But just that which would save me; these things flit.

"Nevertheless you, O Sir Gauwaine, lie,
Whatever may have happen'd these long years,
God knows I speak truth, saying that you lie!

"All I have said is truth, by Christ's dear tears."
She would not speak another word, but stood
Turn'd sideways; listening, like a man who hears

His brother's trumpet sounding through the wood
Of his foes' lances. She lean'd eagerly,
And gave a slight spring sometimes, as she could

At last hear something really; joyfully
Her cheek grew crimson, as the headlong speed
Of the roan charger drew all men to see,
The knight who came was Launcelot at good need.

KING ARTHUR'S TOMB

Hot August noon—already on that day
  Since sunrise through the Wiltshire downs, most sad
Of mouth and eye, he had gone leagues of way;
  Ay and by night, till whether good or bad

He was, he knew not, though he knew perchance
  That he was Launcelot, the bravest knight
Of all who since the world was, have borne lance,
  Or swung their swords in wrong cause or in right.

Nay, he knew nothing now, except that where
  The Glastonbury gilded towers shine,
A lady dwelt, whose name was Guenevere;
  This he knew also; that some fingers twine,

Not only in a man's hair, even his heart,
  (Making him good or bad I mean,) but in his life,
Skies, earth, men's looks and deeds, all that has part,
  Not being ourselves, in that half-sleep, half-strife,

(Strange sleep, strange strife,) that men call living; so
  Was Launcelot most glad when the moon rose,
Because it brought new memories of her—" Lo,
  Between the trees a large moon, the wind lows

" Not loud, but as a cow begins to low,
  Wishing for strength to make the herdsman hear:
The ripe corn gathereth dew; yea, long ago,
  In the old garden life, my Guenevere

" Loved to sit still among the flowers, till night
  Had quite come on, hair loosen'd, for she said,
Smiling like heaven, that its fairness might
  Draw up the wind sooner to cool her head.

"Now while I ride how quick the moon gets small,
  As it did then—I tell myself a tale
That will not last beyond the whitewashed wall,
  Thoughts of some joust must help me through the vale,

"Keep this till after—How Sir Gareth ran
  A good course that day under my Queen's eyes,
And how she sway'd laughing at Dinadan—
  No—back again, the other thoughts will rise,

"And yet I think so fast 'twill end right soon—
  Verily then I think, that Guenevere,
Made sad by dew and wind, and tree-barred moon,
  Did love me more than ever, was more dear

"To me than ever, she would let me lie
  And kiss her feet, or, if I sat behind,
Would drop her hand and arm most tenderly,
  And touch my mouth.   And she would let me wind

"Her hair around my neck, so that it fell
  Upon my red robe, strange in the twilight
With many unnamed colours, till the bell
  Of her mouth on my cheek sent a delight

"Through all my ways of being; like the stroke
  Wherewith God threw all men upon the face
When he took Enoch, and when Enoch woke
  With a changed body in the happy place.

"Once, I remember, as I sat beside,
  She turn'd a little, and laid back her head,
And slept upon my breast: I almost died
  In those night-watches with my love and dread,

"There lily-like she bow'd her head and slept,
  And I breathed low, and did not dare to move,
But sat and quiver'd inwardly, thoughts crept,
  And frighten'd me with pulses of my Love.

"The stars shone out above the doubtful green
  Of her boddice, in the green sky overhead;
Pale in the green sky were the stars I ween,
  Because the moon shone like a star she shed

" When she dwelt up in heaven a while ago,
   And ruled all things but God : the night went on,
The wind grew cold, and the white moon grew low,
   One hand had fallen down, and now lay on

" My cold stiff palm ; there were no colours then
   For near an hour, and I fell asleep
In spite of all my striving, even when
   I held her whose name-letters make me leap.

" I did not sleep long, feeling that in sleep
   I did some loved one wrong, so that the sun
Had only just arisen from the deep
   Still land of colours, when before me one

" Stood whom I knew, but scarcely dared to touch,
   She seemed to have changed so in the night ;
Moreover she held scarlet lilies, such
   As Maiden Margaret bears upon the light

" Of the great church walls, natheless did I walk
   Through the fresh wet woods, and the wheat that
      morn,
Touching her hair and hand and mouth, and talk
   Of love we held, nigh hid among the corn.

" Back to the palace, ere the sun grew high,
   We went, and in a cool green room all day
I gazed upon the arras giddily,
   Where the wind set the silken kings a-sway.

" I could not hold her hand, or see her face ;
   For which may God forgive me ! but I think,
Howsoever, that she was not in that place."
   These memories Launcelot was quick to drink ;

And when these fell, some paces past the wall,
   There rose yet others, but they wearied more,
And tasted not so sweet ; they did not fall
   So soon, but vaguely wrenched his strained heart sore

In shadowy slipping from his grasp ; these gone,
   A longing followed ; if he might but touch
That Guenevere at once !   Still night, the lone
   Grey horse's head before him vex'd him much,

King Arthur's Tomb

In steady nodding over the grey road—
　　Still night, and night, and night, and emptied heart
Of any stories; what a dismal load
　　Time grew at last, yea, when the night did part,

And let the sun flame over all, still there
　　The horse's grey ears turn'd this way and that,
And still he watch'd them twitching in the glare
　　Of the morning sun, behind them still he sat,

Quite wearied out with all the wretched night,
　　Until about the dustiest of the day,
On the last down's brow he drew his rein in sight
　　Of the Glastonbury roofs that choke the way.

And he was now quite giddy as before,
　　When she slept by him, tired out and her hair
Was mingled with the rushes on the floor,
　　And he, being tired too, was scarce aware

Of her presence; yet as he sat and gazed,
　　A shiver ran throughout him, and his breath
Came slower, he seem'd suddenly amazed,
　　As though he had not heard of Arthur's death.

This for a moment only, presently
　　He rode on giddy still, until he reach'd
A place of apple-trees, by the thorn-tree
　　Wherefrom St. Joseph in the days past preached.

Dazed there he laid his head upon a tomb,
　　Not knowing it was Arthur's, at which sight
One of her maidens told her, "he is come,"
　　And she went forth to meet him; yet a blight

Had settled on her, all her robes were black,
　　With a long white veil only; she went slow,
As one walks to be slain, her eyes did lack
　　Half her old glory, yea, alas! the glow

Had left her face and hands; this was because
　　As she lay last night on her purple bed,
Wishing for morning, grudging every pause
　　Of the palace clocks, until that Launcelot's head

Should lie on her breast, with all her golden hair
    Each side—when suddenly the thing grew drear,
In morning twilight, when the grey downs bare
    Grew into lumps of sin to Guenevere.

At first she said no word, but lay quite still,
    Only her mouth was open, and her eyes
Gazed wretchedly about from hill to hill ;
    As though she asked, not with so much surprise

As tired disgust, what made them stand up there
    So cold and grey.   After, a spasm took
Her face, and all her frame, she caught her hair,
    All her hair, in both hands, terribly she shook,

And rose till she was sitting in the bed,
    Set her teeth hard, and shut her eyes and seem'd
As though she would have torn it from her head,
    Natheless she dropp'd it, lay down, as she deem'd

It matter'd not whatever she might do—
    O Lord Christ ! pity on her ghastly face !
Those dismal hours while the cloudless blue
    Drew the sun higher—He did give her grace ;

Because at last she rose up from her bed,
    And put her raiment on, and knelt before
The blessed rood, and with her dry lips said,
    Muttering the words against the marble floor :

" Unless you pardon, what shall I do, Lord,
    But go to hell ? and there see day by day
Foul deed on deed, hear foulest word on word,
    For ever and ever, such as on the way

" To Camelot I heard once from a churl,
    That curled me up upon my jennet's neck
With bitter shame ; how then, Lord, should I curl
    For ages and for ages ? dost thou reck

" That I am beautiful, Lord, even as you
    And your dear Mother ? why did I forget
You were so beautiful, and good, and true,
    That you loved me so, Guenevere ?   O yet

" If even I go hell, I cannot choose
    But love you, Christ, yea, though I cannot keep
From loving Launcelot; O Christ! must I lose
    My own heart's love? see, though I cannot weep,

" Yet am I very sorry for my sin;
    Moreover, Christ, I cannot bear that hell,
I am most fain to love you, and to win
    A place in heaven some time—I cannot tell—

"Speak to me, Christ! I kiss, kiss, kiss your feet;
    Ah! now I weep!"—The maid said, " By the tomb
He waiteth for you, lady," coming fleet,
    Not knowing what woe filled up all the room.

So Guenevere rose and went to meet him there,
    He did not hear her coming, as he lay
On Arthur's head, till some of her long hair
    Brush'd on the new-cut stone—" Well done! to pray

" For Arthur, my dear lord, the greatest king
    That ever lived."   " Guenevere! Guenevere!
Do you not know me, are you gone mad? fling
    Your arms and hair about me, lest I fear

" You are not Guenevere, but some other thing."
    " Pray you forgive me, fair lord Launcelot!
I am not mad, but I am sick; they cling,
    God's curses, unto such as I am; not

" Ever again shall we twine arms and lips."
    " Yea, she is mad: thy heavy law, O Lord,
Is very tight about her now, and grips
    Her poor heart, so that no right word

" Can reach her mouth; so, Lord, forgive her now,
    That she not knowing what she does, being mad,
Kills me in this way—Guenevere, bend low
    And kiss me once! for God's love kiss me! sad

" Though your face is, you look much kinder now;
    Yea once, once for the last time kiss me, lest I die."
" Christ! my hot lips are very near his brow,
    Help me to save his soul!—Yea, verily,

" Across my husband's head, fair Launcelot !
    Fair serpent mark'd with V upon the head !
This thing we did while yet he was alive,
    Why not, O twisting knight, now he is dead?

" Yea, shake ! shake now and shiver ! if you can
    Remember anything for agony,
Pray you remember how when the wind ran
    One cool spring evening through fair aspen-tree,

" And elm and oak about the palace there,
    The king came back from battle, and I stood
To meet him, with my ladies, on the stair,
    My face made beautiful with my young blood."

" Will she lie now, Lord God?"   " Remember too,
    Wrung heart, how first before the knights there came
A royal bier, hung round with green and blue,
    About it shone great tapers with sick flame.

" And thereupon Lucius, the Emperor,
    Lay royal-robed, but stone-cold now and dead,
Not able to hold sword or sceptre more,
    But not quite grim ; because his cloven head

" Bore no marks now of Launcelot's bitter sword,
    Being by embalmers deftly solder'd up ;
So still it seem'd the face of a great lord,
    Being mended as a craftsman mends a cup.

" Also the heralds sung rejoicingly
    To their long trumpets ; ' Fallen under shield,
Here lieth Lucius, King of Italy,
    Slain by Lord Launcelot in open field.'

" Thereat the people shouted 'Launcelot !'
    And through the spears I saw you drawing nigh,
You and Lord Arthur—nay, I saw you not,
    But rather Arthur, God would not let die,

" I hoped, these many years, he should grow great,
    And in his great arms still encircle me,
Kissing my face, half blinded with the heat
    Of king's love for the queen I used to be.

"Launcelot, Launcelot, why did he take your hand,
  When he had kissed me in his kingly way?
Saying, 'This is the knight whom all the land
  Calls Arthur's banner, sword, and shield to-day;

" 'Cherish him, love.' Why did your long lips cleave
  In such strange way unto my fingers then?
So eagerly glad to kiss, so loath to leave
  When you rose up? Why among helmed men

"Could I always tell you by your long strong arms,
  And sway like an angel's in your saddle there?
Why sicken'd I so often with alarms
  Over the tilt-yard? Why were you more fair

"Than aspens in the autumn at their best?
  Why did you fill all lands with your great fame,
So that Breuse even, as he rode, fear'd lest
  At turning of the way your shield should flame?

"Was it nought then, my agony and strife?
  When as day passed by day, year after year,
I found I could not live a righteous life?
  Didst ever think that queens held their truth dear.

"O, but your lips say, 'Yea, but she was cold
  Sometimes, always uncertain as the spring;
When I was sad she would be overbold,
  Longing for kisses;' when war-bells did ring,

"The back-toll'd bells of noisy Camelot."—
  "Now, Lord God, listen! listen, Guenevere,
Though I am weak just now, I think there's not
  A man who dares to say, 'You hated her,

" 'And left her moaning while you fought your fill
  In the daisied meadows;' lo you her thin hand,
That on the carven stone can not keep still,
  Because she loves me against God's command,

"Has often been quite wet with tear on tear,
  Tears Launcelot keeps somewhere, surely not
In his own heart, perhaps in Heaven, where
  He will not be these ages."—"Launcelot!

"Loud lips, wrung heart! I say, when the bells rang,
  The noisy back-toll'd bells of Camelot,
There were two spots on earth, the thrushes sang
  In the lonely gardens where my love was not,

"Where I was almost weeping; I dared not
  Weep quite in those days, lest one maid should say,
In tittering whispers; 'Where is Launcelot
  To wipe with some kerchief those tears away?'

"Another answer sharply with brows knit,
  And warning hand up, scarcely lower though,
'You speak too loud, see you, she heareth it,
  This tigress fair has claws, as I well know,

"'As Launcelot knows too, the poor knight! well-a-day!
  Why met he not with Iseult from the West,
Or, better still, Iseult of Brittany,
  Perchance indeed quite ladyless were best.'

"Alas, my maids, you loved not overmuch
  Queen Guenevere, uncertain as sunshine
In March; forgive me! for my sin being such,
  About my whole life, all my deeds did twine,

"Made me quite wicked; as I found out then,
  I think; in the lonely palace, where each morn
We went, my maids and I, to say prayers when
  They sang mass in the chapel on the lawn.

"And every morn I scarce could pray at all,
  For Launcelot's red-golden hair would play,
Instead of sunlight, on the painted wall,
  Mingled with dreams of what the priest did say;

"Grim curses out of Peter and of Paul;
  Judging of strange sins in Leviticus;
Another sort of writing on the wall,
  Scored deep across the painted heads of us,

"Christ sitting with the woman at the well,
  And Mary Magdalen repenting there,
Her dimmed eyes scorch'd and red at sight of hell
  So hardly scaped, no gold light on her hair.

" And if the priest said anything that seem'd
 To touch upon the sin they said we did,—
(This in their teeth) they look'd as if they deem'd
 That I was spying what thoughts might be hid

" Under green-cover'd bosoms, heaving quick
 Beneath quick thoughts; while they grew red with
  shame,
And gazed down at their feet—while I felt sick,
 And almost shriek'd if one should call my name,

" The thrushes sang in the lone garden there—
 But where you were the birds were scared I trow—
Clanging of arms about pavilions fair,
 Mixed with the knight's laughs; there, as I well know,

" Rode Launcelot, the king of all the band,
 And scowling Gauwaine, like the night in day,
And handsome Gareth, with his great white hand
 Curl'd round the helm-crest, ere he join'd the fray;

" And merry Dinadan with sharp dark face,
 All true knights loved to see; and in the fight
Great Tristram, and though helmed you could trace
 In all his bearing the frank noble knight;

" And by him Palomydes, helmet off,
 He fought, his face brush'd by his hair,
Red heavy swinging hair; he fear'd a scoff
 So overmuch, though what true knight would dare

" To mock that face, fretted with useless care,
 And bitter useless striving after love ?
O Palomydes, with much honour bear
 Beast Glatysaunt upon your shield, above

" Your helm that hides the swinging of your hair,
 And think of Iseult, as your sword drives through
Much mail and plate—O God, let me be there
 A little time, as I was long ago !

" Because stout Gareth lets his spear fall low,
 Gauwaine, and Launcelot, and Dinadan
Are helm'd and waiting; let the trumpets go !
 Bend over, ladies, to see all you can !

"Clench teeth, dames, yea, clasp hands, for Gareth's spear
　　Throws Kay from out his saddle, like a stone
From a castle-window when the foe draws near—
　　'Iseult!'—Sir Dinadan rolleth overthrown.

"'Iseult!'—again—the pieces of each spear
　　Fly fathoms up, and both the great steeds reel;
'Tristram for Iseult!' 'Iseult!' and 'Guenevere,'
　　The ladies' names bite verily like steel.

"They bite—bite me, Lord God—I shall go mad,
　　Or else die kissing him, he is so pale,
He thinks me mad already, O bad! bad!
　　Let me lie down a little while and wail."

"No longer so, rise up, I pray you, love,
　　And slay me really, then we shall be heal'd,
Perchance, in the aftertime by God above."
　　"Banner of Arthur—with black-bended shield

"Sinister-wise across the fair gold ground!
　　Here let me tell you what a knight you are,
O sword and shield of Arthur! you are found
　　A crooked sword, I think, that leaves a scar

"On the bearer's arm, so be he thinks it straight,
　　Twisted Malay's crease beautiful blue-grey,
Poison'd with sweet fruit; as he found too late,
　　My husband Arthur, on some bitter day!

"O sickle cutting hemlock the day long!
　　That the husbandman across his shoulder hangs,
And, going homeward about evensong,
　　Dies the next morning, struck through by the fangs!

"Banner, and sword, and shield, you dare not pray to die,
　　Lest you meet Arthur in the other world,
And, knowing who you are, he pass you by,
　　Taking short turns that he may watch you curl'd

"Body and face and limbs in agony,
　　Lest he weep presently and go away,
Saying, 'I loved him once,' with a sad sigh—
　　Now I have slain him, Lord, let me go too, I pray.
　　　　　　　　　　　　　　[LAUNCELOT *falls*.

" Alas, alas ! I know not what to do,
  If I run fast it is perchance that I
May fall and stun myself, much better so,
  Never, never again ! not even when I die."

LAUNCELOT, *on awaking.*

" I stretch'd my hands towards her and fell down,
  How long I lay in swoon I cannot tell :
My head and hands were bleeding from the stone,
  When I rose up, also I heard a bell."

SIR GALAHAD, A CHRISTMAS
MYSTERY

It is the longest night in all the year,
    Near on the day when the Lord Christ was born;
Six hours ago I came and sat down here,
    And ponder'd sadly, wearied and forlorn.

The winter wind that pass'd the chapel-door,
    Sang out a moody tune, that went right well
With mine own thoughts: I look'd down on the floor,
    Between my feet, until I heard a bell

Sound a long way off through the forest deep,
    And toll on steadily; a drowsiness
Came on me, so that I fell half asleep,
    As I sat there not moving: less and less

I saw the melted snow that hung in beads
    Upon my steel-shoes; less and less I saw
Between the tiles the bunches of small weeds:
    Heartless and stupid, with no touch of awe

Upon me, half-shut eyes upon the ground,
    I thought; O! Galahad, the days go by,
Stop and cast up now that which you have found,
    So sorely you have wrought and painfully.

Night after night your horse treads down alone
    The sere damp fern, night after night you sit
Holding the bridle like a man of stone,
    Dismal, unfriended, what thing comes of it.

And what if Palomydes also ride,
    And over many a mountain and bare heath
Follow the questing beast with none beside?
    Is he not able still to hold his breath

With thoughts of Iseult? doth he not grow pale
  With weary striving, to seem best of all
To her, "as she is best," he saith? to fail
  Is nothing to him, he can never fall.

For unto such a man love-sorrow is
  So dear a thing unto his constant heart,
That even if he never win one kiss,
  Or touch from Iseult, it will never part.

And he will never know her to be worse
  Than in his happiest dreams he thinks she is:
Good knight, and faithful, you have 'scaped the curse
  In wonderful-wise; you have great store of bliss.

Yea, what if Father Launcelot ride out,
  Can he not think of Guenevere's arms, round,
Warm and lithe, about his neck, and shout
  Till all the place grows joyful with the sound?

And when he lists can often see her face,
  And think, "Next month I kiss you, or next week,
And still you think of me:" therefore the place
  Grows very pleasant, whatsoever he seek.

But me, who ride alone, some carle shall find
  Dead in my arms in the half-melted snow,
When all unkindly with the shifting wind,
  The thaw comes on at Candlemas: I know

Indeed that they will say: "This Galahad
  If he had lived had been a right good knight;
Ah! poor chaste body!" but they will be glad,
  Not most alone, but all, when in their sight

That very evening in their scarlet sleeves
  The gay-dress'd minstrels sing; no maid will talk
Of sitting on my tomb, until the leaves,
  Grown big upon the bushes of the walk,

East of the Palace-pleasaunce, make it hard
  To see the minster therefrom: well-a-day!
Before the trees by autumn were well bared,
  I saw a damozel with gentle play,

Within that very walk say last farewell
    To her dear knight, just riding out to find
(Why should I choke to say it?) the Sangreal,
    And their last kisses sunk into my mind,

Yea, for she stood lean'd forward on his breast,
    Rather, scarce stood ; the back of one dear hand,
That it might well be kiss'd, she held and press'd
    Against his lips ; long time they stood there, fann'd

By gentle gusts of quiet frosty wind,
    Till Mador de la porte a-going by,
And my own horsehoofs roused them ; they untwined,
    And parted like a dream.   In this way I,

With sleepy face bent to the chapel floor,
    Kept musing half asleep, till suddenly
A sharp bell rang from close beside the door,
    And I leapt up when something pass'd me by,

Shrill ringing going with it, still half blind
    I stagger'd after, a great sense of awe
At every step kept gathering on my mind,
    Thereat I have no marvel, for I saw

One sitting on the altar as a throne,
    Whose face no man could say he did not know,
And though the bell still rang, he sat alone,
    With raiment half blood-red, half white as snow.

Right so I fell upon the floor and knelt,
    Not as one kneels in church when mass is said,
But in a heap, quite nerveless, for I felt
    The first time what a thing was perfect dread.

But mightily the gentle voice came down :
    " Rise up, and look and listen, Galahad,
Good knight of God, for you will see no frown
    Upon my face ; I come to make you glad.

" For that you say that you are all alone,
    I will be with you always, and fear not
You are uncared for, though no maiden moan
    Above your empty tomb ; for Launcelot,

" He in good time shall be my servant too,
    Meantime, take note whose sword first made him
        knight,
And who has loved him alway, yea, and who
    Still trusts him alway, though in all men's sight,

" He is just what you know, O Galahad,
    This love is happy even as you say,
But would you for a little time be glad,
    To make ME sorry long day after day?

" Her warm arms round his neck half throttle Me,
    The hot love-tears burn deep like spots of lead,
Yea, and the years pass quick: right dismally
    Will Launcelot at one time hang his head;

" Yea, old and shrivell'd he shall win my love.
    Poor Palomydes fretting out his soul!
Not always is he able, son, to move
    His love, and do it honour: needs must roll

" The proudest destrier sometimes in the dust,
    And then 'tis weary work; he strives beside
Seem better than he is, so that his trust
    Is always on what chances may betide;

" And so he wears away, my servant, too,
    When all these things are gone, and wretchedly
He sits and longs to moan for Iseult, who
    Is no care now to Palomydes: see,

" O good son Galahad, upon this day,
    Now even, all these things are on your side,
But these you fight not for; look up, I say,
    And see how I can love you, for no pride

" Closes your eyes, no vain lust keeps them down.
    See now you have ME always; following
That holy vision, Galahad, go on,
    Until at last you come to Me to sing

" In Heaven always, and to walk around
    The garden where I am:" he ceased, my face
And wretched body fell upon the ground;
    And when I look'd again, the holy place

Was empty; but right so the bell again
    Came to the chapel-door, there entered
Two angels first, in white, without a stain,
    And scarlet wings, then, after them a bed,

Four ladies bore, and set it down beneath
    The very altar-step, and while for fear
I scarcely dared to move or draw my breath,
    Those holy ladies gently came a-near,

And quite unarm'd me, saying: " Galahad,
    Rest here awhile and sleep, and take no thought
Of any other thing than being glad;
    Hither the Sangreal will be shortly brought,

" Yet must you sleep the while it stayeth here."
    Right so they went away, and I, being weary,
Slept long and dream'd of Heaven : the bell comes near,
    I doubt it grows to morning.   Miserere!

*Enter Two Angels in white, with scarlet wings ; also Four
    Ladies in gowns of red and green ; also an Angel, bear-
    ing in his hands a surcoat of white, with a red cross.*

AN ANGEL.

O servant of the high God, Galahad!
    Rise and be arm'd, the Sangreal is gone forth
Through the great forest, and you must be had
    Unto the sea that lieth on the north:

There shall you find the wondrous ship wherein
    The spindles of King Solomon are laid,
And the sword that no man draweth without sin,
    But if he be most pure: and there is stay'd

Hard by, Sir Launcelot, whom you will meet
    In some short space upon that ship : first, though,
Will come here presently that lady sweet,
    Sister of Percival, whom you well know,

And with her Bors and Percival: stand now,
    These ladies will to arm you.

FIRST LADY, *putting on the hauberke.*
Galahad,
That I may stand so close beneath your brow,
  I, Margaret of Antioch, am glad.

SECOND LADY, *girding him with the sword.*
That I may stand and touch you with my hand,
  O Galahad, I, Cecily, am glad.

THIRD LADY, *buckling on the spurs.*
That I may kneel while up above you stand,
  And gaze at me, O holy Galahad,
I, Lucy, am most glad.

FOURTH LADY, *putting on the basnet.*
O gentle knight,
That you bow down to us in reverence,
We are most glad, I, Katherine, with delight
  Must needs fall trembling.

ANGEL, *putting on the crossed surcoat.*
Galahad, we go hence,
For here, amid the straying of the snow,
  Come Percival's sister, Bors, and Percival.
    [*The Four Ladies carry out the bed,
      and all go but* Galahad.

GALAHAD.

How still and quiet everything seems now:
  They come, too, for I hear the horsehoofs fall.

Enter Sir Bors, Sir Percival, *and* his Sister.

Fair friends and gentle lady, God you save!
  A many marvels have been here to-night;
Tell me what news of Launcelot you have,
  And has God's body ever been in sight.

SIR BORS.

Why, as for seeing that same holy thing,
  As we were riding slowly side by side,
An hour ago, we heard a sweet voice sing,
  And through the bare twigs saw a great light glide,

With many-colour'd raiment, but far off,
    And so pass'd quickly—from the court nought good;
Poor merry Dinadan, that with jape and scoff
    Kept us all merry, in a little wood

Was found all hack'd and dead: Sir Lionel
    And Gauwaine have come back from the great quest,
Just merely shamed; and Lauvaine, who loved well
    Your father Launcelot, at the king's behest

Went out to seek him, but was almost slain,
    Perhaps is dead now; everywhere
The knights come foil'd from the great quest, in vain;
    In vain they struggle for the vision fair.

THE CHAPEL IN LYONESS

<small>Sir Ozana le cure Hardy. Sir Galahad.
Sir Bors de Ganys.</small>

Sir Ozana.

All day long and every day,
From Christmas-Eve to Whit-Sunday,
Within that Chapel-aisle I lay,
    And no man came a-near.

Naked to the waist was I,
And deep within my breast did lie,
Though no man any blood could spy,
    The truncheon of a spear.

No meat did ever pass my lips.
Those days—(Alas! the sunlight slips
From off the gilded parclose, dips,
    And night comes on apace.)

My arms lay back behind my head;
Over my raised-up knees was spread
A samite cloth of white and red;
    A rose lay on my face.

Many a time I tried to shout;
But as in dream of battle-rout,
My frozen speech would not well out;
    I could not even weep.

With inward sigh I see the sun
Fade off the pillars one by one,
My heart faints when the day is done,
    Because I cannot sleep.

Sometimes strange thoughts pass through my head;
Not like a tomb is this my bed,
Yet oft I think that I am dead;
    That round my tomb is writ,

" Ozana of the hardy heart,
Knight of the Table Round,
Pray for his soul, lords, of your part;
    A true knight he was found."
Ah! me, I cannot fathom it.   [*He sleeps.*

SIR GALAHAD.

All day long and every day,
Till his madness pass'd away,
I watch'd Ozana as he lay
    Within the gilded screen.

All my singing moved him not;
As I sung my heart grew hot,
With the thought of Launcelot
    Far away, I ween.

So I went a little space
From out the chapel, bathed my face
In the stream that runs apace
    By the churchyard wall.

There I pluck'd a faint wild rose,
Hard by where the linden grows,
Sighing over silver rows
    Of the lilies tall.

I laid the flower across his mouth;
The sparkling drops seem'd good for drouth;
He smiled, turn'd round toward the south,
    Held up a golden tress.

The light smote on it from the west:
He drew the covering from his breast,
Against his heart that hair he prest;
    Death him soon will bless.

Sir Bors.

I enter'd by the western door;
    I saw a knight's helm lying there:
I raised my eyes from off the floor,
    And caught the gleaming of his hair.

I stept full softly up to him;
    I laid my chin upon his head;
I felt him smile; my eyes did swim,
    I was so glad he was not dead.

I heard Ozana murmur low,
    "There comes no sleep nor any love."
But Galahad stoop'd and kiss'd his brow:
    He shiver'd; I saw his pale lips move.

Sir Ozana.

There comes no sleep nor any love;
    Ah me! I shiver with delight.
I am so weak I cannot move;
    God move me to thee, dear, to-night!
Christ help! I have but little wit:
My life went wrong; I see it writ,

"Ozana of the hardy heart,
    Knight of the Table Round,
Pray for his soul, lords, on your part;
    A good knight he was found."
Now I begin to fathom it.   [*He dies.*

Sir Bors.

Galahad sits dreamily:
What strange things may his eyes see,
Great blue eyes fix'd full on me?
On his soul, Lord, have mercy.

Sir Galahad.

Ozana, shall I pray for thee?
   Her cheek is laid to thine;
No long time hence, also I see
   Thy wasted fingers twine

Within the tresses of her hair
   That shineth gloriously,
Thinly outspread in the clear air
   Against the jasper sea.

SIR PETER HARPDON'S END

In an English Castle in Poictou.

Sir Peter Harpdon, *a Gascon knight in the English service,* and John Curzon, *his lieutenant.*

JOHN CURZON.

OF those three prisoners, that before you came
We took down at St. John's hard by the mill,
Two are good masons; we have tools enough,
And you have skill to set them working.

SIR PETER.

So—

What are their names?

JOHN CURZON.

Why, Jacques Aquadent,
And Peter Plombiere, but—

SIR PETER.

What colour'd hair
Has Peter now? has Jacques got bow legs?

JOHN CURZON.

Why, sir, you jest—what matters Jacques' hair,
Or Peter's legs to us?

SIR PETER.

O! John, John, John!
Throw all your mason's tools down the deep well,
Hang Peter up and Jacques; they're no good,
We shall not build, man.

35

JOHN CURZON (*going*).

                   Shall I call the guard
To hang them, sir? and yet, sir, for the tools,
We'd better keep them still; sir, fare you well.
                 [*Muttering as he goes.*
What have I done that he should jape at me?
And why not build? the walls are weak enough,
And we've two masons and a heap of tools.
                 [*Goes, still muttering.*

SIR PETER.

To think a man should have a lump like that
For his lieutenant! I must call him back,
Or else, as surely as St. George is dead,
He'll hang our friends the masons—here, John! John!

JOHN CURZON.

At your good service, sir.

SIR PETER.

               Come now, and talk
This weighty matter out; there—we've no stone
To mend our walls with,—neither brick nor stone.

JOHN CURZON.

There is a quarry, sir, some ten miles off.

SIR PETER.

We are not strong enough to send ten men
Ten miles to fetch us stone enough to build,
In three hours' time they would be taken or slain,
The cursed Frenchmen ride abroad so thick.

JOHN CURZON.

But we can send some villaynes to get stone.

SIR PETER.

Alas! John, that we cannot bring them back,
They would go off to Clisson or Sanxere,
And tell them we were weak in walls and men,
Then down go we; for, look you, times are changed,

And now no longer does the country shake
At sound of English names; our captains fade
From off our muster-rolls. At Lusac bridge
I dare say you may even yet see the hole
That Chandos beat in dying; far in Spain
Pembroke is prisoner; Phelton prisoner here;
Manny lies buried in the Charterhouse;
Oliver Clisson turn'd these years agone;
The Captal died in prison; and, over all,
Edward the prince lies underneath the ground,
Edward the king is dead, at Westminster
The carvers smooth the curls of his long beard.
Everything goes to rack—eh! and we too.
Now, Curzon, listen; if they come, these French,
Whom have I got to lean on here, but you?
A man can die but once, will you die then,
Your brave sword in your hand, thoughts in your heart
Of all the deeds we have done here in France—
And yet may do? So God will have your soul,
Whoever has your body.

John Curzon.

Why, sir, I
Will fight till the last moment, until then
Will do whate'er you tell me. Now I see
We must e'en leave the walls; well, well, perhaps
They're stronger than I think for; pity, though!
For some few tons of stone, if Guesclin comes.

Sir Peter.

Farewell, John, pray you watch the Gascons well,
I doubt them.

John Curzon.

Truly, sir, I will watch well. [Goes.

Sir Peter.

Farewell, good lump! and yet, when all is said,
'Tis a good lump. Why then, if Guesclin comes;
Some dozen stones from his petrariae,
And, under shelter of his crossbows, just

An hour's steady work with pickaxes,
Then a great noise—some dozen swords and glaives
A-playing on my basnet all at once,
And little more cross purposes on earth
For me.
　　　　　Now this is hard: a month ago,
And a few minutes' talk had set things right
'Twixt me and Alice ;—if she had a doubt,
As (may Heaven bless her !) I scarce think she had,
'Twas but their hammer, hammer in her ears,
Of "how Sir Peter fail'd at Lusac bridge :"
And "how he was grown moody of late days ;"
And "how Sir Lambert" (think now !) "his dear friend,
His sweet, dear cousin, could not but confess
That Peter's talk tended towards the French,
Which he " (for instance Lambert) "was glad of,
Being " (Lambert, you see) " on the French side."
　　　　　　　　　　　　　　　　　　　Well,

If I could but have seen her on that day,
Then, when they sent me off !
　　　　　　　　　　　I like to think,
Although it hurts me, makes my head twist, what,
If I had seen her, what I should have said,
What she, my darling, would have said and done.
As thus perchance—
　　　　　　　　To find her sitting there,
In the window-seat, not looking well at all,
Crying perhaps, and I say quietly ;
"Alice !" she looks up, chokes a sob, looks grave,
Changes from pale to red, but, ere she speaks,
Straightway I kneel down there on both my knees,
And say : "O lady, have I sinn'd, your knight ?
That still you ever let me walk alone
In the rose garden, that you sing no songs
When I am by, that ever in the dance
You quietly walk away when I come near ?
Now that I have you, will you go, think you ?"

Ere she could answer I would speak again,
Still kneeling there.
　　　　　　　　"What ! they have frighted you,
By hanging burs, and clumsily carven puppets,

Round my good name; but afterwards, my love,
I will say what this means; this moment, see!
Do I kneel here, and can you doubt me?   Yea,"
(For she would put her hands upon my face,)
"Yea, that is best, yea feel, love, am I changed?"
And she would say: "Good knight, come, kiss my lips!"
And afterwards as I sat there would say:

"Please a poor silly girl by telling me
What all those things they talk of really were,
For it is true you did not help Chandos,
And true, poor love! you could not come to me
When I was in such peril."

                                   I should say:
"I am like Balen, all things turn to blame—
I did not come to you?   At Bergerath
The constable had held us close shut up,
If from the barriers I had made three steps,
I should have been but slain; at Lusac, too,
We struggled in a marish half the day,
And came too late at last: you know, my love,
How heavy men and horses are all arm'd.
All that Sir Lambert said was pure, unmix'd,
Quite groundless lies; as you can think, sweet love."

She, holding tight my hand as we sat there,
Started a little at Sir Lambert's name,
But otherwise she listen'd scarce at all
To what I said.   Then with moist, weeping eyes,
And quivering lips, that scarcely let her speak,
She said, "I love you."

                            Other words were few,
The remnant of that hour; her hand smooth'd down
My foolish head; she kiss'd me all about
My face, and through the tangles of my beard
Her little fingers crept.

                            O! God, my Alice,
Not this good way: my lord but sent and said
That Lambert's sayings were taken at their worth,
Therefore that day I was to start, and keep
This hold against the French; and I am here,—
                            [*Looks out of the window.*

A sprawling lonely gard with rotten walls,
And no one to bring aid if Guesclin comes,
Or any other.
                There's a pennon now!
At last.
                But not the constable's, whose arms,
I wonder, does it bear?   Three golden rings
On a red ground; my cousin's by the rood!
Well, I should like to kill him, certainly,
But to be kill'd by him—
                  [*A trumpet sounds.*
                That's for a herald;
I doubt this does not mean assaulting yet.

Enter JOHN CURZON.

What says the herald of our cousin, sir?

JOHN CURZON.

So please you, sir, concerning your estate,
He has good will to talk with you.

SIR PETER.

                      Outside,
I'll talk with him, close by the gate St. Ives.
Is he unarm'd?

JOHN CURZON.

        Yea, sir, in a long gown.

SIR PETER.

Then bid them bring me hither my furr'd gown
With the long sleeves, and under it I'll wear,
By Lambert's leave, a secret coat of mail;
And will you lend me, John, your little axe?
I mean the one with Paul wrought on the blade?
And I will carry it inside my sleeve,
Good to be ready always—you, John, go
And bid them set up many suits of arms,
Bows, archgays, lances, in the base-court, and
Yourself, from the south postern setting out,
With twenty men, be ready to break through
Their unguarded rear when I cry out "St. George!"

JOHN CURZON.

How, sir! will you attack him unawares,
And slay him unarm'd?

SIR PETER.

Trust me, John, I know
The reason why he comes here with sleeved gown,
Fit to hide axes up.   So, let us go.

[*They go.*

Outside the castle by the great gate ; Sir Lambert *and* Sir Peter
seated ; guards attending each, the rest of Sir Lambert's
men drawn up about a furlong off.

SIR PETER.

And if I choose to take the losing side
Still, does it hurt you?

SIR LAMBERT.

O! no hurt to me;
I see you sneering, "Why take trouble then,
Seeing you love me not?" look you, our house
(Which, taken altogether, I love much)
Had better be upon the right side now,
If, once for all, it wishes to bear rule
As such a house should : cousin, you're too wise
To feed your hope up fat, that this fair France
Will ever draw two ways again ; this side
The French, wrong-headed, all a-jar
With envious longings ; and the other side
The order'd English, orderly led on
By those two Edwards through all wrong and right,
And muddling right and wrong to a thick broth
With that long stick, their strength.   This is all changed,
The true French win, on either side you have
Cool-headed men, good at a tilting match,
And good at setting battles in array,
And good at squeezing taxes at due time ;

Therefore by nature we French being here
Upon our own big land—
                    [*Sir Peter laughs aloud.*
                         Well, Peter! well!
What makes you laugh?

                    SIR PETER.

                         Hearing you sweat to prove
All this I know so well; but you have read
The siege of Troy?

                    SIR LAMBERT.

                    O! yea, I know it well.

                    SIR PETER.

There! they were wrong, as wrong as men could be;
For, as I think, they found it such delight
To see fair Helen going through their town:
Yea, any little common thing she did
(As stooping to pick a flower) seem'd so strange,
So new in its great beauty, that they said;
"Here we will keep her living in this town,
Till all burns up together."   And so, fought,
In a mad whirl of knowing they were wrong;
Yea, they fought well, and ever, like a man
That hangs legs off the ground by both his hands,
Over some great height, did they struggle sore,
Quite sure to slip at last; wherefore, take note
How almost all men, reading that sad siege,
Hold for the Trojans; as I did at least,
Thought Hector the best knight a long way:
                                        Now
Why should I not do this thing that I think,
For even when I come to count the gains,
I have them my side: men will talk, you know,
(We talk of Hector, dead so long agone,)
When I am dead, of how this Peter clung
To what he thought the right; of how he died,
Perchance, at last, doing some desperate deed
Few men would care do now, and this is gain

To me, as ease and money is to you,
Moreover, too, I like the straining game
Of striving well to hold up things that fall ;
So one becomes great ; see you ! in good times
All men live well together, and you, too,
Live dull and happy—happy ? not so quick,
Suppose sharp thoughts begin to burn you up.
Why then, but just to fight as I do now,
A halter round my neck, would be great bliss.
O ! I am well off.   [*Aside.*
         Talk, and talk, and talk,
I know this man has come to murder me,
And yet I talk still.

Sir Lambert.

         If your side were right,
You might be, though you lost ; but if I said,
"You are a traitor, being, as you are,
Born Frenchman."   What are Edwards unto you,
Or Richards ?

Sir Peter.

         Nay, hold there, my Lambert, hold !
For fear your zeal should bring you to some harm,
Don't call me traitor.

Sir Lambert.

         Furthermore, my knight.
Men call you slippery on your losing side,
When at Bordeaux I was ambassador,
I heard them say so, and could scarce say " Nay."
       [*He takes hold of something in his
         sleeve, and rises.*

Sir Peter (*rising*).

They lied—and you lie, not for the first time.
What have you got there, fumbling up your sleeve,
A stolen purse ?

Sir Lambert.

         Nay, liar in your teeth !
Dead liar too ; St. Dennis and St. Lambert !
       [*Strikes at* Sir Peter *with a dagger.*

SIR PETER (*striking him flatlings with his axe*).

How thief! thief! thief! so there, fair thief, so there,
St. George Guienne! glaives for the castellan!
You French, you are but dead, unless you lay
Your spears upon the earth.   St. George Guienne!

Well done, John Curzon, how he has them now

In the Castle.

JOHN CURZON.

What shall we do with all these prisoners, sir?

SIR PETER.

Why put them all to ransom, those that can
Pay anything, but not too light though, John,
Seeing we have them on the hip: for those
That have no money, that being certified,
Why turn them out of doors before they spy;
But bring Sir Lambert guarded unto me.

JOHN CURZON.

I will, fair sir.   [*He goes.*

SIR PETER.

              I do not wish to kill him,
Although I think I ought; he shall go mark'd,
By all the saints, though!

Enter Lambert (*guarded*).

                    Now, Sir Lambert, now!
What sort of death do you expect to get,
Being taken this way?

SIR LAMBERT.

                    Cousin! cousin! think!
I am your own blood; may God pardon me!
I am not fit to die; if you knew all,
All I have done since I was young and good.
O! you would give me yet another chance,

As God would, that I might wash all clear out,
By serving you and Him.   Let me go now!
And I will pay you down more golden crowns
Of ransom than the king would!

Sir Peter.

            Well, stand back,
And do not touch me!   No, you shall not die,
Nor yet pay ransom.   You, John Curzon, cause
Some carpenters to build a scaffold, high,
Outside the gate; when it is built, sound out
To all good folks, "Come, see a traitor punish'd!"
Take me my knight, and set him up thereon,
And let the hangman shave his head quite clean,
And cut his ears off close up to the head;
And cause the minstrels all the while to play
Soft music, and good singing; for this day
Is my high day of triumph; is it not,
Sir Lambert?

Sir Lambert.

        Ah! on your own blood,
Own name, you heap this foul disgrace? you dare,
With hands and fame thus sullied, to go back
And take the Lady Alice—

Sir Peter.

            Say her name
Again, and you are dead, slain here by me.
Why should I talk with you, I'm master here,
And do not want your schooling; is it not
My mercy that you are not dangling dead
There in the gateway with a broken neck?

Sir Lambert.

Such mercy! why not kill me then outright?
To die is nothing; but to live that all
May point their fingers! yea, I'd rather die.

John Curzon.

Why, will it make you any uglier man
To lose your ears? they're much too big for you,
You ugly Judas!

SIR PETER.

Hold, John !   [*To* Lambert.
                    That's your choice,
To die, mind !   Then you shall die—Lambert mine,
I thank you now for choosing this so well,
It saves me much perplexity and doubt ;
Perchance an ill deed too, for half I count
This sparing traitors is an ill deed.
                              Well,
Lambert, die bravely, and we're almost friends.

SIR LAMBERT, *grovelling.*

O God ! this is a fiend and not a man ;
Will some one save me from him ? help, help, help !
I will not die.

SIR PETER.

                Why, what is this I see ?
A man who is a knight, and bandied words
So well just now with me, is lying down,
Gone mad for fear like this !   So, so, you thought
You knew the worst, and might say what you pleased.
I should have guess'd this from a man like you.
Eh ! righteous Job would give up skin for skin,
Yea, all a man can have for simple life,
And we talk fine, yea, even a hound like this,
Who needs must know that when he dies, deep hell
Will hold him fast for ever—so fine we talk,
" Would rather die "—all that.   Now sir, get up !
And choose again : shall it be head sans ears,
Or trunk sans head ?
                      John Curzon, pull him up !
What, life then ? go and build the scaffold, John.

    Lambert, I hope that never on this earth
We meet again ; that you'll turn out a monk,
And mend the life I give you, so farewell,
I'm sorry you're a rascal.   John, despatch.

In the French camp before the Castle.

Sir Peter *prisoner*, Guesclin, Clisson, Sir Lambert.

SIR PETER.

So now is come the ending of my life ;
If I could clear this sickening lump away
That sticks in my dry throat, and say a word,
Guesclin might listen.

GUESCLIN.

           Tell me, fair sir knight,
If you have been clean liver before God,
And then you need not fear much ; as for me,
I cannot say I hate you, yet my oath,
And cousin Lambert's ears here clench the thing.

SIR PETER.

I knew you could not hate me, therefore I
Am bold to pray for life ; 'twill harm your cause
To hang knights of good name, harm here in France
I have small doubt, at any rate hereafter
Men will remember you another way
Than I should care to be remember'd, ah !
Although hot lead runs through me for my blood,
All this falls cold as though I said, " Sweet lords,
Give back my falcon ! "
           See how young I am,
Do you care altogether more than France,
Say rather one French faction, than for all
The state of Christendom ? a gallant knight,
As (yea, by God !) I have been, is more worth
Than many castles ; will you bring this death,
For a mere act of justice, on my head ?

Think how it ends all, death ! all other things
Can somehow be retrieved, yea, send me forth
Naked and maimed, rather than slay me here ;
Then somehow will I get me other clothes,
And somehow will I get me some poor horse,
And, somehow clad in poor old rusty arms,
Will ride and smite among the serried glaives,

Fear not death so ; for I can tilt right well,
Let me not say " I could ; " I know all tricks,
That sway the sharp sword cunningly ; ah you,
You, my Lord Clisson, in the other days
Have seen me learning these, yea, call to mind,
How in the trodden corn by Chartrés town,
When you were nearly swooning from the back
Of your black horse, those three blades slid at once
From off my sword's edge ; pray for me, my lord !

CLISSON.

Nay, this is pitiful, to see him die.
My Lord the Constable, I pray you note
That you are losing some few thousand crowns
By slaying this man ; also think ; his lands
Along the Garonne river lie for leagues,
And are right rich, a many mills he has,
Three abbeys of grey monks do hold of him,
Though wishing well for Clement, as we do ;
I know the next heir, his old uncle, well,
Who does not care two deniers for the knight
As things go now, but slay him, and then see,
How he will bristle up like any perch,
With curves of spears.   What ! do not doubt, my lord,
You'll get the money, this man saved my life,
And I will buy him for two thousand crowns ;
Well, five then—eh ! what !   " No " again ? well then,
Ten thousand crowns ?

GUESCLIN.

        My sweet lord, much I grieve
I cannot please you, yea, good sooth, I grieve
This knight must die, as verily he must ;
For I have sworn it, so men take him out,
Use him not roughly.

SIR LAMBERT, *coming forward.*

        Music, do you know,
Music will suit you well, I think, because
You look so mild, like Laurence being grill'd ;
Or perhaps music soft and low, because
This is high day of triumph unto me,

Is it not, Peter?
                You are frighten'd, though,
Eh! you are pale, because this hurts you much,
Whose life was pleasant to you, not like mine,
You ruin'd wretch! Men mock me in the streets,
Only in whispers loud, because I am
Friend of the constable; will this please you,
Unhappy Peter? once a-going home,
Without my servants, and a little drunk,
At midnight through the lone dim lamp-lit streets,
A whore came up and spat into my eyes,
(Rather to blind me than to make me see,)
But she was very drunk, and tottering back,
Even in the middle of her laughter, fell
And cut her head against the pointed stones,
While I lean'd on my staff, and look'd at her,
And cried, being drunk.
                Girls would not spit at you,
You are so handsome, I think verily
Most ladies would be glad to kiss your eyes,
And yet you will be hung like a cur dog
Five minutes hence, and grow black in the face,
And curl your toes up. Therefore I am glad.

Guess why I stand and talk this nonsense now,
With Guesclin getting ready to play chess,
And Clisson doing something with his sword,
I can't see what, talking to Guesclin though,
I don't know what about, perhaps of you.
But, cousin Peter, while I stroke your beard,
Let me say this, I'd like to tell you now
That your life hung upon a game of chess,
That if, say, my squire Robert here should beat,
Why you should live, but hang if I beat him;
Then guess, clever Peter, what I should do then;
Well, give it up? why, Peter, I should let
My squire Robert beat me, then you would think
That you were safe, you know; Eh? not at all,
But I should keep you three days in some hold,
Giving you salt to eat, which would be kind,
Considering the tax there is on salt;
And afterwards should let you go, perhaps?
No I should not, but I should hang you, sir,

With a red rope in lieu of mere grey rope.

But I forgot, you have not told me yet
If you can guess why I talk nonsense thus,
Instead of drinking wine while you are hang'd?
You are not quick at guessing, give it up.
This is the reason; here I hold your hand,
And watch you growing paler, see you writhe,
And this, my Peter, is a joy so dear,
I cannot by all striving tell you how
I love it, nor I think, good man, would you
Quite understand my great delight therein;
You, when you had me underneath you once,
Spat as it were, and said, " Go take him out,"
(That they might do that thing to me whereat,
E'en now this long time off I could well shriek,)
And then you tried forget I ever lived,
And sunk your hating into other things;
While I—St. Dennis! though, I think you'll faint,
Your lips are grey so; yes, you will, unless
You let it out and weep like a hurt child;
Hurrah! you do now.   Do not go just yet,
For I am Alice, am right like her now;
Will you not kiss me on the lips, my love?—

CLISSON.

You filthy beast, stand back and let him go,
Or by God's eyes I'll choke you.
                              [*Kneeling to* Sir Peter.
                                        Fair sir knight,
I kneel upon my knees and pray to you
That you would pardon me for this your death;
God knows how much I wish you still alive,
Also how heartily I strove to save
Your life at this time; yea, he knows quite well,
(I swear it, so forgive me!) how I would,
If it were possible, give up my life
Upon this grass for yours; fair knight, although,
He knowing all things knows this thing too, well,
Yet when you see his face some short time hence,
Tell him I tried to save you.

SIR PETER.

                    O! my lord,
I cannot say this is as good as life,
But yet it makes me feel far happier now,
And if at all, after a thousand years,
I see God's face, I will speak loud and bold,
And tell Him you were kind, and like Himself;
Sir, may God bless you!
                    Did you note how I
Fell weeping just now? pray you, do not think
That Lambert's taunts did this, I hardly heard
The base things that he said, being deep in thought
Of all things that have happen'd since I was
A little child; and so at last I thought
Of my true lady: truly, sir, it seem'd
No longer gone than yesterday, that this
Was the sole reason God let me be born
Twenty-five years ago, that I might love
Her, my sweet lady, and be loved by her;
This seem'd so yesterday, to-day death comes,
And is so bitter strong, I cannot see
Why I was born.
              But as a last request,
I pray you, O kind Clisson, send some man,
Some good man, mind you, to say how I died,
And take my last love to her: fare-you-well,
And may God keep you; I must go now, lest
I grow too sick with thinking on these things;
Likewise my feet are wearied of the earth,
From whence I shall be lifted upright soon.
                      [As he goes.
Ah me! shamed too, I wept at fear of death;
And yet not so, I only wept because
There was no beautiful lady to kiss me
Before I died, and sweetly wish good speed
From her dear lips. O for some lady, though
I saw her ne'er before; Alice, my love,
I do not ask for; Clisson was right kind,
If he had been a woman, I should die
Without this sickness: but I am all wrong,
So wrong and hopelessly afraid to die.

There, I will go.
            My God! how sick I am,
If only she could come and kiss me now.

The Hotel de la Barde, Bordeaux.

The Lady Alice de la Barde *looking out of a window
into the street.*

No news yet! surely, still he holds his own;
That garde stands well; I mind me passing it
Some months ago; God grant the walls are strong!
I heard some knights say something yestereve,
I tried hard to forget: words far apart
Struck on my heart; something like this; one said
"What eh! a Gascon with an English name,
Harpdon?" then nought, but afterwards, "Poictou."
As one who answers to a question ask'd;
Then carelessly regretful came, "No, no."
Whereto in answer loud and eagerly,
One said, "Impossible? Christ, what foul play!"
And went off angrily; and while thenceforth
I hurried gaspingly afraid, I heard,
"Guesclin;" "Five thousand men-at-arms;" "Clisson."
My heart misgives me it is all in vain
I send these succours; and in good time there!
Their trumpet sounds, ah! here they are; good knights,
God up in Heaven keep you.
                 If they come
And find him prisoner—for I can't believe
Guesclin will slay him, even though they storm—
(The last horse turns the corner.)
                   God in Heaven!
What have I got to thinking of at last!
That thief I will not name is with Guesclin,
Who loves him for his lands. My love! my love!
O, if I lose you after all the past,
What shall I do?
              I cannot bear the noise
And light street out there, with this thought alive,
Like any curling snake within my brain;
Let me just hide my head within these soft

Deep cushions, there to try and think it out.

[Lying in the window-seat.

I cannot hear much noise now, and I think
That I shall go to sleep: it all sounds dim
And faint, and I shall soon forget most things;
Yea, almost that I am alive and here;
It goes slow, comes slow, like a big mill-wheel
On some broad stream, with long green weeds a-sway,
And soft and slow it rises and it falls,
Still going onward.

           Lying so, one kiss,
And I should be in Avalon asleep,
Among the poppies, and the yellow flowers;
And they should brush my cheek, my hair being spread
Far out among the stems; soft mice and small
Eating and creeping all about my feet,
Red shod and tired; and the flies should come
Creeping o'er my broad eyelids unafraid;
And there should be a noise of water going,
Clear blue, fresh water breaking on the slates,
Likewise the flies should creep—God's eyes! God help,
A trumpet? I will run fast, leap adown
The slippery sea-stairs, where the crabs fight.

                          Ah!
I was half dreaming, but the trumpet's true,
He stops here at our house.   The Clisson arms?
Ah, now for news.   But I must hold my heart,
And be quite gentle till he is gone out;
And afterwards,—but he is still alive,
He must be still alive.

        Enter a Squire *of* Clisson's.

           Good day, fair sir,
I give you welcome, knowing whence you come.

        SQUIRE.

My Lady Alice de la Barde, I come
From Oliver Clisson, knight and mighty lord,
Bringing you tidings: I make bold to hope
You will not count me villain, even if
They wring your heart; nor hold me still in hate.

For I am but a mouthpiece after all,
A mouthpiece, too, of one who wishes well
To you and your's.

ALICE.

            Can you talk faster, sir,
Get over all this quicker? fix your eyes
On mine, I pray you, and whate'er you see,
Still go on talking fast, unless I fall,
Or bid you stop.

SQUIRE.

            I pray your pardon then,
And, looking in your eyes, fair lady, say
I am unhappy that your knight is dead.
Take heart, and listen! let me tell you all.
We were five thousand goodly men-at-arms,
And scant five hundred had he in that hold;
His rotten sand-stone walls were wet with rain,
And fell in lumps wherever a stone hit;
Yet for three days about the barrier there
The deadly glaives were gather'd, laid across,
And push'd and pull'd; the fourth our engines came;
But still amid the crash of falling walls,
And roar of lombards, rattle of hard bolts,
The steady bow-strings flash'd, and still stream'd out
St. George's banner, and the seven swords,
And still they cried, "St. George Guienne," until
Their walls were flat as Jericho's of old,
And our rush came, and cut them from the keep.

ALICE.

Stop, sir, and tell me if you slew him then,
And where he died, if you can really mean
That Peter Harpdon, the good knight, is dead?

SQUIRE.

Fair lady, in the base-court—

ALICE.

What base-court?
What do you talk of?   Nay, go on, go on;
'Twas only something gone within my head:
Do you not know, one turns one's head round quick,
And something cracks there with sore pain? go on,
And still look at my eyes.

SQUIRE.

Almost alone,
There in the base-court fought he with his sword,
Using his left hand much, more than the wont
Of most knights now-a-days; our men gave back,
For wheresoever he hit a downright blow,
Some one fell bleeding, for no plate could hold
Against the sway of body and great arm;
Till he grew tired, and some man (no! not I,
I swear not I, fair lady, as I live!)
Thrust at him with a glaive between the knees,
And threw him; down he fell, sword undermost;
Many fell on him, crying out their cries,
Tore his sword from him, tore his helm off, and—

ALICE.

Yea, slew him; I am much too young to live,
Fair God, so let me die.
You have done well,
Done all your message gently, pray you go,
Our knights will make you cheer; moreover, take
This bag of franks for your expenses.
[*The* Squire *kneels.*

But
You do not go; still looking at my face,
You kneel! what, squire, do you mock me then?
You need not tell me who has set you on,
But tell me only, 'tis a made-up tale.
You are some lover may-be, or his friend;
Sir, if you loved me once, or your friend loved,
Think, is it not enough that I kneel down

And kiss your feet, your jest will be right good
If you give in now, carry it too far,
And 'twill be cruel; not yet? but you weep
Almost, as though you loved me; love me then,
And go to Heaven by telling all your sport,
And I will kiss you, then with all my heart,
Upon the mouth; O! what can I do then
To move you?

SQUIRE.

Lady fair, forgive me still!
You know I am so sorry, but my tale
Is not yet finish'd:
So they bound his hands,
And brought him tall and pale to Guesclin's tent,
Who, seeing him, leant his head upon his hand,
And ponder'd somewhile, afterwards, looking up—
Fair dame, what shall I say?

ALICE.

Yea, I know now,
Good squire, you may go now with my thanks.

SQUIRE.

Yet, lady, for your own sake I say this,
Yea, for my own sake, too, and Clisson's sake.
When Guesclin told him he must be hanged soon,
Within a while he lifted up his head
And spoke for his own life; not crouching, though,
As abjectly afraid to die, nor yet
Sullenly brave as many a thief will die;
Nor yet as one that plays at japes with God:
Few words he spoke; not so much what he said
Moved us, I think, as, saying it, there played
Strange tenderness from that big soldier there
About his pleading; eagerness to live
Because folk loved him, and he loved them back,
And many gallant plans unfinish'd now
For ever. Clisson's heart, which may God bless!

Was moved to pray for him, but all in vain;
Wherefore I bring this message:

That he waits,

Still loving you, within the little church
Whose windows, with the one eye of the light
Over the altar, every night behold
The great dim broken walls he strove to keep!

There my Lord Clisson did his burial well.
Now, lady, I will go; God give you rest!

ALICE.

Thank Clisson from me, squire, and farewell!
And now to keep myself from going mad.
Christ! I have been a many times to church,
And, ever since my mother taught me prayers,
Have used them daily, but to-day I wish
To pray another way; come face to face,
O Christ, that I may clasp your knees and pray,
I know not what, at any rate come now
From one of many places where you are;
Either in Heaven amid thick angel wings,
Or sitting on the altar strange with gems,
Or high up in the dustiness of the apse;
Let us go, You and I, a long way off,
To the little damp, dark, Poitevin church;
While you sit on the coffin in the dark,
Will I lie down, my face on the bare stone
Between your feet, and chatter anything
I have heard long ago, what matters it
So I may keep you there, your solemn face
And long hair even-flowing on each side,
Until you love me well enough to speak,
And give me comfort; yea, till o'er your chin,
And cloven red beard the great tears roll down
In pity for my misery, and I die,
Kissed over by you.

Eh Guesclin! if I were

Like Countess Mountfort now, that kiss'd the knight,
Across the salt sea come to fight for her;
Ah! just to go about with many knights,

Wherever you went, and somehow on one day,
In a thick wood to catch you off your guard,
Let you find, you and your some fifty friends,
Nothing but arrows wheresoe'er you turn'd,
Yea, and red crosses, great spears over them;
And so, between a lane of my true men,
To walk up pale and stern and tall, and with
My arms on my surcoat, and his therewith,
And then to make you kneel, O knight Guesclin;
And then—alas! alas! when all is said,
What could I do but let you go again,
Being pitiful woman?   I get no revenge,
Whatever happens; and I get no comfort,
I am but weak, and cannot move my feet,
But as men bid me.
              Strange I do not die.
Suppose this had not happen'd after all;
I will lean out again and watch for news.

I wonder how long I can still feel thus,
As though I watch'd for news, feel as I did
Just half-an-hour ago, before this news.
How all the street is humming, some men sing,
And some men talk; some look up at the house,
Then lay their heads together and look grave;
Their laughter pains me sorely in the heart,
Their thoughtful talking makes my head turn round,
Yea, some men sing, what is it then they sing?
Eh Launcelot, and love and fate and death;
They ought to sing of him who was as wight
As Launcelot or Wade, and yet avail'd
Just nothing, but to fail and fail and fail,
And so at last to die and leave me here,
Alone and wretched; yea, perhaps they will,
When many years are past, make songs of us;
God help me, though, truly I never thought
That I should make a story in this way,
A story that his eyes can never see.

[One sings from outside.]

Therefore be it believed
Whatsoever he grieved,
Whan his horse was relieved,
*   This Launcelot,*

Beat down on his knee.
Right valiant was he
God's body to see,
*   Though he saw it not.*

Right valiant to move,
But for his sad love
The high God above
*   Stinted his praise.*

Yet so he was glad
That his son Lord Galahad
That high joyaunce had
*   All his life-days.*

Sing we therefore then
Launcelot's praise again,
For he wan crownés ten,
*   If he wan not twelve.*

To his death from his birth
He was muckle of worth,
Lay him in the cold earth,
*   A long grave ye may delve.*

Omnes homines benedicite!
This last fitte ye may see,
All men pray for me,
Who made this history
Cunning and fairly.

RAPUNZEL

The Prince, *being in the wood near the tower,*
in the evening.

I could not even think
    What made me weep that day
When out of the council-hall
    The courtiers pass'd away,—

The Witch.

    Rapunzel, Rapunzel,
    Let down your hair!

Rapunzel.

Is it not true that every day
She climbeth up the same strange way,
Her scarlet cloak spread broad and gay,
    Over my golden hair?

The Prince.

And left me there alone,
    To think on what they said;
"Thou art a king's own son,
    'Tis fit that thou should'st wed."

The Witch.

    Rapunzel, Rapunzel,
    Let down your hair!

Rapunzel.

When I undo the knotted mass,
Fathoms below the shadows pass
Over my hair along the grass.
    O my golden hair!

THE PRINCE.

I put my armour on,
   Thinking on what they said;
" Thou art a king's own son,
   'Tis fit that thou should'st wed."

THE WITCH.

   Rapunzel, Rapunzel,
   Let down your hair !

RAPUNZEL.

See on the marble parapet
I lean my brow, strive to forget
That fathoms below my hair grows wet
   With the dew, my golden hair.

THE PRINCE.

I rode throughout the town,
   Men did not bow the head,
Though I was the king's own son;
   " He rides to dream," they said.

THE WITCH.

   Rapunzel, Rapunzel,
   Wind up your hair !

RAPUNZEL.

See, on the marble parapet
The faint red stains with tears are wet ;
The long years pass, no help comes yet
   To free my golden hair.

THE PRINCE.

For leagues and leagues I rode,
   Till hot my armour grew,
Till underneath the leaves
   I felt the evening dew.

THE WITCH.

   Rapunzel, Rapunzel,
   Weep through your hair !

RAPUNZEL.

And yet—but I am growing old,
For want of love my heart is cold,
Years pass, the while I loose and fold
  The fathoms of my hair.

THE PRINCE, *in the morning*.

I have heard tales of men, who in the night
  Saw paths of stars let down to earth from heaven,
Who follow'd them until they reach'd the light
  Wherein they dwell, whose sins are all forgiven;

But who went backward when they saw the gate
  Of diamond, nor dared to enter in;
All their life long they were content to wait,
  Purging them patiently of every sin.

I must have had a dream of some such thing,
  And now am just awaking from that dream;
For even in grey dawn those strange words ring
  Through heart and brain, and still I see that gleam.

For in my dream at sunset-time I lay
  Beneath these beeches, mail and helmet off,
Right full of joy that I had come away
  From court; for I was patient of the scoff

That met me always there from day to day,
  From any knave or coward of them all;
I was content to live that wretched way;
  For truly till I left the council-hall,

And rode forth arm'd beneath the burning sun,
  My gleams of happiness were faint and few,
But then I saw my real life had begun,
  And that I should be strong quite well I knew.

For I was riding out to look for love,
  Therefore the birds within the thickets sung,
Even in hot noontide, as I pass'd, above
  The elms o'ersway'd with longing towards me hung.

Now some few fathoms from the place where I
    Lay in the beech-wood, was a tower fair,
The marble corners faint against the sky ;
    And dreamily I wonder'd what lived there :

Because it seem'd a dwelling for a queen,
    No belfry for the swinging of great bells ;
No bolt or stone had ever crush'd the green
    Shafts, amber and rose walls, no soot that tells

Of the Norse torches burning up the roofs,
    On the flower-carven marble could I see ;
But rather on all sides I saw the proofs
    Of a great loneliness that sicken'd me ;

Making me feel a doubt that was not fear,
    Whether my whole life long had been a dream,
And I should wake up soon in some place, where
    The piled-up arms of the fighting angels gleam ;

Not born as yet, but going to be born,
    No naked baby as I was at first,
But an armèd knight, whom fire, hate and scorn
    Could turn from nothing : my heart almost burst

Beneath the beeches, as I lay a-dreaming,
    I tried so hard to read this riddle through,
To catch some golden cord that I saw gleaming
    Like gossamer against the autumn blue.

But while I ponder'd these things, from the wood
    There came a black-hair'd woman, tall and bold,
Who strode straight up to where the tower stood,
    And cried out shrilly words, whereon behold—

THE WITCH, *from the tower.*

Rapunzel, Rapunzel,
Let down you hair !

THE PRINCE.

Ah Christ ! it was no dream then, but there stood
    (She comes again) a maiden passing fair,
Against the roof, with face turn'd to the wood,
    Bearing within her arms waves of her yellow hair.

I read my riddle when I saw her stand,
    Poor love ! her face quite pale against her hair,
Praying to all the leagues of empty land
    To save her from the woe she suffer'd there.

To think ! they trod upon her golden hair
    In the witches' sabbaths ; it was a delight
For these foul things, while she, with thin feet bare,
    Stood on the roof upon the winter night.

To plait her dear hair into many plaits,
    And then, while God's eye look'd upon the thing,
In the very likenesses of Devil's bats,
    Upon the ends of her long hair to swing.

And now she stood above the parapet,
    And, spreading out her arms, let her hair flow,
Beneath that veil her smooth white forehead set
    Upon the marble, more I do not know ;

Because before my eyes a film of gold
    Floated, as now it floats.   O, unknown love,
Would that I could thy yellow stair behold,
    If still thou standest with lead roof above !

THE WITCH, *as she passes.*

Is there any who will dare
To climb up the yellow stair,
Glorious Rapunzel's golden hair ?

THE PRINCE.

If it would please God make you sing again,
    I think that I might very sweetly die,
My soul somehow reach heaven in joyous pain,
    My heavy body on the beech-nuts lie.

Now I remember ; what a most strange year,
    Most strange and awful, in the beechen wood
I have pass'd now ; I still have a faint fear
    It is a kind of dream not understood.

I have seen no one in this wood except
   The witch and her; have heard no human tones,
But when the witches' revelry has crept
   Between the very jointing of my bones.

Ah! I know now; I could not go away,
   But needs must stop to hear her sing that song
She always sings at dawning of the day.
   I am not happy here, for I am strong,

And every morning do I whet my sword,
   Yet Rapunzel still weeps within the tower,
And still God ties me down to the green sward,
   Because I cannot see the gold stair floating lower.

RAPUNZEL *sings from the tower.*

My mother taught me prayers
To say when I had need;
I have so many cares,
That I can take no heed
Of many words in them;
But I remember this:
Christ, bring me to thy bliss.
Mary, maid withouten wem,
Keep me! I am lone, I wis,
Yet besides I have made this
By myself: *Give me a kiss,*
Dear God, dwelling up in heaven!
Also: *Send me a true knight,*
Lord Christ, with a steel sword, bright,
Broad, and trenchant; yea, and seven
Spans from hilt to point, O Lord!
And let the handle of his sword
Be gold on silver, Lord in heaven!
Such a sword as I see gleam
Sometimes, when they let me dream.

Yea, besides, I have made this:
Lord, give Mary a dear kiss,
And let gold Michael, who looked down,
When I was there, on Rouen town
From the spire, bring me that kiss
On a lily! Lord, do this!

These prayers on the dreadful nights
When the witches plait my hair,
And the fearfullest of sights
On the earth and in the air,
Will not let me close my eyes,
I murmur often, mix'd with sighs,
That my weak heart will not hold
At some things that I behold.
Nay, not sighs, but quiet groans,
That swell out the little bones
Of my bosom; till a trance
God sends in middle of that dance,
And I behold the countenance
Of Michael, and can feel no more
The bitter east wind biting sore
My naked feet; can see no more
The crayfish on the leaden floor,
That mock with feeler and grim claw.

Yea, often in that happy trance,
Beside the blessed countenance
Of golden Michael, on the spire
Glowing all crimson in the fire
Of sunset, I behold a face,
Which sometime, if God give me grace,
May kiss me in this very place.

Evening in the tower.

RAPUNZEL.

It grows half way between the dark and light;
    Love, we have been six hours here alone,
I fear that she will come before the night,
    And if she finds us thus we are undone.

THE PRINCE.

Nay, draw a little nearer, that your breath
    May touch my lips, let my cheek feel your arm;
Now tell me, did you ever see a death,
    Or ever see a man take mortal harm?

RAPUNZEL.

Once came two knights and fought with swords below,
   And while they fought I scarce could look at all,
My head swam so, after a moaning low
   Drew my eyes down ; I saw against the wall

One knight lean dead, bleeding from head and breast,
   Yet seem'd it like a line of poppies red
In the golden twilight, as he took his rest,
   In the dusky time he scarcely seemed dead.

But the other, on his face six paces off,
   Lay moaning, and the old familiar name
He mutter'd through the grass, seem'd like a scoff
   Of some lost soul remembering his past fame.

His helm all dinted lay beside him there,
   The visor-bars were twisted towards the face,
The crest, which was a lady very fair,
   Wrought wonderfully, was shifted from its place.

The shower'd mail-rings on the speed-walk lay,
   Perhaps my eyes were dazzled with the light
That blazed in the west, yet surely on that day
   Some crimson thing had changed the grass from bright

Pure green I love so. But the knight who died
   Lay there for days after the other went ;
Until one day I heard a voice that cried,
   " Fair knight, I see Sir Robert we were sent

"To carry dead or living to the king."
   So the knights came and bore him straight away
On their lance truncheons, such a batter'd thing,
   His mother had not known him on that day,

But for his helm-crest, a gold lady fair
   Wrought wonderfully.

THE PRINCE.

              Ah, they were brothers then,
And often rode together, doubtless where
   The swords were thickest, and were loyal men,

Until they fell in these same evil dreams.

RAPUNZEL.

Yea, love; but shall we not depart from hence?
The white moon groweth golden fast, and gleams
 Between the aspen stems; I fear—and yet a sense

Of fluttering victory comes over me,
 That will not let me fear aright; my heart—
Feel how it beats, love, strives to get to thee,
 I breathe so fast that my lips needs must part;

Your breath swims round my mouth, but let us go.

THE PRINCE.

I, Sebald, also, pluck from off the staff
The crimson banner, let it lie below,
 Above it in the wind let grasses laugh.

Now let us go, love, down the winding stair,
 With fingers intertwined: ay, feel my sword!
I wrought it long ago, with golden hair
 Flowing about the hilts, because a word,

Sung by a minstrel old, had set me dreaming
 Of a sweet bow'd-down face with yellow hair,
Betwixt green leaves I used to see it gleaming,
 A half smile on the lips, though lines of care

Had sunk the cheeks, and made the great eyes hollow;
 What other work in all the world had I,
But through all turns of fate that face to follow?
 But wars and business kept me there to die.

O child, I should have slain my brother, too,
 My brother, Love, lain moaning in the grass,
Had I not ridden out to look for you,
 When I had watch'd the gilded courtiers pass

From the golden hall. But it is strange your name
 Is not the same the minstrel sung of yore;
You call'd it Rapunzel, 'tis not the name.
 See, love, the stems shine through the open door.

Morning in the woods.

RAPUNZEL.

O Love! me and my unknown name you have well won;
　The witch's name was Rapunzel; eh! not so sweet?
No!—but is this real grass, love, that I tread upon?
　What call they these blue flowers that lean across my feet?

THE PRINCE.

Dip down your dear face in the dewy grass, O love!
　And ever let the sweet slim harebells, tenderly hung,
Kiss both your parted lips; and I will hang above,
　And try to sing that song the dreamy harper sung.

He sings.

　　'Twixt the sunlight and the shade
　　Float up memories of my maid,
　　　　God, remember Guendolen!

　　Gold or gems she did not wear,
　　But her yellow rippled hair,
　　　　Like a veil, hid Guendolen!

　　'Twixt the sunlight and the shade,
　　My rough hands so strangely made,
　　　　Folded Golden Guendolen;

　　Hands used to grip the sword-hilt hard,
　　Framed her face, while on the sward,
　　　　Tears fell down from Guendolen.

　　Guendolen now speaks no word,
　　Hands fold round about the sword,
　　　　Now no more of Guendolen.

　　Only 'twixt the light and shade
　　Floating memories of my maid
　　　　Make me pray for Guendolen.

GUENDOLEN.

I kiss thee, new-found name; but I will never go:
　Your hands need never grip the hammer'd sword again,
But all my golden hair shall ever round you flow,
　Between the light and shade from Golden Guendolen.

Afterwards, in the Palace.

KING SEBALD.

I took my armour off,
   Put on king's robes of gold,
Over her kirtle green
   The gold fell fold on fold.

THE WITCH, *out of hell.*

Guendolen! Guendolen!
One lock of hair!

GUENDOLEN.

I am so glad, for every day
He kisses me much the same way
As in the tower; under the sway
   Of all my golden hair.

KING SEBALD.

We rode throughout the town,
   A gold crown on my head,
Through all the gold-hung streets,
   "Praise God!" the people said.

THE WITCH.

Guendolen! Guendolen!
Lend me your hair!

GUENDOLEN.

Verily, I seem like one
Who, when day is almost done,
Through a thick wood meets the sun
   That blazes in her hair.

KING SEBALD.

Yea, at the palace gates,
   "Praise God!" the great knights said,
"For Sebald the high king,
   And the lady's golden head."

THE WITCH.

Woe is me! Guendolen
Sweeps back her hair.

GUENDOLEN.

Nothing wretched now, no screams;
I was unhappy once in dreams,
And even now a harsh voice seems
    To hang about my hair.

THE WITCH.

WOE! THAT ANY MAN COULD DARE
TO CLIMB UP THE YELLOW STAIR,
GLORIOUS GUENDOLEN'S GOLDEN HAIR.

CONCERNING GEFFRAY
TESTE NOIRE

AND if you meet the Canon of Chimay,
    As going to Ortaise you well may do,
Greet him from John of Castel Neuf, and say,
    All that I tell you, for all this is true.

This Geffray Teste Noire was a Gascon thief,
    Who, under shadow of the English name,
Pilled all such towns and countries as were lief
    To King Charles and St. Dennis; thought it blame

If anything escaped him; so my lord,
    The Duke of Berry, sent Sir John Bonne Lance,
And other knights, good players with the sword,
    To check this thief, and give the land a chance.

Therefore we set our bastides round the tower
    That Geffray held, the strong thief! like a king,
High perch'd upon the rock of Ventadour,
    Hopelessly strong by Christ! it was mid spring,

When first I joined the little army there
    With ten good spears; Auvergne is hot, each day
We sweated armed before the barrier,
    Good feats of arms were done there often—eh?

Your brother was slain there? I mind me now
    A right, good man-at-arms, God pardon him!
I think 'twas Geffray smote him on the brow
    With some spiked axe, and while he totter'd, dim

About the eyes, the spear of Alleyne Roux
    Slipped through his camaille and his throat; well, well!
Alleyne is paid now; your name Alleyne too?
    Mary! how strange—but this tale I would tell—

For spite of all our bastides, damned blackhead
　　Would ride abroad whene'er he chose to ride,
We could not stop him ; many a burgher bled
　　Dear gold all round his girdle ; far and wide

The villaynes dwelt in utter misery
　　'Twixt us and thief Sir Geffray ; hauled this way
By Sir Bonne Lance at one time, he gone by,
　　Down comes this Teste Noire on another day.

And therefore they dig up the stone, grind corn,
　　Hew wood, draw water, yea, they lived, in short,
As I said just now, utterly forlorn,
　　Till this our knave and blackhead was out-fought.

So Bonne Lance fretted, thinking of some trap
　　Day after day, till on a time he said ;
" John of Newcastle, if we have good hap,
　　We catch our thief in two days." " How ? " I said.

" Why, Sir, to-day he rideth out again,
　　Hoping to take well certain sumpter mules
From Carcassonne, going with little train,
　　Because, forsooth, he thinketh us mere fools ;

" But if we set an ambush in some wood,
　　He is but dead : so, Sir, take thirty spears
To Verville forest, if it seem you good."
　　Then felt I like the horse in Job, who hears

The dancing trumpet sound, and we went forth;
　　And my red lion on the spear-head flapped,
As faster than the cool wind we rode North,
　　Towards the wood of Verville ; thus it happed.

We rode a soft space on that day while spies
　　Got news about Sir Geffray ; the red wine
Under the road-side bush was clear ; the flies,
　　The dragon-flies I mind me most, did shine

In brighter arms than ever I put on ;
　　So—" Geffray," said our spies, " would pass that way
Next day at sundown ; " then he must be won ;
　　And so we enter'd Verville wood next day,

In the afternoon; through it the highway runs,
   'Twixt copses of green hazel, very thick,
And underneath, with glimmering of suns,
   The primroses are happy; the dews lick

The soft green moss. "Put cloths about your arms,
   Lest they should glitter; surely they will go
In a long thin line, watchful for alarms,
   With all their carriages of booty, so—

"Lay down my pennon in the grass—Lord God!
   What have we lying here? will they be cold,
I wonder, being so bare, above the sod,
   Instead of under? This was a knight too, fold

"Lying on fold of ancient rusted mail;
   No plate at all, gold rowels to the spurs,
And see the quiet gleam of turquoise pale
   Along the ceinture; but the long time blurs

"Even the tinder of his coat to nought,
   Except these scraps of leather; see how white
The skull is, loose within the coif! He fought
   A good fight, maybe, ere he was slain quite.

"No armour on the legs too; strange in faith—
   A little skeleton for a knight though—ah!
This one is bigger, truly without scathe
   His enemies escaped not—ribs driven out far,—

"That must have reach'd the heart, I doubt—how now,
   What say you, Aldovrand—a woman? why?"
"Under the coif a gold wreath on the brow,
   Yea, see the hair not gone to powder, lie,

"Golden, no doubt, once—yea, and very small—
   This for a knight; but for a dame, my lord,
These loose-hung bones seem shapely still, and tall,—
   Didst ever see a woman's bones, my lord?"

Often, God help me! I remember when
   I was a simple boy, fifteen years old,
The Jacquerie froze up the blood of men
   With their fell deeds, not fit now to be told:

God help again! we enter'd Beauvais town,
   Slaying them fast, whereto I help'd, mere boy
As I was then; we gentles cut them down,
   These burners and defilers, with great joy.

Reason for that, too, in the great church there
   These fiends had lit a fire, that soon went out,
The church at Beauvais being so great and fair—
   My father, who was by me, gave a shout

Between a beast's howl and a woman's scream,
   Then, panting, chuckled to me : "John, look! look!
Count the dames' skeletons!"   From some bad dream
   Like a man just awaked, my father shook;

And I, being faint with smelling the burnt bones,
   And very hot with fighting down the street,
And sick of such a life, fell down, with groans
   My head went weakly nodding to my feet.—

—An arrow had gone through her tender throat,
   And her right wrist was broken ; then I saw
The reason why she had on that war-coat,
   Their story came out clear without a flaw;

For when he knew that they were being waylaid,
   He threw it over her, yea, hood and all;
Whereby he was much hack'd, while they were stay'd
   By those their murderers ; many an one did fall

Beneath his arm, no doubt, so that he clear'd
   Their circle, bore his death-wound out of it ;
But as they rode, some archer least afear'd
   Drew a strong bow, and thereby she was hit.

Still as he rode he knew not she was dead,
   Thought her but fainted from her broken wrist,
He bound with his great leathern belt—she bled?
   Who knows! he bled too, neither was there miss'd

The beating of her heart, his heart beat well
   For both of them, till here, within this wood,
He died scarce sorry ; easy this to tell ;
   After these years the flowers forget their blood.—

How could it be ? never before that day,
   However much a soldier I might be,
Could I look on a skeleton and say
   I care not for it, shudder not—now see,

Over those bones I sat and pored for hours,
   And thought, and dream'd, and still I scarce could see
The small white bones that lay upon the flowers,
   But evermore I saw the lady ; she

With her dear gentle walking leading in,
   By a chain of silver twined about her wrists,
Her loving knight, mounted and arm'd to win
   Great honour for her, fighting in the lists.

O most pale face, that brings such joy and sorrow
   Into men's hearts—yea, too, so piercing sharp
That joy is, that it marcheth nigh to sorrow
   For ever—like an overwinded harp.

Your face must hurt me always ; pray you now,
   Doth it not hurt you too ? seemeth some pain
To hold you always, pain to hold your brow
   So smooth, unwrinkled ever ; yea again,

Your long eyes where the lids seem like to drop,
   Would you not, lady, were they shut fast, feel
Far merrier ? there so high they will not stop,
   They are most sly to glide forth and to steal

Into my heart ; *I kiss their soft lids there,*
   And in green gardens scarce can stop my lips
From wandering on your face, but that your hair
   Falls down and tangles me, back my face slips.

Or say your mouth—I saw you drink red wine
   Once at a feast ; how slowly it sank in,
As though you fear'd that some wild fate might twine
   Within that cup, and slay you for a sin.

And when you talk your lips do arch and move
   In such wise that a language new I know
Besides their sound ; they quiver, too, with love
   When you are standing silent ; know this, too,

I saw you kissing once, like a curved sword
   That bites with all its edge, did your lips lie,
Curled gently, slowly, long time could afford
   For caught-up breathings : like a dying sigh

They gather'd up their lines and went away,
   And still kept twitching with a sort of smile,
As likely to be weeping presently,—
   Your hands too—how I watch'd them all the while!

"Cry out St. Peter now," quoth Aldovrand;
   I cried, "St. Peter," broke out from the wood
With all my spears; we met them hand to hand,
   And shortly slew them; natheless, by the rood,

We caught not blackhead then, or any day;
   Months after that he died at last in bed,
From a wound pick'd up at a barrier-fray;
   That same year's end a steel bolt in the head,

And much bad living kill'd Teste Noire at last;
   John Froissart knoweth he is dead by now,
No doubt, but knoweth not this tale just past;
   Perchance then you can tell him what I show.

In my new castle, down beside the Eure,
   There is a little chapel of squared stone,
Painted inside and out; in green nook pure
   There did I lay them, every wearied bone;

And over it they lay, with stone-white hands
   Clasped fast together, hair made bright with gold
This Jaques Picard, known through many lands,
   Wrought cunningly; he's dead now—I am old.

A GOOD KNIGHT IN PRISON

SIR GUY, *being in the court of a Pagan castle.*

THIS castle where I dwell, it stands
A long way off from Christian lands,
A long way off my lady's hands,
A long way off the aspen trees,
And murmur of the lime-tree bees.

But down the Valley of the Rose
My lady often hawking goes,
Heavy of cheer; oft turns behind,
Leaning towards the western wind,
Because it bringeth to her mind
Sad whisperings of happy times,
The face of him who sings these rhymes.

King Guilbert rides beside her there,
Bends low and calls her very fair,
And strives, by pulling down his hair,
To hide from my dear lady's ken
The grisly gash I gave him, when
I cut him down at Camelot;
However he strives, he hides it not,
That tourney will not be forgot,
Besides, it is King Guilbert's lot,
Whatever he says she answers not.

Now tell me, you that are in love,
From the king's son to the wood-dove,
Which is the better, he or I?

For this king means that I should die
In this lone Pagan castle, where
The flowers droop in the bad air
On the September evening.

Look, now I take mine ease and sing,
Counting as but a little thing
The foolish spite of a bad king.

For these vile things that hem me in,
These Pagan beasts who live in sin,
The sickly flowers pale and wan,
The grim blue-bearded castellan,
The stanchions half worn-out with rust,
Whereto their banner vile they trust—
Why, all these things I hold them just
Like dragons in a missal-book,
Wherein, whenever we may look,
We see no horror, yea, delight
We have, the colours are so bright;
Likewise we note the specks of white,
And the great plates of burnish'd gold.

Just so this Pagan castle old,
And everything I can see there,
Sick-pining in the marshland air,
I note; I will go over now,
Like one who paints with knitted brow,
The flowers and all things one by one,
From the snail on the wall to the setting sun.

Four great walls, and a little one
That leads down to the barbican,
Which walls with many spears they man,
When news comes to the castellan
Of Launcelot being in the land.

And as I sit here, close at hand
Four spikes of sad sick sunflowers stand,
The castellan with a long wand
Cuts down their leaves as he goes by,
Ponderingly, with screw'd-up eye,
And fingers twisted in his beard—
Nay, was it a knight's shout I heard?
I have a hope makes me afeard:
It cannot be, but if some dream
Just for a minute made me deem

I saw among the flowers there
My lady's face with long red hair,
Pale, ivory-colour'd dear face come,
As I was wont to see her some
Fading September afternoon,
And kiss me, saying nothing, soon
To leave me by myself again;
    Could I get this by longing: vain!

    The castellan is gone: I see
On one broad yellow flower a bee
Drunk with much honey—
                  Christ! again,
Some distant knight's voice brings me pain,
I thought I had forgot to feel,
I never heard the blissful steel
These ten years past; year after year,
Through all my hopeless sojourn here,
No Christian pennon has been near;
Laus Deo! the dragging wind draws on
Over the marshes, battle won,
Knights' shouts, and axes hammering,
Yea, quicker now the dint and ring
Of flying hoofs; ah! castellan,
When they come back count man for man,
Say whom you miss.

THE PAGANS, *from the battlements.*

               Mahound to aid!
Why flee ye so like men dismay'd?

THE PAGANS, *from without.*

Nay, haste! for here is Launcelot,
Who follows quick upon us, hot
And shouting with his men-at-arms.

SIR GUY.

Also the Pagans raise alarms,
And ring the bells for fear; at last
My prison walls will be well past.

SIR LAUNCELOT, *from outside.*

Ho ! in the name of the Trinity,
Let down the drawbridge quick to me,
And open doors, that I may see
Guy the good knight.

THE PAGANS, *from the battlements.*

                Nay, Launcelot,
With mere big words ye win us not.

SIR LAUNCELOT.

Bid Miles bring up la perriere,
And archers clear the vile walls there,
Bring back the notches to the ear,
Shoot well together ! God to aid !
These miscreants will be well paid.

Hurrah ! all goes together ; Miles
Is good to win my lady's smiles
For his good shooting—Launcelot !
On knights a-pace ! this game is hot !

SIR GUY *sayeth afterwards.*

I said, I go to meet her now,
And saying so, I felt a blow
From some clench'd hand across my brow,
And fell down on the sunflowers
Just as a hammering smote my ears,
After which this I felt in sooth ;
My bare hands throttling without ruth
The hairy-throated castellan ;
Then a grim fight with those that ran
To slay me, while I shouted, "God
For the Lady Mary !" deep I trod
That evening in my own red blood ;
Nevertheless so stiff I stood,
That when the knights burst the old wood
Of the castle-doors, I was not dead.

I kiss the Lady Mary's head,
Her lips, and her hair golden red,
Because to-day we have been wed.

OLD LOVE

"You must be very old, Sir Giles,"
  I said ; he said : " Yea, very old : "
Whereat the mournfullest of smiles
  Creased his dry skin with many a fold.

" They hammer'd out my basnet point
  Into a round salade," he said,
" The basnet being quite out of joint,
  Natheless the salade rasps my head."

He gazed at the great fire awhile :
  " And you are getting old, Sir John ; "
(He said this with that cunning smile
  That was most sad ;) " we both wear on,

" Knights come to court and look at me,
  With eyebrows up, except my lord,
And my dear lady, none I see
  That know the ways of my old sword."

(My lady ! at that word no pang
  Stopp'd all my blood.)   " But tell me, John,
Is it quite true that pagans hang
  So thick about the east, that on

" The eastern sea no Venice flag
  Can fly unpaid for ? "   " True," I said,
" And in such way the miscreants drag
  Christ's cross upon the ground, I dread

" That Constantine must fall this year."
  Within my heart ; " These things are small ;
This is not small, that things outwear
  I thought were made for ever, yea, all,

Old Love

" All things go soon or late ; " I said—
   I saw the duke in court next day ;
Just as before, his grand great head
   Above his gold robes dreaming lay,

Only his face was paler ; there
   I saw his duchess sit by him ;
And she—she was changed more ; her hair
   Before my eyes that used to swim,

And make me dizzy with great bliss
   Once, when I used to watch her sit—
Her hair is bright still, yet it is
   As though some dust were thrown on it.

Her eyes are shallower, as though
   Some grey glass were behind ; her brow
And cheeks the straining bones show through,
   Are not so good for kissing now.

Her lips are drier now she is
   A great duke's wife these many years,
They will not shudder with a kiss
   As once they did, being moist with tears.

Also her hands have lost that way
   Of clinging that they used to have ;
They look'd quite easy, as they lay
   Upon the silken cushions brave

With broidery of the apples green
   My Lord Duke bears upon his shield.
Her face, alas ! that I have seen
   Look fresher than an April field,

This is all gone now ; gone also
   Her tender walking ; when she walks
She is most queenly I well know,
   And she is fair still :—as the stalks

Of faded summer-lilies are,
   So is she grown now unto me
This spring-time, when the flowers star
   The meadows, birds sing wonderfully.

I warrant once she used to cling
   About his neck, and kiss'd him so,
And then his coming step would ring
   Joy-bells for her,—some time ago.

Ah! sometimes like an idle dream
   That hinders true life overmuch,
Sometimes like a lost heaven, these seem—
   This love is not so hard to smutch.

THE GILLIFLOWER OF GOLD

A GOLDEN gilliflower to-day
I wore upon my helm alway,
And won the prize of this tourney.
    Hah! hah! la belle jaune giroflée.

However well Sir Giles might sit,
His sun was weak to wither it,
Lord Miles's blood was dew on it:
    Hah! hah! la belle jaune giroflée.

Although my spear in splinters flew,
From John's steel-coat my eye was true;
I wheel'd about, and cried for you,
    Hah! hah! la belle jaune giroflée.

Yea, do not doubt my heart was good,
Though my sword flew like rotten wood,
To shout, although I scarcely stood,
    Hah! hah! la belle jaune giroflée.

My hand was steady too, to take
My axe from round my neck, and break
John's steel-coat up for my love's sake.
    Hah! hah! la belle jaune giroflée.

When I stood in my tent again,
Arming afresh, I felt a pain
Take hold of me, I was so fain—
    Hah! hah! la belle jaune giroflée.

To hear: "*Honneur aux fils des preux!*"
Right in my ears again, and shew
The gilliflower blossom'd new.
    Hah! hah! la belle jaune giroflée.

The Sieur Guillaume against me came,
His tabard bore three points of flame
From a red heart: with little blame—
    Hah! hah! la belle jaune giroflée.

Our tough spears crackled up like straw;
He was the first to turn and draw
His sword, that had nor speck nor flaw,—
    Hah! hah! la belle jaune giroflée.

But I felt weaker than a maid,
And my brain, dizzied and afraid,
Within my helm a fierce tune play'd,—
    Hah! hah! la belle jaune giroflée.

Until I thought of your dear head,
Bow'd to the gilliflower bed,
The yellow flowers stain'd with red;—
    Hah! hah! la belle jaune giroflée.

Crash! how the swords met, *"giroflée!"*
The fierce tune in my helm would play,
"La belle! la belle! jaune giroflée!"
    Hah! hah! la belle jaune giroflée.

Once more the great swords met again,
"La belle! la belle!" but who fell then?
Le Sieur Guillaume, who struck down ten;—
    Hah! hah! la belle jaune giroflée.

And as with mazed and unarm'd face,
Toward my own crown and the Queen's place,
They led me at a gentle pace—
    Hah! hah! la belle jaune giroflée.

I almost saw your quiet head
Bow'd o'er the gilliflower bed,
The yellow flowers stain'd with red—
    Hah! hah! la belle jaune giroflée.

SHAMEFUL DEATH

THERE were four of us about that bed;
   The mass-priest knelt at the side,
I and his mother stood at the head,
   Over his feet lay the bride;
We were quite sure that he was dead,
   Though his eyes were open wide.

He did not die in the night,
   He did not die in the day,
But in the morning twilight
   His spirit pass'd away,
When neither sun nor moon was bright,
   And the trees were merely grey.

He was not slain with the sword,
   Knight's axe, or the knightly spear,
Yet spoke he never a word
   After he came in here;
I cut away the cord
   From the neck of my brother dear.

He did not strike one blow,
   For the recreants came behind,
In a place where the hornbeams grow,
   A path right hard to find,
For the hornbeam boughs swing so,
   That the twilight makes it blind.

They lighted a great torch then,
   When his arms were pinion'd fast,
Sir John the knight of the Fen,
   Sir Guy of the Dolorous Blast,
With knights threescore and ten,
   Hung brave Lord Hugh at last.

I am threescore and ten,
  And my hair is all turn'd grey,
But I met Sir John of the Fen
  Long ago on a summer day,
And am glad to think of the moment when
  I took his life away.

I am threescore and ten,
  And my strength is mostly pass'd,
But long ago I and my men,
  When the sky was overcast,
And the smoke roll'd over the reeds of the fen,
  Slew Guy of the Dolorous Blast.

And now, knights all of you,
  I pray you pray for Sir Hugh,
A good knight and a true,
  And for Alice, his wife, pray too.

THE EVE OF CRECY

GOLD on her head, and gold on her feet,
And gold where the hems of her kirtle meet,
And a golden girdle round my sweet ;—
    Ah ! qu'elle est belle La Marguerite.

Margaret's maids are fair to see,
Freshly dress'd and pleasantly ;
Margaret's hair falls down to her knee ;—
    Ah ! qu'elle est belle La Marguerite.

If I were rich I would kiss her feet,
I would kiss the place where the gold hems meet,
And the golden girdle round my sweet—
    Ah ! qu'elle est belle La Marguerite.

Ah me ! I have never touch'd her hand ;
When the arriere-ban goes through the land,
Six basnets under my pennon stand ;—
    Ah ! qu'elle est belle La Marguerite.

And many an one grins under his hood :
" Sir Lambert de Bois, with all his men good,
Has neither food nor firewood ;"—
    Ah ! qu'elle est belle La Marguerite.

If I were rich I would kiss her feet,
And the golden girdle of my sweet,
And thereabouts where the gold hems meet ;—
    Ah ! qu'elle est belle La Marguerite.

Yet even now it is good to think,
While my few poor varlets grumble and drink
In my desolate hall, where the fires sink,—
    Ah ! qu'elle est belle La Marguerite.

Of Margaret sitting glorious there,
In glory of gold and glory of hair,
And glory of glorious face most fair ;—
    Ah ! qu'elle est belle La Marguerite.

Likewise to-night I make good cheer,
Because this battle draweth near :
For what have I to lose or fear ?—
    Ah ! qu'elle est belle La Marguerite.

For, look you, my horse is good to prance
A right fair measure in this war-dance,
Before the eyes of Philip of France ;—
    Ah ! qu'elle est belle La Marguerite.

And sometime it may hap, perdie,
While my new towers stand up three and three,
And my hall gets painted fair to see—
    Ah ! qu'elle est belle La Marguerite.

That folks may say : " Times change, by the rood,
For Lambert, banneret of the wood,
Has heaps of food and firewood ;—
    Ah ! qu'elle est belle La Marguerite.

" And wonderful eyes, too, under the hood
Of a damsel of right noble blood : "
St. Ives, for Lambert of the wood !—
    Ah ! qu'elle est belle La Marguerite.

THE JUDGMENT OF GOD

SWERVE to the left, son Roger," he said,
   " When you catch his eyes through the helmet-slit,
Swerve to the left, then out at his head,
   And the Lord God give you joy of it !"

The blue owls on my father's hood
   Were a little dimm'd as I turn'd away;
This giving up of blood for blood
   Will finish here somehow to-day.

So—when I walk'd out from the tent,
   Their howling almost blinded me;
Yet for all that I was not bent
   By any shame.   Hard by, the sea

Made a noise like the aspens where
   We did that wrong, but now the place
Is very pleasant, and the air
   Blows cool on any passer's face.

And all the wrong is gather'd now
   Into the circle of these lists—
Yea, howl out, butchers ! tell me how
   His hands were cut off at the wrists;

And how Lord Roger bore his face
   A league above his spear-point, high
Above the owls, to that strong place
   Among the waters—yea, yea, cry:

"What a brave champion we have got!
   Sir Oliver, the flower of all
The Hainault knights."   The day being hot,
   He sat beneath a broad white pall,

White linen over all his steel ;
　　What a good knight he look'd ! his sword
Laid thwart his knees ; he liked to feel
　　Its steadfast edge clear as his word.

And he look'd solemn ; how his love
　　Smiled whitely on him, sick with fear !
How all the ladies up above
　　Twisted their pretty hands ! so near

The fighting was—Ellayne ! Ellayne !
　　They cannot love like you can, who
Would burn your hands off, if that pain
　　Could win a kiss—am I not true

To you for ever ? therefore I
　　Do not fear death or anything ;
If I should limp home wounded, why,
　　While I lay sick you would but sing,

And soothe me into quiet sleep.
　　If they spat on the recreaunt knight,
Threw stones at him, and cursed him deep,
　　Why then—what then ; your hand would light

So gently on his drawn-up face,
　　And you would kiss him, and in soft
Cool scented clothes would lap him, pace
　　The quiet room and weep oft,—oft

Would turn and smile, and brush his cheek
　　With your sweet chin and mouth ; and in
The order'd garden you would seek
　　The biggest roses—any sin.

And these say : " No more now my knight,
　　Or God's knight any longer "—you,
Being than they so much more white,
　　So much more pure and good and true, ¹

Will cling to me for ever—there,
　　Is not that wrong turn'd right at last
Through all these years, and I wash'd clean ?
　　Say, yea, Ellayne ; the time is past,

Since on that Christmas-day last year
    Up to your feet the fire crept,
And the smoke through the brown leaves sere
    Blinded your dear eyes that you wept;

Was it not I that caught you then,
    And kiss'd you on the saddle-bow?
Did not the blue owl mark the men
    Whose spears stood like the corn a-row?

This Oliver is a right good knight,
    And must needs beat me, as I fear,
Unless I catch him in the fight,
    My father's crafty way—John, here!

Bring up the men from the south gate,
    To help me if I fall or win,
For even if I beat, their hate
    Will grow to more than this mere grin.

THE LITTLE TOWER

Up and away through the drifting rain !
Let us ride to the Little Tower again,

Up and away from the council-board !
Do on the hauberk, gird on the sword.

The king is blind with gnashing his teeth,
Change gilded scabbard to leather sheath :

Though our arms are wet with the slanting rain,
This is joy to ride to my love again :

I laugh in his face when he bids me yield ;
Who knows one field from the other field,

For the grey rain driveth all astray ?—
Which way through the floods, good carle, I pray ?

"The left side yet ! the left side yet !
Till your hand strikes on the bridge parapet."

"Yea so : the causeway holdeth good
Under the water ? "   " Hard as wood ;

"Right away to the uplands ; speed, good knight."
Seven hours yet before the light.

Shake the wet off on the upland road ;
My taberd has grown a heavy load.

What matter ? up and down hill after hill ;
Dead grey night for five hours still.

The hill-road droppeth lower again,
Lower, down to the poplar plain.

No furlong farther for us to-night,
The Little Tower draweth in sight;

They are ringing the bells, and the torches glare,
Therefore the roofs of wet slate stare.

There she stands, and her yellow hair slantingly
Drifts the same way that the rain goes by.

Who will be faithful to us to-day,
With little but hard glaive-strokes for pay?

The grim king fumes at the council-board:
" Three more days, and then the sword;

Three more days, and my sword through his head;
And above his white brows, pale and dead,

A paper crown on the top of the spire;
And for her the stake and the witches' fire."

Therefore though it be long ere day,
Take axe and pick and spade, I pray.

Break the dams down all over the plain:
God send us three more days such rain:

Block all the upland roads with trees;
The Little Tower with no great ease

Is won, I warrant; bid them bring
Much sheep and oxen, everything

The spits are wont to turn with; wine
And wheaten bread, that we may dine

In plenty each day of the siege;
Good friends, ye know me no hard liege;

My lady is right fair, see ye!
Pray God to keep you frank and free.

Love Isabeau, keep goodly cheer;
The Little Tower will stand well here

Many a year when we are dead,
And over it our green and red,
Barred with the Lady's golden head;
From mere old age when we are dead.

THE SAILING OF THE SWORD

Across the empty garden-beds,
  When the Sword went out to sea,
I scarcely saw my sisters' heads
  Bowed each beside a tree.
I could not see the castle leads,
  When the Sword went out to sea.

Alicia wore a scarlet gown,
  When the Sword went out to sea,
But Ursula's was russet brown:
  For the mist we could not see
The scarlet roofs of the good town,
  When the Sword went out to sea.

Green holly in Alicia's hand,
  When the Sword went out to sea;
With sere oak-leaves did Ursula stand;
  O! yet alas for me!
I did but bear a peel'd white wand,
  When the Sword went out to sea.

O, russet brown and scarlet bright,
  When the Sword went out to sea,
My sisters wore; I wore but white:
  Red, brown, and white, are three;
Three damozels; each had a knight,
  When the Sword went out to sea.

Sir Robert shouted loud, and said,
  When the Sword went out to sea,
" Alicia, while I see thy head,
  What shall I bring for thee?"
" O, my sweet lord, a ruby red:"
  The Sword went out to sea.

Sir Miles said, while the sails hung down,
   When the Sword went out to sea,
"Oh, Ursula! while I see the town,
   What shall I bring for thee?"
"Dear knight, bring back a falcon brown:"
   The Sword went out to sea.

But my Roland, no word he said
   When the Sword went out to sea;
But only turn'd away his head,—
   A quick shriek came from me:
"Come back, dear lord, to your white maid;"—
   The Sword went out to sea.

The hot sun bit the garden-beds,
   When the Sword came back from sea;
Beneath an apple-tree our heads
   Stretched out toward the sea;
Grey gleam'd the thirsty castle-leads,
   When the Sword came back from sea.

Lord Robert brought a ruby red,
   When the Sword came back from sea;
He kissed Alicia on the head:
   "I am come back to thee;
'Tis time, sweet love, that we were wed,
   Now the Sword is back from sea!"

Sir Miles he bore a falcon brown,
   When the Sword came back from sea;
His arms went round tall Ursula's gown,—
   "What joy, O love, but thee?
Let us be wed in the good town,
   Now the Sword is back from sea!"

My heart grew sick, no more afraid,
   When the Sword came back from sea;
Upon the deck a tall white maid
   Sat on Lord Roland's knee;
His chin was press'd upon her head,
   When the Sword came back from sea!

SPELL-BOUND

How weary is it none can tell,
    How dismally the days go by!
I hear the tinkling of the bell,
    I see the cross against the sky.

The year wears round to autumn-tide,
    Yet comes no reaper to the corn;
The golden land is like a bride
    When first she knows herself forlorn—

She sits and weeps with all her hair
    Laid downward over tender hands;
For stained silk she hath no care,
    No care for broken ivory wands;

The silver cups beside her stand;
    The golden stars on the blue roof
Yet glitter, though against her hand
    His cold sword presses for a proof

He is not dead, but gone away.
    How many hours did she wait
For me, I wonder? Till the day
    Had faded wholly, and the gate

Clanged to behind returning knights?
    I wonder did she raise her head
And go away, fleeing the lights;
    And lay the samite on her bed,

The wedding samite strewn with pearls:
    Then sit with hands laid on her knees,
Shuddering at half-heard sound of girls
    That chatter outside in the breeze?

I wonder did her poor heart throb
　　At distant tramp of coming knight?
How often did the choking sob
　　Raise up her head and lips?　The light,

Did it come on her unawares,
　　And drag her sternly down before
People who loved her not? in prayers
　　Did she say one name and no more?

And once—all songs they ever sung,
　　All tales they ever told to me,
This only burden through them rung:
　　O ! golden love that waitest me,

The days pass on, pass on a pace,
　　Sometimes I have a little rest
In fairest dreams, when on thy face
　　My lips lie, or thy hands are prest

About my forehead, and thy lips
　　Draw near and nearer to mine own ;
But when the vision from me slips,
　　In colourless dawn I lie and moan,

And wander forth with fever'd blood,
　　That makes me start at little things,
The blackbird screaming from the wood,
　　The sudden whirr of pheasants' wings.

O ! dearest, scarcely seen by me—
　　But when that wild time had gone by,
And in these arms I folded thee,
　　Who ever thought those days could die?

Yet now I wait, and you wait too,
　　For what perchance may never come ;
You think I have forgotten you,
　　That I grew tired and went home.

But what if some day as I stood
　　Against the wall with strained hands,
And turn'd my face toward the wood,
　　Away from all the golden lands ;

And saw you come with tired feet,
   And pale face thin and wan with care,
And stained raiment no more neat,
   The white dust lying on your hair :—

Then I should say, I could not come ;
   This land was my wide prison, dear ;
I could not choose but go ; at home
   There is a wizard whom I fear :

He bound me round with silken chains
   I could not break ; he set me here
Above the golden-waving plains,
   Where never reaper cometh near.

And you have brought me my good sword,
   Wherewith in happy days of old
I won you well from knight and lord ;
   My heart upswells and I grow bold.

But I shall die unless you stand,
   —Half lying now, you are so weak,—
Within my arms, unless your hand
   Pass to and fro across my cheek.

THE WIND

Ah! no, no, it is nothing, surely nothing at all,
Only the wild-going wind round by the garden-wall,
For the dawn just now is breaking, the wind beginning to
fall.

> *Wind, wind! thou art sad, art thou kind?*
> *Wind, wind, unhappy! thou art blind,*
> *Yet still thou wanderest the lily-seed to find.*

So I will sit, and think and think of the days gone by,
Never moving my chair for fear the dogs should cry,
Making no noise at all while the flambeau burns awry.

For my chair is heavy and carved, and with sweeping green
behind
It is hung, and the dragons thereon grin out in the gusts of
the wind ;
On its folds an orange lies, with a deep gash cut in the rind.

> *Wind, wind! thou art sad, art thou kind?*
> *Wind, wind, unhappy! thou art blind,*
> *Yet still thou wanderest the lily-seed to find.*

If I move my chair it will scream, and the orange will roll
out far,
And the faint yellow juice ooze out like blood from a wizard's
jar ;
And the dogs will howl for those who went last month to the
war.

> *Wind, wind! thou art sad, art thou kind?*
> *Wind, wind, unhappy! thou art blind,*
> *Yet still thou wanderest the lily-seed to find.*

So I will sit and think of love that is over and past,
O! so long ago—yes, I will be quiet at last ;
Whether I like it or not, a grim half-slumber is cast

Over my worn old brains, that touches the roots of my heart,
And above my half-shut eyes the blue roof 'gins to part,
And show the blue spring sky, till I am ready to start

From out of the green-hung chair; but something keeps me
  still,
And I fall in a dream that I walk'd with her on the side of a
  hill,
Dotted—for was it not spring?—with tufts of the daffodil.

> *Wind, wind! thou art sad, art thou kind?*
> *Wind, wind, unhappy! thou art blind,*
> *Yet still thou wanderest the lily-seed to find.*

And Margaret as she walk'd held a painted book in her
  hand;
Her finger kept the place; I caught her, we both did stand
Face to face, on the top of the highest hill in the land.

> *Wind, wind! thou art sad, art thou kind?*
> *Wind, wind, unhappy! thou art blind,*
> *Yet still thou wanderest the lily-seed to find.*

I held to her long bare arms, but she shudder'd away from
  me,
While the flush went out of her face as her head fell back on
  a tree,
And a spasm caught her mouth, fearful for me to see;

And still I held to her arms till her shoulder touch'd my
  mail,
Weeping she totter'd forward, so glad that I should prevail,
And her hair went over my robe, like a gold flag over a sail.

> *Wind, wind! thou art sad, art thou kind?*
> *Wind, wind, unhappy! thou art blind,*
> *Yet still thou wanderest the lily-seed to find.*

I kiss'd her hard by the ear, and she kiss'd me on the brow,
And then lay down on the grass, where the mark on the moss
  is now,
And spread her arms out wide while I went down below.

> *Wind, wind! thou art sad, art thou kind?*
> *Wind, wind, unhappy! thou art blind,*
> *Yet still thou wanderest the lily-seed to find.*

And then I walk'd for a space to and fro on the side of the
    hill,
Till I gather'd and held in my arms great sheaves of the
    daffodil,
And when I came again my Margaret lay there still.

I piled them high and high above her heaving breast,
How they were caught and held in her loose ungirded vest!
But one beneath her arm died, happy so to be prest!

> *Wind, wind! thou art sad, art thou kind?*
> *Wind, wind, unhappy! thou art blind,*
> *Yet still thou wanderest the lily-seed to find.*

Again I turn'd my back and went away for an hour;
She said no word when I came again, so, flower by flower,
I counted the daffodils over, and cast them languidly lower.

> *Wind, wind! thou art sad, art thou kind?*
> *Wind, wind, unhappy! thou art blind,*
> *Yet still thou wanderest the lily-seed to find.*

My dry hands shook and shook as the green gown show'd
    again,
Clear'd from the yellow flowers, and I grew hollow with pain,
And on to us both there fell from the sun-shower drops of
    rain.

> *Wind, wind! thou art sad, art thou kind?*
> *Wind, wind, unhappy! thou art blind,*
> *Yet still thou wanderest the lily-seed to find.*

Alas! alas! there was blood on the very quiet breast,
Blood lay in the many folds of the loose ungirded vest,
Blood lay upon her arm where the flower had been prest.

I shriek'd and leapt from my chair, and the orange roll'd out
    far,
The faint yellow juice oozed out like blood from a wizard's
    jar;
And then in march'd the ghosts of those that had gone to
    the war.

I knew them by the arms that I was used to paint
Upon their long thin shields; but the colours were all grown
    faint,
And faint upon their banner was Olaf, king and saint.

> *Wind, wind! thou art sad, art thou kind?*
> *Wind, wind, unhappy! thou art blind,*
> *Yet still thou wanderest the lily-seed to find.*

THE BLUE CLOSET

THE DAMOZELS.

LADY ALICE, Lady Louise,
Between the wash of the tumbling seas
We are ready to sing, if so ye please;
So lay your long hands on the keys;
        Sing, " *Laudate pueri.*"

And ever the great bell overhead
Boom'd in the wind a knell for the dead,
Though no one toll'd it, a knell for the dead.

LADY LOUISE.

Sister, let the measure swell
Not too loud; for you sing not well
If you drown the faint boom of the bell;
        He is weary, so am I.

And ever the chevron overhead
Flapp'd on the banner of the dead;
(Was he asleep, or was he dead?)

LADY ALICE.

Alice the Queen, and Louise the Queen,
Two damozels wearing purple and green,
Four lone ladies dwelling here
From day to day and year to year;
And there is none to let us go;
To break the locks of the doors below,
Or shovel away the heaped-up snow;
And when we die no man will know
That we are dead; but they give us leave,
Once every year on Christmas-eve,

To sing in the Closet Blue one song;
And we should be so long, so long,
If we dared, in singing; for dream on dream,
They float on in a happy stream;
Float from the gold strings, float from the keys,
Float from the open'd lips of Louise;
But, alas! the sea-salt oozes through
The chinks of the tiles of the Closet Blue;
And ever the great bell overhead
Booms in the wind a knell for the dead,
The wind plays on it a knell for the dead.

[*They sing all together.*]

How long ago was it, how long ago,
He came to this tower with hands full of snow?

"Kneel down, O love Louise, kneel down," he said,
And sprinkled the dusty snow over my head.

He watch'd the snow melting, it ran through my hair,
Ran over my shoulders, white shoulders and bare.

"I cannot weep for thee, poor love Louise,
For my tears are all hidden deep under the seas;

"In a gold and blue casket she keeps all my tears,
But my eyes are no longer blue, as in old years;

"Yea, they grow grey with time, grow small and dry,
I am so feeble now, would I might die.'

And in truth the great bell overhead
Left off his pealing for the dead,
Perchance, because the wind was dead.

Will he come back again, or is he dead?
O! is he sleeping, my scarf round his head?

Or did they strangle him as he lay there,
With the long scarlet scarf I used to wear?

Only I pray thee, Lord, let him come here!
Both his soul and his body to me are most dear.

Dear Lord, that loves me, I wait to receive
Either body or spirit this wild Christmas-eve.

Through the floor shot up a lily red,
With a patch of earth from the land of the dead,
For he was strong in the land of the dead.

What matter that his cheeks were pale,
  His kind kiss'd lips all grey?
"O, love Louise, have you waited long?"
  "O, my lord Arthur, yea."

What if his hair that brush'd her cheek
  Was stiff with frozen rime?
His eyes were grown quite blue again,
  As in the happy time.

"O, love Louise, this is the key
  Of the happy golden land!
O, sisters, cross the bridge with me,
  My eyes are full of sand.
What matter that I cannot see,
  If ye take me by the hand?"

And ever the great bell overhead,
And the tumbling seas mourn'd for the dead;
For their song ceased, and they were dead.

THE TUNE OF SEVEN TOWERS

No one goes there now:
   For what is left to fetch away
From the desolate battlements all arow,
   And the lead roof heavy and grey?
" *Therefore,*" *said fair Yoland of the flowers,*
" *This is the tune of Seven Towers.*"

No one walks there now;
   Except in the white moonlight
The white ghosts walk in a row;
   If one could see it, an awful sight,—
" *Listen!*" *said fair Yoland of the flowers,*
" *This is the tune of Seven Towers.*"

But none can see them now,
   Though they sit by the side of the moat,
Feet half in the water, there in a row,
   Long hair in the wind afloat.
" *Therefore,*" *said fair Yoland of the flowers,*
" *This is the tune of Seven Towers.*"

If any will go to it now,
   He must go to it all alone,
Its gates will not open to any row
   Of glittering spears—will *you* go alone?
" *Listen!*" *said fair Yoland of the flowers,*
" *This is the tune of Seven Towers.*"

By my love go there now,
   To fetch me my coif away,
My coif and my kirtle, with pearls arow,
   Oliver, go to-day!
" *Therefore,*" *said fair Yoland of the flowers,*
" *This is the tune of Seven Towers.*"

I am unhappy now,
  I cannot tell you **why**;
If you go, the priests and I in a **row**
  Will pray that you may not die.
" *Listen!*" *said fair Yoland of the flowers,*
" *This is the tune of Seven Towers.*"

If you will go for me now,
  I will kiss your mouth at last;
    [*She sayeth inwardly.*]
(*The graves stand grey in a row,*)
  Oliver, hold me fast!
" *Therefore,*" *said fair Yoland of the flowers,*
" *This is the tune of Seven Towers.*"

GOLDEN WINGS

MIDWAYS of a walled garden,
  In the happy poplar land,
  Did an ancient castle stand,
With an old knight for a warden.

Many scarlet bricks there were
  In its walls, and old grey stone;
  Over which red apples shone
At the right time of the year.

On the bricks the green moss grew,
  Yellow lichen on the stone,
  Over which red apples shone;
Little war that castle knew.

Deep green water fill'd the moat,
  Each side had a red-brick lip,
  Green and mossy with the drip
Of dew and rain; there was a boat

Of carven wood, with hangings green
  About the stern; it was great bliss
  For lovers to sit there and kiss
In the hot summer noons, not seen.

Across the moat the fresh west wind
  In very little ripples went;
  The way the heavy aspens bent
Towards it, was a thing to mind.

The painted drawbridge over it
  Went up and down with gilded chains,
  'Twas pleasant in the summer rains
Within the bridge-house there to sit.

There were five swans that ne'er did eat
 The water-weeds, for ladies came
 Each day, and young knights did the same,
And gave them cakes and bread for meat.

They had a house of painted wood,
 A red roof gold-spiked over it,
 Wherein upon their eggs to sit
Week after week; no drop of blood,

Drawn from men's bodies by sword-blows,
 Came ever there, or any tear;
 Most certainly from year to year
'Twas pleasant as a Provence rose.

The banners seem'd quite full of ease,
 That over the turret-roofs hung down;
 The battlements could get no frown
From the flower-moulded cornices.

Who walked in that garden there?
 Miles and Giles and Isabeau,
 Tall Jehane du Castel beau,
Alice of the golden hair,

Big Sir Gervaise, the good knight,
 Fair Ellayne le Violet,
 Mary, Constance fille de fay,
Many dames with footfall light.

Whosoever wander'd there,
 Whether it be dame or knight,
 Half of scarlet, half of white
Their raiment was; of roses fair

Each wore a garland on the head,
 At Ladies' Gard the way was so:
 Fair Jehane du Castel beau
Wore her wreath till it was dead.

Little joy she had of it,
 Of the raiment white and red,
 Or the garland on her head,
She had none with whom to sit

Golden Wings

In the carven boat at noon;
  None the more did Jehane weep,
  She would only stand and keep
Saying, "He will be here soon."

Many times in the long day
  Miles and Giles and Gervaise past,
  Holding each some white hand fast,
Every time they heard her say:

"Summer cometh to an end,
  Undern cometh after noon;
  Golden wings will be here soon,
What if I some token send?"

Wherefore that night within the hall,
  With open mouth and open eyes,
  Like some one listening with surprise,
She sat before the sight of all.

Stoop'd down a little she sat there,
  With neck stretch'd out and chin thrown up,
  One hand around a golden cup;
And strangely with her fingers fair

She beat some tune upon the gold;
  The minstrels in the gallery
  Sung: "Arthur, who will never die,
In Avallon he groweth old."

And when the song was ended, she
  Rose and caught up her gown and ran;
  None stopp'd her eager face and wan
Of all that pleasant company.

Right so within her own chamber
  Upon her bed she sat; and drew
  Her breath in quick gasps; till she knew
That no man follow'd after her:

She took the garland from her head,
  Loosed all her hair, and let it lie
  Upon the coverlit; thereby
She laid the gown of white and red;

And she took off her scarlet shoon,
  And bared her feet; still more and more
  Her sweet face redden'd; evermore
She murmur'd: "He will be here soon;

" Truly he cannot fail to know
  My tender body waits him here;
  And if he knows, I have no fear
For poor Jehane du Castel beau."

She took a sword within her hand,
  Whose hilts were silver, and she sung,
  Somehow like this, wild words that rung
A long way over the moonlit land:—

    Gold wings across the sea!
    Grey light from tree to tree,
    Gold hair beside my knee,
    I pray thee come to me,
    Gold wings!

            The water slips,
    The red-bill'd moorhen dips.
    Sweet kisses on red lips;
    Alas! the red rust grips,
    And the blood-red dagger rips,
    Yet, O knight, come to me!

    Are not my blue eyes sweet?
    The west wind from the wheat
    Blows cold across my feet;
    Is it not time to meet
    Gold wings across the sea?

    White swans on the green moat,
    Small feathers left afloat
    By the blue-painted boat;
    Swift running of the stoat;
    Sweet gurgling note by note
    Of sweet music.

            O gold wings,
    Listen how gold hair sings,
    And the Ladies' Castle rings,
    Gold wings across the sea.

I sit on a purple bed,
Outside, the wall is red,
Thereby the apple hangs,
And the wasp, caught by the fangs,

Dies in the autumn night,
And the bat flits till light,
And the love-crazed knight

Kisses the long wet grass:
The weary days pass,—
Gold wings across the sea!

Gold wings across the sea!
Moonlight from tree to tree,
Sweet hair laid on my knee,
O, sweet knight, come to me!

Gold wings, the short night slips,
The white swan's long neck drips,
I pray thee, kiss my lips,
Gold wings across the sea.

No answer through the moonlit night;
No answer in the cold grey dawn;
No answer when the shaven lawn
Grew green, and all the roses bright.

Her tired feet look'd cold and thin,
Her lips were twitch'd, and wretched tears,
Some, as she lay, roll'd past her ears,
Some fell from off her quivering chin.

Her long throat, stretch'd to its full length,
Rose up and fell right brokenly;
As though the unhappy heart was nigh
Striving to break with all its strength.

And when she slipp'd from off the bed,
Her cramp'd feet would not hold her; she
Sank down and crept on hand and knee,
On the window-sill she laid her head.

There, with crooked arm upon the sill,
    She look'd out, muttering dismally:
    "There is no sail upon the sea,
No pennon on the empty hill.

"I cannot stay here all alone,
    Or meet their happy faces here,
    And wretchedly I have no fear;
A little while, and I am gone."

Therewith she rose upon her feet,
    And totter'd; cold and misery
    Still made the deep sobs come, till she
At last stretch'd out her fingers sweet,

And caught the great sword in her hand;
    And, stealing down the silent stair,
    Barefooted in the morning air,
And only in her smock, did stand

Upright upon the green lawn grass;
    And hope grew in her as she said:
    "I have thrown off the white and red,
And pray God it may come to pass

"I meet him; if ten years go by
    Before I meet him; if, indeed,
    Meanwhile both soul and body bleed,
Yet there is end of misery,

"And I have hope.   He could not come,
    But I can go to him and show
    These new things I have got to know,
And make him speak, who has been dumb."

O Jehane! the red morning sun
    Changed her white feet to glowing gold,
    Upon her smock, on crease and fold,
Changed that to gold which had been dun.

O Miles, and Giles, and Isabeau,
    Fair Ellayne le Violet,
    Mary, Constance fille de fay!
Where is Jehane du Castel beau?

O big Gervaise ride apace!
   Down to the hard yellow sand,
   Where the water meets the land.
This is Jehane by her face;

Why has she a broken sword?
   Mary! she is slain outright;
   Verily a piteous sight;
Take her up without a word!

Giles and Miles and Gervaise there,
   Ladies' Gard must meet the war;
   Whatsoever knights these are,
Man the walls withouten fear!

Axes to the apple-trees,
   Axes to the aspens tall!
   Barriers without the wall
May be lightly made of these.

O poor shivering Isabeau;
   Poor Ellayne le Violet,
   Bent with fear! we miss to-day
Brave Jehane du Castel beau.

O poor Mary, weeping so!
   Wretched Constance fille de fay!
   Verily we miss to-day
Fair Jehane du Castel beau.

The apples now grow green and sour
   Upon the mouldering castle-wall,
   Before they ripen there they fall:
There are no banners on the tower.

The draggled swans most eagerly eat
   The green weeds trailing in the moat;
   Inside the rotting leaky boat
You see a slain man's stiffen'd feet.

THE HAYSTACK IN THE FLOODS

HAD she come all the way for this,
To part at last without a kiss?
Yea, had she borne the dirt and rain
That her own eyes might see him slain
Beside the haystack in the floods?

Along the dripping leafless woods,
The stirrup touching either shoe,
She rode astride as troopers do;
With kirtle kilted to her knee,
To which the mud splash'd wretchedly;
And the wet dripp'd from every tree
Upon her head and heavy hair,
And on her eyelids broad and fair;
The tears and rain ran down her face.

By fits and starts they rode apace,
And very often was his place
Far off from her; he had to ride
Ahead, to see what might betide
When the roads cross'd; and sometimes, when
There rose a murmuring from his men,
Had to turn back with promises;
Ah me! she had but little ease;
And often for pure doubt and dread
She sobb'd, made giddy in the head
By the swift riding; while, for cold,
Her slender fingers scarce could hold
The wet reins: yea, and scarcely, too,
She felt the foot within her shoe
Against the stirrup: all for this,
To part at last without a kiss
Beside the haystack in the floods.

For when they near'd that old soak'd hay,
They saw across the only way
That Judas, Godmar, and the three
Red running lions dismally
Grinn'd from his pennon, under which,
In one straight line along the ditch,
They counted thirty heads.

                              So then,
While Robert turn'd round to his men,
She saw at once the wretched end,
And, stooping down, tried hard to rend
Her coif the wrong way from her head,
And hid her eyes ; while Robert said :
" Nay, love, 'tis scarcely two to one,
At Poictiers where we made them run
So fast—why, sweet my love, good cheer,
The Gascon frontier is so near,
Nought after this."

                    But, " O," she said,
" My God ! my God ! I have to tread
The long way back without you ; then
The court at Paris ; those six men ;
The gratings of the Chatelet ;
The swift Seine on some rainy day
Like this, and people standing by,
And laughing, while my weak hands try
To recollect how strong men swim.
All this, or else a life with him,
For which I should be damned at last,
Would God that this next hour were past !"

He answer'd not, but cried his cry,
" St. George for Marny ! " cheerily ;
And laid his hand upon her rein.
Alas ! no man of all his train
Gave back that cheery cry again ;
And, while for rage his thumb beat fast
Upon his sword-hilt, some one cast
About his neck a kerchief long,
And bound him.

                    Then they went along
To Godmar; who said: "Now, Jehane,
Your lover's life is on the wane
So fast, that, if this very hour
You yield not as my paramour,
He will not see the rain leave off—
Nay, keep your tongue from gibe and scoff,
Sir Robert, or I slay you now."

She laid her hand upon her brow,
Then gazed upon the palm, as though
She thought her forehead bled, and—"No."
She said, and turn'd her head away,
As there were nothing else to say,
And everything were settled: red
Grew Godmar's face from chin to head:
"Jehane, on yonder hill there stands
My castle, guarding well my lands:
What hinders me from taking you,
And doing that I list to do
To your fair wilful body, while
Your knight lies dead?"

                        A wicked smile
Wrinkled her face, her lips grew thin,
A long way out she thrust her chin:
"You know that I should strangle you
While you were sleeping; or bite through
Your throat, by God's help—ah!" she said,
"Lord Jesus, pity your poor maid!
For in such wise they hem me in,
I cannot choose but sin and sin,
Whatever happens: yet I think
They could not make me eat or drink,
And so should I just reach my rest."
"Nay, if you do not my behest,
O Jehane! though I love you well,"
Said Godmar, "would I fail to tell
All that I know." "Foul lies," she said.
"Eh? lies my Jehane? by God's head,
At Paris folks would deem them true!
Do you know, Jehane, they cry for you,

' Jehane the brown ! Jehane the brown !
Give us Jehane to burn or drown ! '—
Eh—gag me, Robert !—sweet my friend,
This were indeed a piteous end
For those long fingers, and long feet,
And long neck, and smooth shoulders sweet ;
An end that few men would forget
That saw it—So, an hour yet :
Consider, Jehane, which to take
Of life or death ! "

                              So, scarce awake,
Dismounting, did she leave that place,
And totter some yards : with her face
Turn'd upward to the sky she lay,
Her head on a wet heap of hay,
And fell asleep : and while she slept,
And did not dream, the minutes crept
Round to the twelve again ; but she,
Being waked at last, sigh'd quietly,
And strangely childlike came, and said :
" I will not."   Straightway Godmar's head,
As though it hung on strong wires, turn'd
Most sharply round, and his face burn'd.

For Robert—both his eyes were dry,
He could not weep, but gloomily
He seem'd to watch the rain ; yea, too,
His lips were firm ; he tried once more
To touch her lips ; she reach'd out, sore
And vain desire so tortured them,
The poor grey lips, and now the hem
Of his sleeve brush'd them.

                              With a start
Up Godmar rose, thrust them apart ;
From Robert's throat he loosed the bands
Of silk and mail ; with empty hands
Held out, she stood and gazed, and saw,
The long bright blade without a flaw
Glide out from Godmar's sheath, his hand
In Robert's hair ; she saw him bend
Back Robert's head ; she saw him send

The thin steel down; the blow told well,
Right backward the knight Robert fell,
And moan'd as dogs do, being half dead,
Unwitting, as I deem: so then
Godmar turn'd grinning to his men,
Who ran, some five or six, and beat
His head to pieces at their feet.

Then Godmar turn'd again and said:
"So, Jehane, the first fitte is read!
Take note, my lady, that your way
Lies backward to the Chatelet!"
She shook her head and gazed awhile
At her cold hands with a rueful smile,
As though this thing had made her mad.

This was the parting that they had
Beside the haystack in the floods.

TWO RED ROSES ACROSS THE MOON

THERE was a lady lived in a hall,
Large in the eyes, and slim and tall;
And ever she sung from noon to noon,
Two red roses across the moon.

There was a knight came riding by
In early spring, when the roads were dry;
And he heard that lady sing at the noon,
Two red roses across the moon.

Yet none the more he stopp'd at all,
But he rode a-gallop past the hall;
And left that lady singing at noon,
Two red roses across the moon.

Because, forsooth, the battle was set,
And the scarlet and blue had got to be met,
He rode on the spur till the next warm noon:—
Two red roses across the moon.

But the battle was scatter'd from hill to hill,
From the windmill to the watermill;
And he said to himself, as it near'd the noon,
Two red roses across the moon.

You scarce could see for the scarlet and blue,
A golden helm or a golden shoe;
So he cried, as the fight grew thick at the noon,
Two red roses across the moon!

Verily then the gold bore through
The huddled spears of the scarlet and blue;
And they cried, as they cut them down at the noon,
Two red roses across the moon!

I trow he stopp'd when he rode again
By the hall, though draggled sore with the rain;
And his lips were pinch'd to kiss at the noon
Two red roses across the moon.

Under the may she stoop'd to the crown,
All was gold, there was nothing of brown;
And the horns blew up in the hall at noon,
Two red roses across the moon.

WELLAND RIVER

FAIR Ellayne she walk'd by Welland river,
  Across the lily lee:
O, gentle Sir Robert, ye are not kind
  To stay so long at sea.

Over the marshland none can see
  Your scarlet pennon fair;
O, leave the Easterlings alone,
  Because of my golden hair.

The day when over Stamford bridge
  That dear pennon I see
Go up toward the goodly street,
  'Twill be a fair day for me.

O, let the bonny pennon bide
  At Stamford, the good town,
And let the Easterlings go free,
  And their ships go up and down.

For every day that passes by
  I wax both pale and green,
From gold to gold of my girdle
  There is an inch between.

I sew'd it up with scarlet silk
  Last night upon my knee,
And my heart grew sad and sore to think
  Thy face I'd never see.

I sew'd it up with scarlet silk,
  As I lay upon my bed:
Sorrow! the man I'll never see
  That had my maidenhead.

But as Ellayne sat on her window-seat
   And comb'd her yellow hair,
She saw come over Stamford bridge
   The scarlet pennon fair.

As Ellayne lay and sicken'd sore,
   The gold shoes on her feet,
She saw Sir Robert and his men
   Ride up the Stamford street.

He had a coat of fine red gold,
   And a bascinet of steel;
Take note his goodly Collayne sword
   Smote the spur upon his heel.

And by his side, on a grey jennet,
   There rode a fair lady,
For every ruby Ellayne wore,
   I count she carried three.

Say, was not Ellayne's gold hair fine,
   That fell to her middle free?
But that lady's hair down in the street,
   Fell lower than her knee.

Fair Ellayne's face, from sorrow and grief,
   Was waxen pale and green:
That lady's face was goodly red,
   She had but little tene.

But as he pass'd by her window
   He grew a little wroth:
O, why does yon pale face look at me
   From out the golden cloth?

It is some burd, the fair dame said
   That aye rode him beside,
Has come to see your bonny face
   This merry summer-tide.

But Ellayne let a lily-flower
   Light on his cap of steel:
O, I have gotten two hounds, fair knight,
   The one has served me well.

But the other, just an hour agone,
   Has come from over sea,
And all his fell is sleek and fine,
   But little he knows of me.

Now, which shall I let go, fair knight,
   And which shall bide with me?
O, lady, have no doubt to keep
   The one that best loveth thee.

O, Robert, see how sick I am!
   Ye do not so by me.
Lie still, fair love! have ye gotten harm
   While I was on the sea?

Of one gift, Robert, that ye gave,
   I sicken to the death,
I pray you nurse-tend me, my knight,
   Whiles that I have my breath.

Six fathoms from the Stamford bridge
   He left that dame to stand,
And whiles she wept, and whiles she cursed
   That she ever had taken land,

He has kiss'd sweet Ellayne on the mouth,
   And fair she fell asleep,
And long and long days after that
   Sir Robert's house she did keep.

RIDING TOGETHER

For many, many days together
　The wind blew steady from the East;
For many days hot grew the weather,
　About the time of our Lady's Feast.

For many days we rode together,
　Yet met we neither friend nor foe;
Hotter and clearer grew the weather,
　Steadily did the East wind blow.

We saw the trees in the hot, bright weather,
　Clear-cut, with shadows very black,
As freely we rode on together
　With helms unlaced and bridles slack.

And often, as we rode together,
　We, looking down the green-bank'd stream,
Saw flowers in the sunny weather,
　And saw the bubble-making bream.

And in the night lay down together,
　And hung above our heads the rood,
Or watch'd night-long in the dewy weather,
　The while the moon did watch the wood.

Our spears stood bright and thick together,
　Straight out the banners stream'd behind,
As we gallop'd on in the sunny weather,
　With faces turn'd towards the wind.

Down sank our threescore spears together,
　As thick we saw the pagans ride;
His eager face in the clear fresh weather,
　Shone out that last time by my side.

Riding Together

Up the sweep of the bridge we dash'd together,
  It lock'd to the crash of the meeting spears,
Down rain'd the buds of the dear spring weather,
  The elm-tree flowers fell like tears.

There, as we roll'd and writhed together,
  I threw my arms above my head,
For close by my side, in the lovely weather,
  I saw him reel and fall back dead.

I and the slayer met together,
  He waited the death-stroke there in his place,
With thoughts of death, in the lovely weather,
  Gapingly mazed at my madden'd face.

Madly I fought as we fought together;
  In vain: the little Christian band
The pagans drown'd, as in stormy weather,
  The river drowns low-lying land.

They bound my blood-stain'd hands together,
  They bound his corpse to nod by my side:
Then on we rode, in the bright March weather,
  With clash of cymbals did we ride.

We ride no more, no more together;
  My prison-bars are thick and strong,
I take no heed of any weather,
  The sweet Saints grant I live not long.

FATHER JOHN'S WAR-SONG

The Reapers.

So many reapers, Father John,
So many reapers and no little son,
To meet you when the day is done,
With little stiff legs to waddle and run?
Pray you beg, borrow, or steal one son.
Hurrah for the corn-sheaves of Father John!

Father John.

O maiden Mary, be wary, be wary!
And go not down to the river,
Lest the kingfisher, your evil wisher,
Lure you down to the river,
Lest your white feet grow muddy,
Your red hair too ruddy
With the river-mud so red:
But when you are wed
Go down to the river;
O maiden Mary, be very wary,
And dwell among the corn!
See, this dame Alice, maiden Mary,
Her hair is thin and white,
But she is a housewife good and wary,
And a great steel key hangs bright
From her gown, as red as the flowers in corn;
She is good and old like the autumn corn.

Maiden Mary.

This is knight Roland, Father John,
Stark in his arms from a field half-won;
Ask him if he has seen your son:
Roland, lay your sword on the corn,
The piled-up sheaves of the golden corn.

KNIGHT ROLAND.

Why does she kiss me, Father John?
She is my true love truly won;
Under my helm is room for one,
But the molten lead-streams trickle and run
From my roof-tree, burning under the sun;
No corn to burn, we had eaten the corn,
There was no waste of the golden corn.

FATHER JOHN.

Ho, you reapers, away from the corn,
To march with the banner of Father John!

THE REAPERS.

We will win a house for Roland his son,
And for maiden Mary with hair like corn,
As red as the reddest of golden corn.

OMNES.

Father John, you have got you a son,
Seven feet high when his helm is on!
Pennon of Roland, banner of John,
Star of Mary, march well on.

SIR GILES' WAR-SONG

Ho! is there any will ride with me,
Sir Giles, le bon des barrières?

The clink of arms is good to hear,
The flap of pennons fair to see;
   Ho! is there any will ride with me,
     Sir Giles, le bon des barrières?

The leopards and lilies are fair to see,
"St. George Guienne" right good to hear:
   Ho! is there any will ride with me,
     Sir Giles, le bon des barrières?

I stood by the barrier,
My coat being blazon'd fair to see;
   Ho! is there any will ride with me,
     Sir Giles, le bon des barrières?

Clisson put out his head to see,
And lifted his basnet up to hear;
   I pull'd him through the bars to ME,
     Sir Giles, le bon des barrières.

NEAR AVALON

A SHIP with shields before the sun,
Six maidens round the mast,
A red-gold crown on every one,
A green gown on the last.

The fluttering green banners there
Are wrought with ladies' heads most fair,
And a portraiture of Guenevere
The middle of each sail doth bear.

A ship with sails before the wind,
And round the helm six knights,
Their heaumes are on, whereby, half blind,
They pass by many sights.

The tatter'd scarlet banners there,
Right soon will leave the spear-heads bare,
Those six knights sorrowfully bear
In all their heaumes some yellow hair.

PRAISE OF MY LADY

My lady seems of ivory
Forehead, straight nose, and cheeks that be
Hollow'd a little mournfully.
    Beata mea Domina!

Her forehead, overshadow'd much
By bows of hair, has a wave such
As God was good to make for me.
    Beata mea Domina!

Nor greatly long my lady's hair,
Nor yet with yellow colour fair,
But thick and crisped wonderfully:
    Beata mea Domina!

Heavy to make the pale face sad,
And dark, but dead as though it had
Been forged by God most wonderfully
    —Beata mea Domina!—

Of some strange metal, thread by thread,
To stand out from my lady's head,
Not moving much to tangle me.
    Beata mea Domina!

Beneath her brows the lids fall slow,
The lashes a clear shadow throw
Where I would wish my lips to be.
    Beata mea Domina!

Her great eyes, standing far apart,
Draw up some memory from her heart,
And gaze out very mournfully;
    —Beata mea Domina!—

So beautiful and kind they are,
But most times looking out afar,
Waiting for something, not for me.
Beata mea Domina!

I wonder if the lashes long
Are those that do her bright eyes wrong,
For always half tears seem to be
—Beata mea Domina!—

Lurking below the underlid,
Darkening the place where they lie hid—
If they should rise and flow for me!
Beata mea Domina!

Her full lips being made to kiss,
Curl'd up and pensive each one is;
This makes me faint to stand and see.
Beata mea Domina!

Her lips are not contented now,
Because the hours pass so slow
Towards a sweet time: (pray for me),
—Beata mea Domina!—

Nay, hold thy peace! for who can tell;
But this at least I know full well,
Her lips are parted longingly,
—Beata mea Domina!—

So passionate and swift to move,
To pluck at any flying love,
That I grow faint to stand and see.
Beata mea Domina!

Yea! there beneath them is her chin,
So fine and round, it were a sin
To feel no weaker when I see
—Beata mea Domina!—

God's dealings; for with so much care
And troublous, faint lines wrought in there,
He finishes her face for me.
Beata mea Domina!

Of her long neck what shall I say?
What things about her body's sway,
Like a knight's pennon or slim tree
          —Beata mea Domina!—

Set gently waving in the wind;
Or her long hands that I may find
On some day sweet to move o'er me?
          Beata mea Domina!

God pity me though, if I miss'd
The telling, how along her wrist
The veins creep, dying languidly
          —Beata mea Domina!—

Inside her tender palm and thin.
Now give me pardon, dear, wherein
My voice is weak and vexes thee.
          Beata mea Domina!

All men that see her any time,
I charge you straightly in this rhyme,
What, and wherever you may be,
          —Beata mea Domina!—

To kneel before her; as for me,
I choke and grow quite faint to see
My lady moving graciously.
          Beata mea Domina!

SUMMER DAWN

Pray but one prayer for me 'twixt thy closed lips,
  Think but one thought of me up in the stars.
The summer night waneth, the morning light slips,
  Faint and grey 'twixt the leaves of the aspen, betwixt
    the cloud-bars,
That are patiently waiting there for the dawn:
  Patient and colourless, though Heaven's gold
Waits to float through them along with the sun.
Far out in the meadows, above the young corn,
  The heavy elms wait, and restless and cold
The uneasy wind rises; the roses are dun;
Through the long twilight they pray for the dawn,
Round the lone house in the midst of the corn.
  Speak but one word to me over the corn,
  Over the tender, bow'd locks of the corn.

IN PRISON

WEARILY, drearily,
Half the day long,
Flap the great banners
High over the stone;
Strangely and eerily
Sounds the wind's song,
Bending the banner-poles.

While, all alone,
Watching the loophole's spark,
Lie I, with life all dark,
Feet tether'd, hands fetter'd
Fast to the stone,
The grim walls, square letter'd
With prison'd men's groan.

Still strain the banner-poles
Through the wind's song,
Westward the banner rolls
Over my wrong.

THE STORY OF THE UNKNOWN CHURCH

AND OTHER PROSE ROMANCES

THE STORY OF THE UNKNOWN CHURCH

I WAS the master-mason of a church that was built more than six hundred years ago; it is now two hundred years since that church vanished from the face of the earth, it was destroyed utterly,—no fragment of it was left; not even the great pillars that bore up the tower at the cross, where the choir used to join the nave. No one knows now even where it stood, only in this very autumn-tide, if you knew the place, you would see the heaps made by the earth-covered ruins heaving the yellow corn into glorious waves, so that the place where my church used to be is as beautiful now as when it stood in all its splendour. I do not remember very much about the land where my church was; I have quite forgotten the name of it, but I know it was very beautiful, and even now, while I am thinking of it, comes a flood of old memories, and I almost seem to see it again,—that old beautiful land! only dimly do I see it in spring and summer and winter, but I see it in autumn-tide clearly now; yes, clearer, clearer, oh! so bright and glorious! yet it was beautiful too in spring, when the brown earth began to grow green: beautiful in summer, when the blue sky looked so much bluer, if you could hem a piece of it in between the new white carving; beautiful in the solemn starry nights, so solemn that it almost reached agony—the awe and joy one had in their great beauty. But of all these beautiful times, I remember the whole only of autumn-tide; the others come in bits to me; I can think only of parts of them, but all of autumn; and of all days and nights in autumn, I remember one more particularly. That autumn day the church was nearly finished, and the monks, for whom we were building the church, and the people, who lived in the town hard by, crowded round us oftentimes to watch us carving.

Now the great Church, and the buildings of the Abbey where the monks lived, were about three miles from the town, and the town stood on a hill overlooking the rich autumn country : it was girt about with great walls that had overhanging battlements, and towers at certain places all along the walls, and often we could see from the churchyard or the Abbey garden, the flash of helmets and spears, and the dim shadowy waving of banners, as the knights and lords and men-at-arms passed to and fro along the battlements ; and we could see too in the town the three spires of the three churches ; and the spire of the Cathedral, which was the tallest of the three, was gilt all over with gold, and always at night-time a great lamp shone from it that hung in the spire midway between the roof of the church and the cross at the top of the spire.   The Abbey where we built the Church was not girt by stone walls, but by a circle of poplar trees, and whenever a wind passed over them, were it ever so little a breath, it set them all a-ripple ; and when the wind was high, they bowed and swayed very low, and the wind, as it lifted the leaves, and showed their silvery white sides, or as again in the lulls of it, it let them drop, kept on changing the trees from green to white, and white to green ; moreover, through the boughs and trunks of the poplars, we caught glimpses of the great golden corn sea, waving, waving, waving for leagues and leagues ; and among the corn grew burning scarlet poppies, and blue corn-flowers ; and the corn-flowers were so blue, that they gleamed, and seemed to burn with a steady light, as they grew beside the poppies among the gold of the wheat.   Through the corn sea ran a blue river, and always green meadows and lines of tall poplars followed its windings.   The old Church had been burned, and that was the reason why the monks caused me to build the new one ; the buildings of the Abbey were built at the same time as the burned-down Church, more than a hundred years before I was born, and they were on the north side of the Church, and joined to it by a cloister of round arches, and in the midst of the cloister was a lawn, and in the midst of that lawn, a fountain of marble, carved round about with flowers and strange beasts ; and at the edge of the lawn, near the round arches, were a great many sun-flowers that were all in blossom on that autumn day ; and up many of the pillars of the cloister crept passion-flowers and roses.

Then farther from the Church, and past the cloister and its buildings, were many detached buildings, and a great garden round them, all within the circle of the poplar trees; in the garden were trellises covered over with roses, and convolvulus, and the great-leaved fiery nasturtium; and specially all along by the poplar trees were there trellises, but on these grew nothing but deep crimson roses; the hollyhocks too were all out in blossom at that time, great spires of pink, and orange, and red, and white, with their soft, downy leaves. I said that nothing grew on the trellises by the poplars but crimson roses, but I was not quite right, for in many places the wild flowers had crept into the garden from without; lush green briony, with green-white blossoms, that grows so fast, one could almost think that we see it grow, and deadly nightshade, La bella donna, O! so beautiful; red berry, and purple, yellow-spiked flower, and deadly, cruel-looking, dark green leaf, all growing together in the glorious days of early autumn. And in the midst of the great garden was a conduit, with its sides carved with histories from the Bible, and there was on it too, as on the fountain in the cloister, much carving of flowers and strange beasts. Now the Church itself was surrounded on every side but the north by the cemetery, and there were many graves there, both of monks and of laymen, and often the friends of those, whose bodies lay there, had planted flowers about the graves of those they loved. I remember one such particularly, for at the head of it was a cross of carved wood, and at the foot of it, facing the cross, three tall sun-flowers; then in the midst of the cemetery was a cross of stone, carved on one side with the Crucifixion of our Lord Jesus Christ, and on the other with Our Lady holding the Divine Child. So that day, that I specially remember, in Autumn-tide, when the Church was nearly finished, I was carving in the central porch of the west front; (for I carved all those bas-reliefs in the west front with my own hand;) beneath me my sister Margaret was carving at the flower-work, and the little quatrefoils that carry the signs of the zodiac and emblems of the months: now my sister Margaret was rather more than twenty years old at that time, and she was very beautiful, with dark brown hair and deep calm violet eyes. I had lived with her all my life, lived with her almost alone latterly, for our father and mother died when she was quite young, and I loved her very much, though I was not thinking of her just then, as she stood beneath me carving. Now the central porch was carved with a bas-relief of the Last Judgment, and it was divided into three parts by horizontal bands of deep flower-work. In the lowest division, just over the doors, was carved The Rising of the Dead; above were angels blowing long trumpets, and Michael the Archangel weighing the souls, and the blessed led into heaven by angels, and the lost into hell by the devil; and in the topmost division was the Judge of the world.

All the figures in the porch were finished except one, and I remember when I woke that morning my exultation at the thought of my Church being so nearly finished; I remember, too, how a kind of misgiving mingled with the exultation, which, try all I could, I was unable to shake off; I thought then it was a rebuke for my pride, well, perhaps it was. The figure I had to carve was Abraham, sitting with a blossoming tree on each side of him, holding in his two hands the corners of his great robe, so that it made a mighty fold, wherein, with their hands crossed over their breasts, were the souls of the faithful, of whom he was called Father: I stood on the scaffolding for some time, while Margaret's chisel worked on bravely down below. I took mine in my hand, and stood so, listening to the noise of the masons inside, and two monks of the Abbey came and stood below me, and a knight, holding his little daughter by the hand, who every now and then looked up at him, and asked him strange questions. I did not think of these long, but began to think of Abraham, yet I could not think of him sitting there, quiet and solemn, while the Judgment-Trumpet was being blown; I rather thought of him as he looked when he chased those kings so far; riding far ahead of any of his company, with his mail-hood off his head, and lying in grim folds down his back, with the strong west wind blowing his wild black hair far out behind him, with the wind rippling the long scarlet pennon of his lance; riding there amid the rocks and the sands alone; with the last gleam of the armour of the beaten kings disappearing behind the winding of the pass; with his company a long, long way behind, quite out of sight, though their trumpets sounded faintly among the clefts of the rocks; and so I thought I saw him, till in his fierce chase he leapt, horse and man, into a deep river, quiet, swift, and smooth; and there was something in the moving of the water-lilies as the breast of the horse swept them aside, that suddenly took away the thought of Abraham and brought a strange dream of lands I had never seen; and the first was of a place where I was quite alone, standing by the side of a river, and there was the sound of singing a very long way off, but no living thing of any kind could be seen, and the land was quite flat, quite without hills, and quite without trees too, and the river wound very much, making all kinds of quaint curves, and on the side where I stood there grew nothing but long grass, but on the other side grew, quite on to the horizon, a great sea of red corn-poppies, only paths of white lilies wound all among them, with here and there a great golden sun-flower.   So I looked down at the river by my feet, and saw how blue it was, and how, as the stream went swiftly by, it swayed to and fro the long green weeds, and I stood and looked at the river for long, till at last I felt some one touch me on the shoulder, and, looking round, I saw standing by me my friend Amyot, whom I love better than any one else in the world, but I thought in my dream that I was frightened when I saw him, for his face had changed so, it was so bright and almost transparent, and his eyes gleamed and shone as I had never seen them do before.   Oh! he was so wondrously beautiful, so fearfully beautiful! and as I looked at him the distant music swelled, and seemed to come close up to me, and then swept by us, and fainted away, at last died off entirely; and then I felt sick at heart, and faint, and parched, and I stooped to drink of the water of the river, and as soon as the water touched my lips, lo! the river vanished, and the flat country with its poppies and lilies, and I dreamed that I was in a boat by myself again, floating in an almost land-locked bay of the northern sea, under a cliff of dark basalt.   I was lying on my back in the boat, looking up at the intensely blue sky, and a long low swell from the outer sea lifted the boat up and let it fall again and carried it gradually nearer and nearer towards the dark cliff; and as I moved on, I saw at last, on the top of the cliff, a castle, with many towers, and on the highest tower of the castle there was a great white banner floating, with a red chevron on it, and three golden stars on the chevron; presently I saw too on one of the towers, growing in a cranny of the worn stones, a great bunch of

golden and blood-red wall-flowers, and I watched the wall-
flowers and banner for long; when suddenly I heard a
trumpet blow from the castle, and saw a rush of armed men
on to the battlements, and there was a fierce fight, till at last
it was ended, and one went to the banner and pulled it down,
and cast it over the cliff into the sea, and it came down
in long sweeps, with the wind making little ripples in it;—
slowly, slowly it came, till at last it fell over me and covered me
from my feet till over my breast, and I let it stay there and
looked again at the castle, and then I saw that there was an
amber-coloured banner floating over the castle in place of
the red chevron, and it was much larger than the other: also
now, a man stood on the battlements, looking towards me;
he had a tilting helmet on, with the visor down, and an
amber-coloured surcoat over his armour: his right hand was
ungauntletted, and he held it high above his head, and in his
hand was the bunch of wall-flowers that I had seen growing
on the wall; and his hand was white and small, like a
woman's, for in my dream I could see even very far off
things much clearer than we see real material things on the
earth: presently he threw the wall-flowers over the cliff, and
they fell in the boat just behind my head, and then I saw,
looking down from the battlements of the castle, Amyot.
He looked down towards me very sorrowfully, I thought,
but, even as in the other dream, said nothing; so I thought
in my dream that I wept for very pity, and for love of him,
for he looked as a man just risen from a long illness, and
who will carry till he dies a dull pain about with him. He
was very thin, and his long black hair drooped all about his
face, as he leaned over the battlements looking at me: he
was quite pale, and his cheeks were hollow, but his eyes
large, and soft, and sad. So I reached out my arms to him,
and suddenly I was walking with him in a lovely garden, and
we said nothing, for the music which I had heard at first was
sounding close to us now, and there were many birds in the
boughs of the trees: oh, such birds! gold and ruby, and
emerald, but they sung not at all, but were quite silent, as
though they too were listening to the music. Now all this
time Amyot and I had been looking at each other, but just
then I turned my head away from him, and as soon as I did
so, the music ended with a long wail, and when I turned
again Amyot was gone; then I felt even more sad and sick

at heart than I had before when I was by the river, and I leaned against a tree, and put my hands before my eyes. When I looked again the garden was gone, and I knew not where I was, and presently all my dreams were gone. The chips were flying bravely from the stone under my chisel at last, and all my thoughts now were in my carving, when I heard my name, "Walter," called, and when I looked down I saw one standing below me, whom I had seen in my dreams just before—Amyot. I had no hopes of seeing him for a long time, perhaps I might never see him again, I thought, for he was away (as I thought) fighting in the holy wars, and it made me almost beside myself to see him standing close by me in the flesh. I got down from my scaffolding as soon as I could, and all thoughts else were soon drowned in the joy of having him by me; Margaret, too, how glad she must have been, for she had been betrothed to him for some time before he went to the wars, and he had been five years away; five years! and how we had thought of him through those many weary days! how often his face had come before me! his brave, honest face, the most beautiful among all the faces of men and women I have ever seen. Yes, I remember how five years ago I held his hand as we came together out of the cathedral of that great, far-off city, whose name I forget now; and then I remember the stamping of the horses' feet; I remember how his hand left mine at last, and then, some one looking back at me earnestly as they all rode on together—looking back, with his hand on the saddle behind him, while the trumpets sang in long solemn peals as they all rode on together, with the glimmer of arms and the fluttering of banners, and the clinking of the rings of the mail, that sounded like the falling of many drops of water into the deep, still waters of some pool that the rocks nearly meet over; and the gleam and flash of the swords, and the glimmer of the lance-heads and the flutter of the rippled banners, that streamed out from them, swept past me, and were gone, and they seemed like a pageant in a dream, whose meaning we know not; and those sounds too, the trumpets, and the clink of the mail, and the thunder of the horse-hoofs, they seemed dream-like too—and it was all like a dream that he should leave me, for we had said that we should always be together; but he went away, and now he is come back again.

We were by his bed-side, Margaret and I; I stood and leaned over him, and my hair fell sideways over my face and touched his face; Margaret kneeled beside me, quivering in every limb, not with pain, I think, but rather shaken by a passion of earnest prayer. After some time (I know not how long), I looked up from his face to the window under-neath which he lay; I do not know what time of the day it was, but I know that it was a glorious autumn day, a day soft with melting, golden haze: a vine and a rose grew together, and trailed half across the window, so that I could not see much of the beautiful blue sky, and nothing of town or country beyond; the vine leaves were touched with red here and there, and three over-blown roses, light pink roses, hung amongst them. I remember dwelling on the strange lines the autumn had made in red on one of the gold-green vine leaves, and watching one leaf of one of the over-blown roses, expecting it to fall every minute; but as I gazed, and felt disappointed that the rose leaf had not fallen yet, I felt my pain suddenly shoot through me, and I remembered what I had lost; and then came bitter, bitter dreams,—dreams which had once made me happy,—dreams of the things I had hoped would be, of the things that would never be now; they came between the fair vine leaves and rose blossoms, and that which lay before the window; they came as before, perfect in colour and form, sweet sounds and shapes. But now in every one was something unutterably miserable; they would not go away, they put out the steady glow of the golden haze, the sweet light of the sun through the vine leaves, the soft leaning of the full blown roses. I wandered in them for a long time; at last I felt a hand put me aside gently, for I was standing at the head of—of the bed; then some one kissed my forehead, and words were spoken—I know not what words. The bitter dreams left me for the bitterer reality at last; for I had found him that morning lying dead, only the morning after I had seen him when he had come back from his long absence—I had found him lying dead, with his hands crossed downwards, with his eyes closed, as though the angels had done that for him; and now when I looked at him he still lay there, and Margaret knelt by him with her face touching his: she was not quivering now, her lips moved not at all as they had done just before; and so, suddenly those words came to my mind which she had spoken when she kissed me, and which at the time I had only heard with my outward hearing, for she had said, "Walter, farewell, and Christ keep you; but for me, I must be with him, for so I promised him last night that I would never leave him any more, and God will let me go." And verily Margaret and Amyot did go, and left me very lonely and sad.

It was just beneath the westernmost arch of the nave, there I carved their tomb: I was a long time carving it; I did not think I should be so long at first, and I said, "I shall die when I have finished carving it," thinking that would be a very short time. But so it happened after I had carved those two whom I loved, lying with clasped hands like husband and wife above their tomb, that I could not yet leave carving it; and so that I might be near them I became a monk, and used to sit in the choir and sing, thinking of the time when we should all be together again. And as I had time I used to go to the westernmost arch of the nave and work at the tomb that was there under the great, sweeping arch; and in process of time I raised a marble canopy that reached quite up to the top of the arch, and I painted it too as fair as I could, and carved it all about with many flowers and histories, and in them I carved the faces of those I had known on earth (for I was not as one on earth now, but seemed quite away out of the world). And as I carved, sometimes the monks and other people too would come and gaze, and watch how the flowers grew; and sometimes too as they gazed, they would weep for pity, knowing how all had been. So my life passed, and I lived in that abbey for twenty years after he died, till one morning, quite early, when they came into the church for matins, they found me lying dead, with my chisel in my hand, underneath the last lily of the tomb.

LINDENBORG POOL[1]

I READ once in lazy humour Thorpe's "Northern Mytho-
logy," on a cold May night when the north wind was blowing;
in lazy humour, but when I came to the tale that is here
amplified there was something in it that fixed my attention
and made me think of it; and whether I would or no, my
thoughts ran in this way, as here follows.

So I felt obliged to write, and wrote accordingly, and by
the time I had done the grey light filled all my room; so I
put out my candles, and went to bed, not without fear and
trembling, for the morning twilight is so strange and lonely.
This is what I wrote.

Yes, on that dark night, with that wild unsteady north
wind howling, though it was Maytime, it was doubtless dis-
mal enough in the forest, where the boughs clashed eerily,
and where, as the wanderer in that place hurried along,
strange forms half showed themselves to him, the more fear-
ful because half seen in that way: dismal enough doubtless
on wide moors where the great wind had it all its own way:
dismal on the rivers creeping on and on between the marsh-
lands, creeping through the willows, the water trickling
through the locks, sounding faintly in the gusts of the wind.

Yet surely nowhere so dismal as by the side of that
still pool.

I threw myself down on the ground there, utterly ex-
hausted with my struggle against the wind, and with bearing
the fathoms and fathoms of the heavily-leaded plumb-line
that lay beside me.

Fierce as the wind was, it could not raise the leaden waters
of that fearful pool, defended as they were by the steep banks
of dripping yellow clay, striped horribly here and there with
ghastly uncertain green and blue.

<hr>

[1] See Thorpe's "Northern Mythology," vol. ii. p. 214.

They said no man could fathom it; and yet all round the edges of it grew a rank crop of dreary reeds and segs, some round, some flat, but none ever flowering as other things flowered, never dying and being renewed, but always the same stiff array of unbroken reeds and segs, some round, some flat. Hard by me were two trees leafless and ugly, made, it seemed, only for the wind to go through with a wild sough on such nights as these; and for a mile from that place were no other trees.

True, I could not see all this at that time, then, in the dark night, but I knew well that it was all there; for much had I studied this pool in the day-time, trying to learn the secret of it; many hours I had spent there, happy with a kind of happiness, because forgetful of the past. And even now, could I not hear the wind going through those trees, as it never went through any trees before or since? could I not see gleams of the dismal moor? could I not hear those reeds just taken by the wind, knocking against each other, the flat ones scraping all along the round ones? Could I not hear, moreover, the slow trickling of the land-springs through the clay banks?

The cold, chill horror of the place was too much for me; I had never been there by night before, nobody had for quite a long time, and now to come on such a night! If there had been any moon, the place would have looked more as it did by day; besides, the moon shining on water is always so beautiful, on any water even: if it had been star-light, one could have looked at the stars and thought of the time when those fields were fertile and beautiful (for such a time was, I am sure), when the cowslips grew among the grass, and when there was promise of yellow-waving corn stained with poppies; that time which the stars had seen, but which we had never seen, which even they would never see again—past time!

Ah! what was that which touched my shoulder?—Yes, I see, only a dead leaf.—Yes, to be here on this eighth of May too of all nights in the year, the night of that awful day when ten years ago I slew him, not undeservedly, God knows, yet how dreadful it was!—Another leaf! and another!—Strange, those trees have been dead this hundred years, I should think. How sharp the wind is too, just as if I were moving along and meeting it;—why, I *am* moving!

what then, I am not there after all; where am I then? there are the trees; no, they are freshly-planted oak saplings, the very ones that those withered last-year's leaves were blown on me from.

I have been dreaming then, and am on my road to the lake: but what a young wood! I must have lost my way; I never saw all this before. Well—I will walk on stoutly.

May the Lord help my senses! I am *riding!*—on a mule; a bell tinkles somewhere on him; the wind blows something about with a flapping sound: something? in Heaven's name, what? *My* long black robes.—Why—when I left my house I was clad in serviceable broadcloth of the nineteenth century.

I shall go mad—I am mad—I am gone to the Devil— I have lost my identity; who knows in what place, in what age of the world I am living now? Yet I will be calm; I have seen all these things before, in pictures surely, or something like them. I am resigned, since it is no worse than that. I am a priest then, in the dim, far-off thirteenth century, riding, about midnight I should say, to carry the blessed sacrament to some dying man.

Soon I found that I was not alone; a man was riding close to me on a horse; he was fantastically dressed, more so than usual for that time, being striped all over in vertical stripes of yellow and green, with quaint birds like exaggerated storks in different attitudes counterchanged on the stripes; all this I saw by the lantern he carried, in the light of which his debauched black eyes quite flashed. On he went, unsteadily rolling, very drunk, though it was the thirteenth century, but being plainly used to that, he sat his horse fairly well.

I watched him in my proper nineteenth-century character, with insatiable curiosity and intense amusement; but as a quiet priest of a long-past age, with contempt and disgust enough, not unmixed with fear and anxiety.

He roared out snatches of doggrel verse as he went along, drinking songs, hunting songs, robbing songs, lust-songs, in a voice that sounded far and far above the roaring of the wind, though that was high, and rolled along the dark road that his lantern cast spikes of light along ever so far, making the devils grin: and meanwhile I, the priest, glanced from him wrathfully every now and then to That which I carried very reverently in my hand, and my blood curdled with

shame and indignation; but being a shrewd priest, I knew
well enough that a sermon would be utterly thrown away on
a man who was drunk every day in the year, and, more
especially, very drunk then. So I held my peace, saying
only under my breath:

"Dixit insipiens in corde suo, Non est Deus. Corrupti sunt
et abominabiles facti sunt in studiis suis; non est qui faciat
bonum, non est usque ad unum: sepulchrum patens est guttur
eorum; linguis suis dolose agebant, venenum aspidum sub labiis
eorum. Dominum non invocaverunt; illic trepidaverunt timore,
ubi non erat timor. Quis dabit ex Sion salutare Israel?"

and so I went on, thinking too at times about the man who
was dying and whom I was soon to see: he had been a bold
bad plundering baron, but was said lately to have altered his
way of life, having seen a miracle or some such thing; he
had departed to keep a tournament near his castle lately, but
had been brought back sore wounded, so this drunken ser-
vant, with some difficulty and much unseasonable merriment,
had made me understand, and now lay at the point of death,
brought about by unskilful tending and such like. Then I
thought of his face—a bad face, very bad, retreating forehead,
small twinkling eyes, projecting lower jaw; and such a voice,
too, he had! like the grunt of a boar mostly.

Now don't you think it strange that this face should be the
same, actually the same as the face of my enemy, slain that
very day ten years ago? I did not hate him, either that
man or the baron, but I wanted to see as little of him as
possible, and I hoped that the ceremony would soon be over,
and that I should be at liberty again.

And so with these thoughts and many others, but all
thought strangely double, we went along, the varlet being too
drunk to take much notice of me, only once, as he was
singing some doggrel, like this, I think, making allowances
for change of language and so forth:

"The Duke went to Treves
  On the first of November
His wife stay'd at Bonn—
  Let me see, I remember;

"When the Duke came back
  To look for his wife,
We came from Cologne,
  And took the Duke's life;

"We hung him mid high
  Between spire and pavement,
From their mouths dropp'd the cabbage
  Of the carles in amazement."

" Boo—hoo ! Church-rat ! Church-mouse !   Hilloa, Priest !
have you brought the pyx, eh ? "

From some cause or other he seemed to think this an
excellent joke, for he almost shrieked with laughter as we
went along ; but by this time we had reached the castle.
Challenge, and counter-challenge, and we passed the outer-
most gate and began to go through some of the courts, in
which stood lime trees here and there, growing green tenderly
with that Maytime, though the north wind bit so keenly.

How strange again ! as I went farther, there seemed no
doubt of it ; here in the aftertime came that pool, how I
knew not ; but in the few moments that we were riding from
the outer gate to the castle-porch I thought so intensely over
the probable cause for the existence of that pool, that (how
strange !) I could almost have thought I was back again
listening to the oozing of the land-springs through the high
clay banks there.   I was wakened from that, before it grew
too strong, by the glare of many torches, and, dismounting,
found myself in the midst of some twenty attendants, with
flushed faces and wildly sparkling eyes, which they were
vainly trying to soften to due solemnity ; mock solemnity I
had almost said, for they did not seem to think it necessary
to appear really solemn, and had difficulty enough apparently
in not prolonging indefinitely the shout of laughter with which
they had at first greeted me.   "Take the holy Father to my
Lord," said one at last, "and we will go with him."

So they led me up the stairs into the gorgeously-furnished
chamber ; the light from the heavy waxen candles was
pleasant to my eyes after the glare and twisted red smoke of
the pine-torches ; but all the essences scattered about the
chamber were not enough to conquer the fiery breath of
those about me.

I put on the alb and stole they brought me, and, before I
went up to the sick man, looked round on those that were in
the rooms ; for the rooms opened one into the other by
many doors, across some of which hung gorgeous tapestry ;
all the rooms seemed to have many people, for some stood
at these doors, and some passed to and fro, swinging aside

the heavy hangings ; once several people at once, seemingly quite by accident, drew aside almost all the veils from the doors, and showed an endless perspective of gorgeousness.

And at these things my heart fainted for horror. " Had not the Jews of late," thought I, the priest, " been very much in the habit of crucifying children in mockery of the Holiest, holding gorgeous feasts while they beheld the poor innocents die ? these men are Atheists, you are in a trap, yet quit yourself like a man."

" Ah, sharp one," thought I, the author, " where are you at last ? try to pray as a test.—Well, well, these things are strangely like devils.—O man, you have talked about bravery often, now is your time to practise it : once for all trust in God, or I fear you are lost."

Moreover it increased my horror that there was no appearance of a woman in all these rooms ; and yet was there not ? there, those things—I looked more intently ; yes, no doubt they were women, but all dressed like men ;—what a ghastly place !

" O man ! do your duty," my angel said ; then in spite of the bloodshot eyes of man and woman there, in spite of their bold looks, they quailed before me.

I stepped up to the bedside, where under the velvet coverlid lay the dying man, his small sparkling eyes only (but dulled now by coming death) showing above the swathings. I was about to kneel down by the bedside to confess him, when one of those—things—called out (now they had just been whispering and sniggering together, but the priest in his righteous, brave scorn would not look at them ; the humbled author, half fearful, half trustful, dared not) : so one called out :

" Sir Priest, for three days our master has spoken no articulate word ; you must pass over all particulars ; ask for a sign only."

Such a strange ghastly suspicion flashed across me just then ; but I choked it, and asked the dying man if he repented of his sins, and if he believed all that was necessary to salvation, and, if so, to make a sign, if he were able : the man moved a little and groaned ; so I took it for a sign, as he was clearly incapable either of speaking or moving, and accordingly began the service for the administration of the sacraments ; and as I began, those behind me and through all the rooms (I know it was through all of them) began to move about, in a bewildering dance-like motion, mazy and intricate ; yes, and presently music struck up through all those rooms, music and singing, lively and gay; many of the tunes I had heard before (in the nineteenth century) ; I could have sworn to half a dozen of the polkas.

The rooms grew fuller and fuller of people ; they passed thick and fast between the rooms, and the hangings were continually rustling ; one fat old man with a big belly crept under the bed where I was, and wheezed and chuckled there, laughing and talking to one who stooped down and lifted up the hangings to look at him.

Still more and more people talking and singing and laughing and twirling about, till my brain went round and round, and I scarce knew what I did ; yet, somehow, I could not leave off ; I dared not even look over my shoulder, fearing lest I should see something so horrible as to make me die.

So I got on with the service, and at last took the Pyx, and took thereout the sacred wafer, whereupon was a deep silence through all those rooms, which troubled me, I think, more than all which had gone before, for I knew well it did not mean reverence.

I held it up, that which I counted so holy, when lo ! great laughter, echoing like thunder-claps through all the rooms, not dulled by the veiling hangings, for they were all raised up together, and, with a slow upheaval of the rich clothes among which he lay, with a sound that was half snarl, half grunt, with helpless body swathed in bedclothes, a huge *swine* that I had been shriving tore from me the Holy Thing, deeply scoring my hand as he did so with tusk and tooth, so that the red blood ran quick on to the floor.

Therewithal he rolled down on to the floor, and lay there helplessly, only able to roll to and fro, because of the swathings.

Then right madly skirled the intolerable laughter, rising to shrieks that were fearfuller than any scream of agony I ever heard ; the hundreds of people through all those grand rooms danced and wheeled about me, shrieking, hemming me in with interlaced arms, the women loosing their long hair and thrusting forward their horribly-grinning unsexed faces toward me till I felt their hot breath.

Oh ! how I hated them all ! almost hated all mankind for

their sakes; how I longed to get right quit of all men; among whom, as it seemed, all sacredest things even were made a mock of. I looked about me fiercely, I sprang forward, and clutched a sword from the gilded belt of one of those who stood near me; with savage blows that threw the blood about the gilded walls and their hangings right over the heads of those—things—I cleared myself from them, and tore down the great stairs madly, yet could not, as in a dream, go fast enough, because of my passion.

I was out in the courtyard, among the lime trees soon, the north wind blowing freshly on my heated forehead in that dawn. The outer gate was locked and bolted; I stooped and raised a great stone and sent it at the lock with all my strength, and I was stronger than ten men then; iron and oak gave way before it, and through the ragged splinters I tore in reckless fury, like a wild horse through a hazel hedge.

And no one had pursued me. I knelt down on the dear green turf outside, and thanked God with streaming eyes for my deliverance, praying Him forgiveness for my unwilling share in that night's mockery.

Then I arose and turned to go, but even as I did so I heard a roar as if the world were coming in two, and looking toward the castle, saw, not a castle, but a great cloud of white lime-dust swaying this way and that in the gusts of the wind.

Then while the east grew bright there arose a hissing, gurgling noise, that swelled into the roar and wash of many waters, and by then the sun had risen a deep black lake lay before my feet.

And this is how I tried to fathom the Lindenborg Pool.

A DREAM

I DREAMED once, that four men sat by the winter fire talking and telling tales, in a house that the wind howled round.

And one of them, the eldest, said: "When I was a boy, before you came to this land, that bar of red sand rock, which makes a fall in our river, had only just been formed; for it used to stand above the river in a great cliff, tunnelled by a cave about midway between the green-growing grass and the green-flowing river; and it fell one night, when you had not yet come to this land, no, nor your fathers.

"Now, concerning this cliff, or pike rather (for it was a tall slip of rock and not part of a range), many strange tales were told; and my father used to say, that in his time many would have explored that cave, either from covetousness (expecting to find gold therein), or from that love of wonders which most young men have, but fear kept them back. Within the memory of man, however, some had entered, and, so men said, were never seen on earth again; but my father said that the tales told concerning such, very far from deterring him (then quite a youth) from the quest of this cavern, made him all the more earnestly long to go; so that one day in his fear, my grandfather, to prevent him, stabbed him in the shoulder, so that he was obliged to keep his bed for long; and somehow he never went, and died at last without ever having seen the inside of the cavern.

"My father told me many wondrous tales about the place, whereof for a long time I have been able to remember nothing; yet, by some means or another, a certain story has grown up in my heart, which I will tell you something of: a story which no living creature ever told me, though I do not remember the time when I knew it not. Yes, I will tell you some of it, not all perhaps, but as much as I am allowed to tell."

The man stopped and pondered awhile, leaning over the fire where the flames slept under the caked coal : he was an old man, and his hair was quite white. He spoke again presently. "And I have fancied sometimes, that in some way, how I know not, I am mixed up with the strange story I am going to tell you." Again he ceased, and gazed at the fire, bending his head down till his beard touched his knees ; then, rousing himself, said in a changed voice (for he had been speaking dreamily hitherto): "That strange-looking old house that you all know, with the limes and yew-trees before it, and the double line of very old yew-trees leading up from the gateway-tower to the porch—you know how no one will live there now because it is so eerie, and how even that bold bad lord that would come there, with his turbulent followers, was driven out in shame and disgrace by invisible agency. Well, in times past there dwelt in that house an old grey man, who was lord of that estate, his only daughter, and a young man, a kind of distant cousin of the house, whom the lord had brought up from a boy, as he was the orphan of a kinsman who had fallen in combat in his quarrel. Now, as the young knight and the young lady were both beautiful and brave, and loved beauty and good things ardently, it was natural enough that they should discover as they grew up that they were in love with one another ; and afterwards, as they went on loving one another, it was, alas! not unnatural that they should sometimes have half-quarrels, very few and far between indeed, and slight to lookers-on, even while they lasted, but nevertheless intensely bitter and unhappy to the principal parties thereto. I suppose their love then, whatever it has grown to since, was not so all-absorbing as to merge all differences of opinion and feeling, for again there were such differences then. So, upon a time it happened, just when a great war had arisen, and Lawrence (for that was the knight's name) was sitting and thinking of war, and his departure from home ; sitting there in a very grave, almost a stern mood, that Ella, his betrothed, came in, gay and sprightly, in a humour that Lawrence often enough could little understand, and this time liked less than ever, yet the bare sight of her made him yearn for her full heart, which he was not to have yet ; so he caught her by the hand, and tried to draw her down to him, but she let her hand lie loose in his, and did not answer the pressure in which his heart flowed to hers; then he arose and stood before her, face to face, but she drew back a little, yet he kissed her on the mouth and said, though a rising in his throat almost choked his voice, 'Ella, are you sorry I am going?' 'Yea,' she said, 'and nay, for you will shout my name among the sword-flashes, and you will fight for me.' 'Yes,' he said, 'for love and duty, dearest.' 'For duty? ah! I think, Lawrence, if it were not for me, you would stay at home and watch the clouds, or sit under the linden-trees singing dismal love ditties of your own making, dear knight: truly, if you turn out a great warrior, I too shall live in fame, for I am certainly the making of your desire to fight.' He let drop his hands from her shoulders, where he had laid them, and said, with a faint flush over his face, 'You wrong me, Ella, for, though I have never wished to fight for the mere love of fighting, and though,' (and here again he flushed a little) 'and though I am not, I well know, so free of the fear of death as a good man would be, yet for this duty's sake, which is really a higher love, Ella, love of God, I trust I would risk life, nay honour, even if not willingly, yet cheerfully at least.' 'Still duty, duty,' she said; 'you lay, Lawrence, as many people do, most stress on the point where you are weakest; moreover, those knights who in time past have done wild, mad things merely at their ladies' word, scarcely did so for duty; for they owed their lives to their country surely, to the cause of good, and should not have risked them for a whim, and yet you praised them the other day.' 'Did I?' said Lawrence; 'well, and in a way they were much to be praised, for even blind love and obedience is well; but reasonable love, reasonable obedience is so far better as to be almost a different thing; yet, I think, if the knights did well partly, the ladies did altogether ill: for if they had faith in their lovers, and did this merely from a mad longing to see them do "noble" deeds, then had they but little faith in God, Who can, and at His good pleasure does give time and opportunity to every man, if he will but watch for it, to serve Him with reasonable service, and gain love and all noble things in greater measure thereby: but if these ladies did as they did, that they might prove their knights, then surely did they lack faith both in God and man. I do not think that two friends even could live together on such terms but for lovers—ah! Ella, Ella, why do you look so at me? on this day, almost the last, we shall be together for long; Ella, your face is changed, your eyes —O Christ! help her and me, help her, good Lord.' 'Lawrence,' she said, speaking quickly and in jerks, 'dare you, for my sake, sleep this night in the cavern of the red pike? for I say to you that, faithful or not, I doubt your courage.' But she was startled when she saw him, and how the fiery blood rushed up to his forehead, then sank to his heart again, and his face became as pale as the face of a dead man: he looked at her and said, 'Yes, Ella, I will go now; for what matter where I go?' He turned and moved toward the door; he was almost gone, when that evil spirit left her, and she cried out aloud, passionately, eagerly: 'Lawrence, Lawrence, come back once more, if only to strike me dead with your knightly sword.' He hesitated, wavered, turned, and in another moment she was lying in his arms weeping into his hair.

"'And yet, Ella, the spoken word, the thought of our hearts cannot be recalled, I must go, and go this night too, only promise one thing.' 'Dearest what? you are always right!' 'Love, you must promise that if I come not again by to-morrow at moonrise, you will go to the red pike, and, having entered the cavern, go where God leads you, and seek me, and never leave that quest, even if it end not but with death.' 'Lawrence, how your heart beats! poor heart! are you afraid that I shall hesitate to promise to perform that which is the only thing I could do? I know I am not worthy to be with you, yet I must be with you in body or soul, or body and soul will die.' They sat silent, and the birds sang in the garden of lilies beyond; then said Ella again; 'Moreover, let us pray God to give us longer life, so that if our natural lives are short for the accomplishment of this quest, we may have more, yea, even many more lives.' 'He will, my Ella,' said Lawrence, 'and I think, nay, I am sure that our wish will be granted; and I, too, will add a prayer, but will ask it very humbly, namely, that he will give me another chance or more to fight in his cause, another life to live instead of this failure.' 'Let us pray too that we may meet, however long the time be before our meeting,' she said: so they knelt down and prayed, hand fast locked in hand meantime; and afterwards they sat in that chamber facing the east, hard by the garden of lilies; and the sun fell from his noontide light gradually, lengthening the shadows, and when he sank below the sky-line all the sky was faint, tender, crimson on a ground of blue; the crimson faded too, and the moon began to rise, but when her golden rim first showed over the wooded hills, Lawrence arose; they kissed one long trembling kiss, and then he went and armed himself; and their lips did not meet again after that, for such a long, long time, so many weary years; for he had said: ' Ella, watch me from the porch, but touch me not again at this time; only, when the moon shows level with the lily-heads, go into the porch and watch me from thence.'

" And he was gone;—you might have heard her heart beating while the moon very slowly rose, till it shone through the rose-covered trellises, level with the lily-heads; then she went to the porch and stood there,—

" And she saw him walking down toward the gateway tower, clad in his mail coat, with a bright, crestless helmet on his head, and his trenchant sword newly grinded, girt to his side; and she watched him going between the yew-trees, which began to throw shadows from the shining of the harvest moon. She stood there in the porch, and round by the corners of the eaves of it looked down towards her and the inside of the porch two serpent-dragons, carved in stone; and on their scales, and about their leering eyes, grew the yellow lichen; she shuddered as she saw them stare at her, and drew closer toward the half-open door; she, standing there, clothed in white from her throat till over her feet, altogether ungirdled; and her long yellow hair, without plait or band, fell down behind and lay along her shoulders, quietly, because the night was without wind, and she too was now standing scarcely moving a muscle.

" She gazed down the line of the yew-trees, and watched how, as he went for the most part with a firm step, he yet shrank somewhat from the shadows of the yews; his long brown hair flowing downward, swayed with him as he walked; and the golden threads interwoven with it, as the fashion was with the warriors in those days, sparkled out from among it now and then; and the faint, far-off moonlight lit up the waves of his mail coat; he walked fast, and was disappearing in the shadows of the trees near the moat, but turned before he was quite lost in them, and waved his ungauntletted hand; then she heard the challenge of the warder, the falling of the drawbridge, the swing of the heavy wicket-gate on its hinges; and, into the brightening lights, and deepening shadows of the moonlight he went from her sight; and she left the porch and went to the chapel, all that night praying earnestly there.

"But he came not back again all the next day, and Ella wandered about that house pale, and fretting her heart away; so when night came and the moon, she arrayed herself in that same raiment that she had worn on the night before, and went toward the river and the red pike.

"The broad moon shone right over it by the time she came to the river; the pike rose up from the other side, and she thought at first that she would have to go back again, cross over the bridge, and so get to it; but, glancing down on the river just as she turned, she saw a little boat fairly gilt and painted, and with a long slender paddle in it, lying on the water, stretching out its silken painter as the stream drew it downwards, she entered it, and taking the paddle made for the other side; the moon meanwhile turning the eddies to silver over the dark green water: she landed beneath the shadow of that great pile of sandstone, where the grass grew green, and the flowers sprang fair right up to the foot of the bare barren rock; it was cut in many steps till it reached the cave, which was overhung by creepers and matted grass; the stream swept the boat downwards, and Ella, her heart beating so as almost to stop her breath, mounted the steps slowly, slowly. She reached at last the platform below the cave, and turning, gave a long gaze at the moonlit country; 'her last,' she said; then she moved, and the cave hid her as the water of the warm seas close over the pearl-diver.

"Just so the night before had it hidden Lawrence. And they never came back, they two:—never, the people say. I wonder what their love has grown to now; ah! they love, I know, but cannot find each other yet: I wonder also if they ever will."

So spoke Hugh the white-haired. But he who sat over against him, a soldier as it seemed, black-bearded, with wild grey eyes that his great brows hung over far; he, while the others sat still, awed by some vague sense of spirits being very near them; this man, Giles, cried out—"Never? old Hugh, it is not so.—Speak! I cannot tell you how it happened, but I know it was not so, not so:—speak quick, Hugh! tell us all, all!"

"Wait a little, my son, wait," said Hugh; "the people indeed said they never came back again at all, but I, but I—Ah! the time is long past over." So he was silent, and sank his head on his breast, though his old thin lips moved, as if he talked softly to himself, and the light of past days flickered in his eyes.

Meanwhile Giles sat with his hands clasped finger over finger, tightly, "till the knuckles whitened;" his lips were pressed firmly together; his breast heaved as though it would burst, as though it must be rid of its secret. Suddenly he sprang up, and in a voice that was a solemn chant, began: "In full daylight, long ago, on a slumberously-wrathful, thunderous afternoon of summer";—then across his chant ran the old man's shrill voice: "On an October day, packed close with heavy-lying mist, which was more than mere autumn-mist":—the solemn stately chanting dropped, the shrill voice went on; Giles sank down again, and Hugh standing there, swaying to and fro to the measured ringing of his own shrill voice, his long beard moving with him, said:—

"On such a day, warm, and stifling so that one could scarcely breathe even down by the sea-shore, I went from bed to bed in the hospital of the pest-laden city with my soothing draughts and medicines. And there went with me a holy woman, her face pale with much watching; yet I think even without those same desolate lonely watchings her face would still have been pale. She was not beautiful, her face being somewhat peevish-looking; apt, she seemed, to be made angry by trifles, and, even on her errand of mercy, she spoke roughly to those she tended:—no, she was not beautiful, yet I could not help gazing at her, for her eyes were very beautiful and looked out from her ugly face as a fair maiden might look from a grim prison between the window-bars of it.

"So, going through that hospital, I came to a bed at last, whereon lay one who had not been struck down by fever or plague, but had been smitten through the body with a sword by certain robbers, so that he had narrowly escaped death. Huge of frame, with stern suffering face he lay there; and I came to him, and asked him of his hurt, and how he fared, while the day grew slowly toward even, in that pest-chamber looking toward the west; the sister came to him soon and knelt down by his bed-side to tend him.

"O Christ! As the sun went down on that dim misty day, the clouds and the thickly-packed mist cleared off, to let him shine on us, on that chamber of woes and bitter unpurifying tears; and the sunlight wrapped those two, the sick man and the ministering woman, shone on them— changed, changed utterly. Good Lord! How was I struck dumb, nay, almost blinded by that change; for there—yes there, while no man but I wondered; there, instead of the unloving nurse, knelt a wonderfully beautiful maiden, clothed all in white, and with long golden hair down her back. Tenderly she gazed at the wounded man, as her hands were put about his head, lifting it up from the pillow but a very little; and he no longer the grim, strong wounded man, but fair, and in the first bloom of youth; a bright polished helmet crowned his head, a mail coat flowed over his breast, and his hair streamed down long from his head, while from among it here and there shone out threads of gold.

"So they spake thus in a quiet tone: 'Body and soul together again, Ella, love; how long will it be now before the last time of all?' 'Long,' she said, 'but the years pass; talk no more, dearest, but let us think only, for the time is short, and our bodies call up memories, change love to better even than it was in the old time.'

"Silence so, while you might count a hundred, then with a great sigh: 'Farewell, Ella, for long,'—'Farewell, Lawrence,' and the sun sank, all was as before.

"But I stood at the foot of the bed pondering, till the sister coming to me, said: 'Master Physician, this is no time for dreaming; act—the patients are waiting, the fell sickness grows worse in this hot close air; feel'—(and she swung open the casement), 'the outer air is no fresher than the air inside; the wind blows dead towards the west, coming from the stagnant marshes; the sea is like a stagnant pool too, you can scarce hear the sound of the long, low surge breaking.' I turned from her and went up to the sick man, and said: 'Sir Knight, in spite of all the sickness about you, you yourself better strangely, and another month will see you with your sword girt to your side again.' 'Thanks, kind master Hugh,' he said, but impatiently, as if his mind were on other things, and he turned in his bed away from me restlessly.

"And till late that night I ministered to the sick in that

hospital; but when I went away, I walked down to the sea, and paced there to and fro over the hard sand: and the moon showed bloody with the hot mist, which the sea would not take on its bosom, though the dull east wind blew it onward continually. I walked there pondering till a noise from over the sea made me turn and look that way; what was that coming over the sea? Laus Deo! the WEST WIND: Hurrah! I feel the joy I felt then over again now, in all its intensity. How came it over the sea? first, far out to sea, so that it was only just visible under the red-gleaming moonlight, far out to sea, while the mists above grew troubled, and wavered, a long level bar of white; it grew nearer quickly, it rushed on toward me fearfully fast, it gathered form, strange, misty, intricate form—the ravelled foam of the green sea; then oh! hurrah! I was wrapped in it,—the cold salt spray—drenched with it, blinded by it, and when I could see again, I saw the great green waves rising, nodding and breaking, all coming on together; and over them from wave to wave leaped the joyous WEST WIND; and the mist and the plague clouds were sweeping back eastward in wild swirls; and right away were they swept at last, till they brooded over the face of the dismal stagnant meres, many miles away from our fair city, and there they pondered wrathfully on their defeat.

"But somehow my life changed from the time when beheld the two lovers, and I grew old quickly." He ceased, then after a short silence said again; "And that was long ago, very long ago, I know not when it happened."

So he sank back again, and for a while no one spoke; till Giles said at last:

"Once in full daylight I saw a vision, while I was waking, while the eyes of men were upon me. long ago on the afternoon of a thunderous summer day, I sat alone in my fair garden near the city; for on that day a mighty reward was to be given to the brave man who had saved us all, leading us so mightily in that battle a few days back; now the very queen, the lady of the land, whom all men reverenced almost as the Virgin Mother, so kind and good and beautiful she was, was to crown him with flowers and gird a sword about him; after the 'Te Deum' had been sung for the victory, and almost all the city were at that time either in the Church, or hard by it, or else were by the hill that was near the river where the crowning was to be: but I sat alone in the garden of my house as I said; sat grieving for the loss of my brave brother, who was slain by my side in that same fight.

" I sat beneath an elm-tree; and as I sat and pondered on that still, windless day, I heard suddenly a breath of air rustle through the boughs of the elm. I looked up, and my heart almost stopped beating, I knew not why, as I watched the path of that breeze over the bowing lilies and the rushes by the fountain; but when I looked to the place whence the breeze had come, I became all at once aware of an appearance that told me why my heart stopped beating. Ah! there they were, those two whom before I had but seen in dreams by night, now before my waking eyes in broad daylight. One, a knight (for so he seemed), with long hair mingled with golden threads, flowing over his mail coat, and a bright crestless helmet on his head, his face sad-looking, but calm; and by his side, but not touching him, walked a wondrously fair maiden, clad in white, her eyelids just shadowing her blue eyes: her arms and hands seeming to float along with her as she moved on quickly, yet very softly; great rest on them both, though sorrow gleamed through it.

" When they came opposite to where I stood, these two stopped for a while, being in nowise shadowy, as I have heard men say ghosts are, but clear and distinct. They stopped close by me, as I stood motionless, unable to pray; they turned to each other, face to face, and the maiden said, ' Love, for this our last true meeting before the end of all, we need a witness; let this man, softened by sorrow, even as we are, go with us.'

" I never heard such music as her words were; though I used to wonder when I was young whether the angels in heaven sung better than the choristers sang in our church, and though, even then the sound of the triumphant hymn came up to me in a breath of wind, and floated round me, making dreams, in that moment of awe and great dread, of the old long-past days in that old church, of her who lay under the pavement of it; whose sweet voice once, once long ago, once only to me—yet I shall see her again." He became silent as he said this, and no man cared to break in upon his thoughts, seeing the choking movement in his throat, the fierce clenching of hand and foot, the stiffening of the muscles all over him; but soon, with an upward jerk of his head, he threw back the long elf locks that had fallen over his eyes while his head was bent down, and went on as before:

"The knight passed his hand across his brow, as if to clear away some mist that had gathered there, and said, in a deep murmurous voice, 'Why the last time, dearest, why the last time? Know you not how long a time remains yet? the old man came last night to the ivory house and told me it would be a hundred years, ay, more, before the happy end.' 'So long,' she said; 'so long; ah! love, what things words are; yet this is the last time; alas! alas! for the weary years! my words, my sin!' 'O love, it is very terrible,' he said; 'I could almost weep, old though I am, and grown cold with dwelling in the ivory house: O, Ella, if you only knew how cold it is there, in the starry nights when the north wind is stirring; and there is no fair colour there, naught but the white ivory, with one narrow line of gleaming gold over every window, and a fathom's-breadth of burnished gold behind the throne. Ella, it was scarce well done of you to send me to the ivory house.' 'Is it so cold, love?' she said, 'I knew it not; forgive me! but as to the matter of a witness, some one we must have, and why not this man?' 'Rather old Hugh,' he said, 'or Cuthbert, his father; they have both been witnesses before.' 'Cuthbert,' said the maiden, solemnly, 'has been dead twenty years; Hugh died last night.'" (Now, as Giles said these words, carelessly, as though not heeding them particularly, a cold sickening shudder ran through the other two men, but he noted it not and went on.) "'This man then be it,' said the knight, and therewith they turned again, and moved on side by side as before; nor said they any word to me, and yet I could not help following them, and we three moved on together, and soon I saw that my nature was changed, and that I was invisible for the time, for, though the sun was high, I cast no shadow, neither did any man that we past notice us, as we made toward the hill by the riverside.

"And by the time we came there the queen was sitting at the top of it, under a throne of purple and gold, with a great band of knights gloriously armed on either side of her; and their many banners floated over them. Then I felt that

those two had left me, and that my own right visible nature
was returned ; yet still did I feel strange, and as if I belonged
not wholly to this earth. And I heard one say, in a low
voice to his fellow, ' See, Sir Giles is here after all ; yet, how
came he here, and why is he not in armour among the noble
knights yonder, he who fought so well ? How wild he looks
too ! ' ' Poor knight,' said the other, ' he is distraught with
the loss of his brother ; let him be ; and see, here comes the
noble stranger knight, our deliverer.' As he spoke, we heard
a great sound of trumpets, and therewithal a long line of
knights on foot wound up the hill towards the throne, and
the queen rose up, and the people shouted ; and, at the end
of all the procession went slowly and majestically the stranger
knight ; a man of noble presence he was, calm, and graceful
to look on ; grandly he went amid the gleaming of their
golden armour ; himself clad in the rent mail and tattered
surcoat he had worn on the battle-day ; bareheaded, too ;
for, in that fierce fight, in the thickest of it, just where he
rallied our men, one smote off his helmet, and another,
coming from behind, would have slain him, but that my
lance bit into his breast.

" So, when they had come within some twenty paces of
the throne, the rest halted, and he went up by himself toward
the queen ; and she, taking the golden hilted sword in her
left hand, with her right hand caught him by the wrist, when
he would have knelt to her, and held him so, tremblingly,
and cried out, ' No, no, thou noblest of all knights, kneel
not to me : have we not heard of thee even before thou
camest hither ? how many widows bless thee, how many
orphans pray for thee, how many happy ones that would be
widows and orphans but for thee, sing to their children, sing
to their sisters, of thy flashing sword, and the heart that
guides it ! And now, O noble one ! thou hast done the very
noblest deed of all, for thou hast kept grown men from
weeping shameful tears ! Oh truly ! the greatest I can do
for thee is very little ; yet, see this sword, golden hilted, and
the stones flash out from it,' (then she hung it round him)
' and see this wreath of lilies and roses for thy head ; lilies
no whiter than thy pure heart, roses no tenderer than thy
true love ; and here, before all these my subjects, I fold
thee, noblest, in my arms, so, so.' Ay, truly it was strange
enough ! those two were together again ; not the queen and

the stranger knight, but the young-seeming knight and the maiden I had seen in the garden. To my eyes they clung together there; though they say, that to the eyes of all else, it was but for a moment that the queen held both his hands in hers; to me also, amid the shouting of the multitude, came an undercurrent of happy song: 'Oh! truly, very truly, my noblest, a hundred years will not be long after this.' 'Hush! Ella, dearest, for talking makes the time speed; think only.'

"Pressed close to each other, as I saw it, their bosoms heaved—but I looked away—alas! when I looked again, I saw naught but the stately stranger knight, descending, hand in hand, with the queen, flushed with joy and triumph, and the people scattering flowers before them.

"And that was long ago, very long ago." So he ceased; then Osric, one of the two younger men, who had been sitting in awe-struck silence all this time, said, with eyes that dared not meet Giles's, in a terrified half whisper, as though he meant not to speak, "How long?" Giles turned round and looked him full in the face, till he dragged his eyes up to his own, then said, "More than a hundred years ago."

So they all sat silent, listening to the roar of the south-west wind; and it blew the windows so, that they rocked in their frames.

Then suddenly, as they sat thus, came a knock at the door of the house; so Hugh bowed his head to Osric, to signify that he should go and open the door; so he arose, trembling, and went.

And as he opened the door the wind blew hard against him, and blew something white against his face, then blew it away again, and his face was blanched, even to his lips; but he plucking up heart of grace, looked out, and there he saw, standing with her face upturned in speech to him, a wonderfully beautiful woman, clothed from her throat till over her feet in long white raiment, ungirt, unbroidered, and with a long veil, that was thrown off from her face, and hung from her head, streaming out in the blast of the wind; which veil was what had struck against his face: beneath her veil her golden hair streamed out too, and with the veil, so that it touched his face now and then. She was very fair, but she did not look young either, because of her statue-like features. She spoke to him slowly and queenly; "I pray you give me shelter in your house for an hour, that I may rest, and so go on my journey again." He was too much terrified to answer in words, and so only bowed his head; and she swept past him in stately wise to the room where the others sat, and he followed her, trembling.

A cold shiver ran through the other men when she entered and bowed low to them, and they turned deadly pale, but dared not move; and there she sat while they gazed at her, sitting there and wondering at her beauty, which seemed to grow every minute; though she was plainly not young, oh no, but rather very, very old, who could say how old? there she sat, and her long, long hair swept down in one curve from her head, and just touched the floor. Her face had the tokens of a deep sorrow on it, ah! a mighty sorrow, yet not so mighty as that it might mar her ineffable loveliness; that sorrow-mark seemed to gather too, and at last the gloriously-slow music of her words flowed from her lips: "Friends, has one with the appearance of a youth come here lately; one with long brown hair, interwoven with threads of gold, flowing down from out of his polished steel helmet; with dark blue eyes and high white forehead, and mail coat over his breast, where the light and shadow lie in waves as he moves; have you seen such an one, very beautiful?"

Then withal as they shook their heads fearfully in answer, a great sigh rose up from her heart, and she said: "Then must I go away again presently, and yet I thought it was the last night of all."

And so she sat awhile with her head resting on her hand; after, she arose as if about to go, and turned her glorious head round to thank the master of the house; and they, strangely enough, though they were terrified at her presence, were yet grieved when they saw that she was going.

Just then the wind rose higher than ever before, yet through the roar of it they could all hear plainly a knocking at the door again; so the lady stopped when she heard it, and, turning, looked full in the face of Herman the youngest, who thereupon, being constrained by that look, rose and went to the door; and as before with Osric, so now the wind blew strong against him; and it blew into his face, so as to blind him, tresses of soft brown hair mingled with glittering threads

of gold; and blinded so, he heard some one ask him musi-
cally, solemnly, if a lady with golden hair and white raiment
was in that house; so Herman, not answering in words,
because of his awe and fear, merely bowed his head; then
he was ware of some one in bright armour passing him, for
the gleam of it was all about him, for as yet he could not see
clearly, being blinded by the hair that had floated about
him.

But presently he followed him into the room, and there
stood such an one as the lady had described; the wavering
flame of the light gleamed from his polished helmet, touched
the golden threads that mingled with his hair, ran along the
rings of his mail.

They stood opposite to each other for a little, he and
the lady, as if they were somewhat shy of each other after
their parting of a hundred years, in spite of the love which
they had for each other; at last he made one step, and took
off his gleaming helmet, laid it down softly, then spread
abroad his arms, and she came to him, and they were clasped
together, her head lying over his shoulder; and the four men
gazed, quite awe-struck.

And as they gazed, the bells of the church began to
ring, for it was New-Year's-eve; and still they clung to-
gether, and the bells rang on, and the old year died.

And there beneath the eyes of those four men the lovers
slowly faded away into a heap of snow-white ashes. Then
the four men kneeled down and prayed, and the next day
they went to the priest, and told him all that had happened.

So the people took those ashes and buried them in their
church, in a marble tomb, and above it they caused to be
carved their figures lying with clasped hands; and on the
sides of it the history of the cave in the red pike.

And in my dream I saw the moon shining on the tomb,
throwing fair colours on it from the painted glass; till a
sound of music rose, deepened, and fainted; then I awoke.

> "No memory labours longer from the deep
>   Gold mines of thought to lift the hidden ore
> That glimpses, moving up, than I from sleep
>   To gather and tell o'er
> Each little sound and sight."

GERTHA'S LOVERS

CHAPTER I

BY THE RIVER

" All thoughts, all passions, all delights,
Whatever stirs this mortal frame,
All are but ministers of love,
And feed his sacred flame."

COLERIDGE.

LONG ago there was a land, never mind where or when, a fair country and good to live in, rich with wealth of golden corn, beautiful with many woods, watered by great rivers, and pleasant trickling streams; moreover, one extremity of it was bounded by the washing of the purple waves, and the other by the solemn watchfulness of the purple mountains.

In a fair lowland valley of this good land sat a maiden, one summer morning early, working with her needle, while she thought of other matters as women use. She was the daughter of a mere peasant, tiller of the kind soil, fisher in the silver waters of the river that flowed down past his cottage to the far-off city; he lived from day to day seeing few people, the one or two neighbours who lived in the cottages hard by, the priest of the little hamlet, now and then an artizan travelling in search of work; except, indeed, when he went to the wars; for he was a fighting man, as were all the people of that country, when need was. His wife was dead these five years, and his daughter alone lived with him; yet she, though of such lowly parentage, was very beautiful; nor merely so, but grand and queen-like also; such a woman as might inspire a whole people to any deed of wise daring for her love.

What thoughts were hers, as she sat working on that summer morning, the song of birds all about her, and the lapping of the low, green river waves on the white sand sounding fresh and pleasantly as the west wind blew them towards her? What thoughts? Good thoughts, surely. For the land wherein she dwelt—so fair a land, so small a land, had never ceased to be desired by the tyrant kings who bore rule round about. Always had they made war against it; never had they conquered, though sometimes they were seemingly victorious in a scattered fight here and there, through sheer force of numbers; for the dwellers in that good land were of a different race to the lazy, slavish people who dwelt about them. Many a song Gertha could sing you of how, long, and long ago, they came from a land far over the sea, where the snow-laden pine-forests, weird halls of strange things, hang over the frozen waters for leagues, and leagues, and leagues along the coasts that were the cradles of mighty nations. Sailing over the sea then, long ago, with their ships all a-blaze with the steel that the heroes carried, they came to this land with their wives and children, and here made desperate war with the wild beasts, with savage swamps, dragon-inhabited, daring famine, and death in all ugly shapes.

And they grew and grew, for God favoured them; and those who dwelt nearest to the "Savage Land," as it used to be called, grew more and more like the strangers, and their good rule spread; and they had a mighty faith withal that they should one day ring the world, going westward ever till they reached their old home in the east, left now so far behind. Judge, therefore, whether the tyrant kings feared these free, brave men! Judge whether, growing more and more cruel as they grew more and more fearful, they strained the chain over the miserable millions of their subjects so that with many it grew intolerable, and was broken asunder; so that, both in well-doing and in wrong-doing, God's kingdom spread.

Think what armies went up against the good land; what plains and valleys were sown with swords and spears and helmets, and the bones of valiant men; and from being nameless once, only thought of as the place where such and such a tree grew very plenteous, where such a river ran, became now to be remembered to all time, nor to be forgotten in eternity.

Think of the desperate fights, in treacherous slippery fords, where the round stones rolled and shifted beneath the hurried trampling of men, fighting for life, and more than life, amid the plash of the reddened waters in the raw, gusty twilight of the February mornings; or in close woods, little lighted up by the low sun just going to sink when the clouds looked thunderous in the summer evenings; or with shouts from crag to crag of the great slate-cliffs, with wrathful thundering of rocks down into the thronged pass below, with unavailing arrow-flights, because arrows cannot pierce the mountains, or leap about among the clefts of the rocks where the mountaineers stand, fiercely joyous.

Think too of the many heads, old and young, beautiful and mean, wept over, not joyously indeed; nay, who knows with what agony, yet at least with love unflecked by any wandering mote of the memory of shame or shrinking; think of the many who, though they fought not at all with spear or sword, yet did, indeed, bear the brunt of many a battle in patiently waiting through heart-sickening watchings, yet never losing hope, in patiently bearing unutterable misery of separation, yet never losing faith.

Had not Gertha then enough to think of, as she sat working hard by where the water lapped the white sand? For this people were so drawn together, that through the love they bore to one another sprung terrible deeds of heroism, any one of which would be enough for a life-time's thought; almost every man of that nation was a hero and a fit companion for the angels; and the glory of their fathers, and how themselves might do deeds that would not shame them, were the things that the men thought of always; and the women, for their part, looked to become wives to brave men, mothers to brave sons.

So now Gertha was singing rough spirit-stirring songs of the deeds of old, and thinking of them, too, with all her heart as she sung. Why she, weak woman as she was, had not she seen the enemies' ships hauled up on the island bank yonder, and burned there? Were not the charred logs, which once, painted red and black, used to carry terror to the peaceful, slothful people of the islands, mouldering there yet, grown over by the long clinging briony? Did not her eyes flash, her brow and cheeks flush with triumph, her heart swell and heave beneath her breast, when the war-music grew nearer and louder every moment; and when she saw at last the little band of her dear countrymen hemming in the dejected prisoners, the white red-crossed banner floating over all, blessing all alike, knight, and sailor, and husbandman; and when she saw, too, her own dear, dear father, brave among the bravest, marching there with bright eyes, and lips curled with joyous triumphant indignation, though the blood that he was marked withal did not come from his enemies' veins only? Did she not then sing, joyously and loud-ringing, remembering these things and many others, while the west wind was joyous about her too, whispering to her softly many things concerning the land of promise? She sang about a king who lived long ago, a man wise and brave beyond all others, slain treacherously in a hunting party by emissaries of the enemy, and slain at the height of his wisdom and good rule; and this was one of the songs that his people had embalmed his memory withal. So, as she sung, behold, the blowing of horns, and trampling as of horse, just as her voice rang clear with,

> "The King rode out in the morning early,
>   Went riding to hunting over the grass;
> Ere the dew fell again that was then bright and pearly,
>   O me!—what a sorrow had come to pass!"

And a great company rode past going to hunt indeed, riding slowly, between her and the river, so that she saw them all clearly enough, the two noble knights especially, who rode at the head of them; one very grand and noble, young withal, yet looking as if he were made to burst asunder the thickest circles of the battle, to gather together from the most hopeless routs men enough to face the foe, and go back fighting, to roll back the line of fight when it wavered, to give strength to all warriors' hearts: fancy such an one, so wise, yet so beautiful, that he moved like the moving of music; such tenderness looked from his eyes, so lovingly the morning sun and the sweet morning haze touched the waves of his golden hair, as they rode on happily. He that rode beside him was smaller and slenderer, smaller both in body and face, and it seemed in mind and heart also; there was a troubled restless look about his eyes; his thin lips were drawn inward tightly, as if he were striving to keep down words which he ought not to speak, or else sometimes very strangely, this look would change, the eyes would glance about no more, yet look more eager and strangely anxious than ever; the thin lips would

part somewhat, as if he were striving to say something which
would not leave his heart; but the great man's eyes were
large and serene, his lips full, his forehead clear, broad, and
white; his companion was sallow, his forehead lower and
rather narrow, his whole face drawn into wrinkles that came
not by age, for he was no older than the other.

They past as they had come, and when the last note of
their horns had died away, Gertha went about her household
duties; yet all that day, whatever she might do, however
much she tried to beat the phantom down, that stately man
with the golden hair floated always before her eyes.

    .   .   .   .

Evening now, the sun was down, the hunt had swept away
past the cottage again, though not within sight of it, and the
two knights having lost their companions were riding on
slowly, their tired horses hanging down their heads.

"Sire, where are we going to?" said the small dark man;
"I mean to say where past that beech-tree? the low swinging
boughs of which will hit you about the end of the nose, I
should think. Ah! his head goes down, somewhat in good
time; he has escaped the beech-bough."

But the other answered no word, for he did not hear his
friend speak, he was singing softly to himself:

> "The King rode out in the morning early,
>   Went riding to hunting over the grass;
> Ere the dew fell again which was then round and pearly,
>   O me!—what a sorrow had come to pass."

He sang this twice or thrice with his head sunk down
towards the saddle-bow, while the other knight gazed at
him with a sad half smile, half sneer on his lips and eyes;
then with a sigh he turned him about and said, "Pardon,
Leuchnar, you said something I did not hear; my mind was
not in this wood, but somewhere else, I know not where.
Leuchnar, we shall not find the hunt to-night; let us, let us
seek rest at that cottage that we passed this morning; it
seems to be the only house near."

"Yea, my Lord Olaf," said Leuchnar, smiling again in
that bitter way, when he saw in spite of the twilight, both
of the sunken sun and of the thick beech-wood, a great
blush come over Olaf's face.

"Yea, for why should we not?" and as he said this,

he fairly burst out into strange explosive laughter, that did not sound merry, yet was not repulsive, but sad only; for Leuchnar was thinking of the ways of man, and found much to amuse him therein; yet his laughter sounded sad in spite of himself, for he was not one who was made to laugh, somehow; but what specially made him laugh now was this, that neither of them had forgotten that hour in the morning, and the maiden sitting alone near the river: each of them, as they burst through the greenest glades of the forest, with cry of hound and sound of horn, had, according to his faith, visions of a dark-haired maiden, sitting and singing, her eyes raised and fixed on one of them; also both wished to go there again, and accordingly had been sad laggards in the hunt, and had lost themselves, not very unwillingly, perhaps; yet now neither liked to confess his longing to the other; Leuchnar would not even do so to himself, and for these reasons he laughed, and his laugh sounded strange and sad.

But Olaf knew that he was in love, and all day long he had been nursing that love delightedly; he blushed yet more at Leuchnar's laugh, for these two seldom needed to tell each other their thoughts in so many words, and certainly not this time. He bowed his head downward in his confusion so low, that his gold curls, falling forward, mingled with the full black of his horse's mane, and growled out therefrom:

" You are a strange fellow, Leuchnar, though a good one; but we will go."

"Yea, to the peasant's cottage, my lord," said Leuchnar, with his head raised, his eyes set straight forward, and his lips curled into something much more like a sneer than a smile; thereat Olaf with a spring sat upright in his saddle, and glanced quickly on either side of him, as though something had stung him unawares; afterwards they both turned their horses' heads aside, and rode slowly in the direction of the cottage, Leuchnar singing in a harsh voice, " The King rode out in the morning early,"—" though the dew has fallen again," he muttered; whereat Olaf gave an uneasy side glance at him.

And soon they heard again the lapping of the river waves on the sand of the silver bay, only lower than before, because the wind had fallen. Then presently they drew rein before the cottage door, when the moon was already growing golden. Sigurd, Gertha's father, came to the door, and courteously held the stirrups of the knights while they dismounted, and they entered, and sat down to such fare as the peasant had, and Gertha served them. But they prayed her so to sit down, that at last it seemed discourteous to refuse them, and she sat down timidly.

Then said Sigurd, when they had eaten enough, " I pray you tell me, fair knights, what news there is from the city, if you come from thence; for there is a rumour of war hereabout, only uncertain as yet."

" Nay, at the city," Leuchnar said, " there is certain news concerning one war, and even beside this, rumours of a great conspiracy between the surrounding rulers of slaves. The Emperor says that this valley always belonged to him; though, indeed, he was not very anxious for it when poisonous swamps spread out on both sides of the river here; or rather his ancestors laid no claim to it; but now, at all events, he is coming to take his own, if he can get it; coming by way (it is his only way, poor fellow!) of the mountain passes. Only, my lord Adolf is off to meet him with ten thousand men, and they are going to try the matter by arbitrement in this fashion; marry, that if the valley belongs to the Emperor, he must know the way to it, and accordingly shall have it if he gets through the mountains in any other way than as a prisoner or dead corpse."

Sigurd and Olaf laughed grimly at Leuchnar's conceit, and Gertha's eyes flashed; while both the knights watched her without seeing how matters went with each other. " Then," said Sigurd again, " Concerning the young king, fair knights, what is he ? " Olaf's eyes twinkled at the question, and Leuchnar seeing that he wanted to answer, let him do so, watching him the while with a quaint amused look on his face. " Why," said Olaf, " he is counted brave and wise, and being young, will, I hope, live long; but he is very ugly." Here he turned, and looked at his friend with a smile. Sigurd started and seemed disappointed, but Gertha turned very pale, and rose from her seat suddenly, nor would she sit down again all that evening. Then Olaf saw that she knew he was the king, and somehow did not feel inclined to laugh any more, but grew stately and solemn, and rather silent too; but Leuchnar talked much with Gertha, and he

seemed to her to be very wise; yet she remembered not
what he said, scarcely heard it indeed, for was not the KING
by her; the king of all that dear people; yet, above all,
whether the other were so or not, *her* king?

Poor maid! she felt it was so hopeless; nay, she said to
herself, "Even if he were to say he loved me, I should be
obliged to deny my love; for what would all the people say,
that the king of so great a nation should marry a peasant
girl, without learning or wealth, or wisdom, with nothing but
a pretty face? Ah! we must be apart always in this world."

And Olaf, the king, said, "So Leuchnar loves her—and I
love her. Well, it will change his life, I think; let him have
her; poor fellow! he has not got many to love him. Be-
sides, she is a peasant's daughter; I am a great king. Yet is
she nobler than I am, for all my kingship. Alas, I fear the
people, not for myself, but for her; they will not understand
her nobility; they will only see that which comes uppermost,
her seeming wisdom, her seeming goodness, which, perchance,
will not show to be so much greater than other women's, as
the queen's ought to do. Then withal to her, if, perchance,
at any time I am not quite sufficient to fill her heart, will
come a weariness of our palace life, a longing for old places,
old habits; then sorrow, then death, through years and years
of tired pining, fought against, bravely indeed, but always a
terrible weight to such an one as she is. Yet, if I knew she
loved me, all this ought to be put aside; and yet, why should
she love me? And, if she does not love me now, what hope
is there; for how can we see each other any more, living such
different far apart lives? But for Leuchnar this is other-
wise; he may come and go often. Then he is wiser; ah!
how much wiser than I am; can think and talk quite won-
derfully, while I am but a mere fighting-man; how it would
change his life too, when he found any one to love him
infinitely, to think his thoughts, be one with him, as people
say. Yes, let Leuchnar have her."

Those three so seeming-calm! what stormy passions, wild
longings, passed through their hearts that evening! Leuchnar
seeming-genial with his good friendly talk, his stories of brave
deeds, told as if his heart were quite in them; speaking so
much more like other men than his wont was; yet saying to
himself, "She must see that I love her; when since I can
remember have I talked so?" Poor fellow; how should she

know that? his voice was to her as the voices of a dream, or perhaps rather like grand music when it wakes a man; for, verily the glory of his tales got quite separated from him, and in some dim way floated in a glory round about Olaf, as far as Gertha was concerned. She heard his name, the hero of every deed, which that far-distant knight, Leuchnar, less present than his own tales, was telling of; whenever danger clung about the brave in those tales, her heart beat for fear of her golden-haired, broad-foreheaded hero; she wondered often, as her heart wandered even from those tales, why she did not fall down before him and win his love or die. How then could she think of Leuchnar? Yet Olaf did think of him, saw well through all his talking what he was thinking of; and, for his own part, though he did not talk aloud, and though even what he said to himself had to do with that subject dearest to him, yet none the less even to himself choked down fiery longings, hardly, very hardly to be restrained.

He tried hard to throw himself into Leuchnar's heart, to think of the loneliness of the man, and his wonderful power of concentrating every thought, every least spark of passion, on some one thing; he remembered how in the years past he had clutched so eagerly at knowledge; how that knowledge had overmastered him, made him more and more lonely year by year; made him despise others because they did not KNOW; he remembered, with a certain pang, how Leuchnar even despised him for one time; yes, he could bear just then to recall all the bitter memories of that time; how he saw it creeping over his friend; how he saw it struggled against, yet still gaining, gaining so surely; he called to mind that day, when Leuchnar spoke his scorn out openly, bitterly despising his own pride and himself the while; he remembered how Leuchnar came back to him afterwards, when knowledge failed him; and yet how it was never the same between them as it had been; he remembered then many a fight wherein they rode side by side together, Leuchnar as brave as he, yet ever with that weight of self-scorn upon him, that made him despise even his bravery; while Olaf rejoiced in his own, reverenced that of others; then he remembered how he was made king, how the love of his countrymen became from that time much more of a passion, true love, than it had been; and through all these things he tried to be Leuchnar, as it were ; not such a hard thing for him ; for, through his unselfishness, he had gained that mighty power of sympathy for others, which no fiercest passion can altogether put aside, even for the time. So he, too, had his thoughts, not easily to be read by others, not to be expressed by himself.

So the night passed ; and they went to rest, or what seemed so, till they were wakened very early in the morning by the sound of a trumpet ringing all about the wooded river-shore ; the knights and Sigurd rose and went forth from the cottage, knowing the trumpet to be a friendly one ; and presently there met them a band of knights fully armed, who drew rein when they saw them.

" King Olaf," said their leader, an old, white-haired knight, " thank God we have found you! When we reached the palace last night, after having lost you, there were waiting for us ambassadors, bringing with them declarations of war from the three Dukes and King Borrace ; so now, I pray you, quick back again! I have sent all about for men, but the time presses, and there is a credible report that King Borrace has already begun his march toward the plain ; as for the three Dukes (whom may the Lord confound !), Lord Hugh's army will account for them, at any rate to hold them in check till we have beaten King Borrace ; but for him we must march presently, if we mean to catch him ; only come King Olaf, and all will be well."

Then knelt Sigurd before the king, as he stood with eyes flashing, and cheek flushing, thinking how God's foes were hastening on to their destruction ; yet for all his joy he longed to see Gertha, perhaps for the last time ; for she was not there, neither did she come at Sigurd's call.

So the King smiled sorrowfully when Sigurd made excuse for her, saying that she feared so great a man as the King ; he could not help wishing she loved him, even though he meant to give her up : so he said ; he could not acknowledge to the full what a difference her love would make to him.

Then would he have given Sigurd presents of money and jewels, but Sigurd would not take them ; only at the last, being constrained, he took the King's dagger, hilted with curiously-wrought steel.

Then they all rode away together ; Barulf, the old man, by the King's side, and talking eagerly with him concerning the

coming wars; but Leuchnar fell into the rear, and said no
word to any.

CHAPTER II

LEUCHNAR'S RIDE

THEN for some days each man wrought his best, that they
might meet the invaders as they ought; yet through all the
work Leuchnar seemed very restless and uneasy, falling into
staring fits, and starting from them suddenly; but the king
was calm and cheerful outwardly, whatever passion strove to
fever him.

But one day when he was resting, leaning out of a window
of the palace that was almost hidden by the heaped jas-
mine and clematis, he heard horse-hoofs, and presently saw
Leuchnar, his sallow face drawn into one frown of eager-
ness, well mounted, lightly armed, just going to ride away,
Olaf well knew whither.

A fierce pang shot through to Olaf's heart; he felt dizzied
and confused; through the clematis stems and curled tendrils,
through the mist rising from his own heart, he dimly saw
Leuchnar gather himself together, raise his bridle-hand, and
bend forward as his horse sprang up to the gallop; he felt
sick, his strong hands trembled; and through the whirling of
his brain, and the buzzing in his ears, he heard himself shout
out: " Good speed, Sir Leuchnar, with your wooing ! "

This was enough; his heart sank, and his passion grew
cool for the second, when he saw how fearfully Leuchnar's
face changed at the well-understood words: troubled before
as it had been, what was it now, when suddenly all the con-
science of the man showed in that small spot of clay, his
face?

He turned his horse, and rode back swiftly; Olaf waited
for him there, scarce knowing what he did at first; yet
within a little, something, thoughts of approaching death
perhaps, had steadied his brain, and kept his passion back:
he heard soon the quick footsteps of some one striding far,
and walked quietly towards the door, where he met Leuchnar,
his teeth set, his lips a little open, that his hard-drawn
breathings might not choke him, his black eyes fixed for-

ward and shining grimly from under his heavy brows like pent-house roofs.

Olaf took him by the arm and gripped him hard; but he tore it away fiercely; he flung himself down before Olaf's feet.

"King Olaf," he said passionately, "I will not go, I will stay here then, if you look at me like that—with your broad white forehead and golden locks—you!—I will die here if I cannot live till I meet the enemy."

Olaf stooped to raise him up, but he drew farther back from him; then said, still kneeling:

"No word—no word yet, king, from you—was it not enough, Olaf, that you should take care of me, and love me in the days before you were king—me, a lonely discontented man, a black spot in the clear whiteness of the most loving people of the earth? was it not enough that, on the day when all the people shouted for Olaf, calling him the wisest and the best, you, with the crown yet on your head, the holy oil not dry there, should take me by the hand, and say to all the knights and all the people, whom you loved so, whom I (God help me!) loved not; 'behold Leuchnar, my friend, who has given me all the wisdom I ever had?' Ah, king! had you looked on me at that moment and seen even then my curling lips saying to my false heart, 'I am so much wiser than these simple ones!'—but your clear eyes only looked straight forward, glancing over the heads of the people that was dear to you, despised by me. Was it not enough, King Olaf, that you, as the days passed, still keeping me the nearest to you, still asking me concerning everything, should be beginning to thaw my hard heart and to shake my faith in the faithlessness of Adam's sons? were not these things enough, that you also, first of all finding pretences to mar the nobleness of your sacrifice even to your own heart, should give your love up to me, not as I do now to you, noisily, but quietly, without a word spoken; then afterwards, when you saw with what base eagerness I caught at that love given up by you, and fearing terrible things for my wretched soul if this went on, stopped me, like my guardian angel, just now when I was sneaking off like a thief in the night, and perhaps now—God help me! God help me!—have perhaps even made me do one thing in the whole course of my life which it is good to have done in His eyes?"

Then, as he knelt there, like a man before the presence of

God, the king spoke slowly, with humble face indeed, and tearfully, but almost smiling, because all things seemed so clear to him in a moment of prophetic vision.

"Dear Knight, your words seem like a bitter satire to me; for I did not call you back just now for your salvation, but because my selfish passion (think of a selfish king, Leuchnar; what a misery!) my passion carried me away: O, forgive me! for indeed I wish you to have her; think now, how many cares, and joys too, I have in tending this people that God has given me; I am sure that I shall not be quite unhappy for long, whatever happens; sometimes, perhaps, when I am weary, sometimes in the dead night, sometimes in the dying autumn, I shall have thoughts of her; but they will never be unbearable, because no power in earth or heaven can keep me from loving her: it will be no shame to you either, Leuchnar; do you not remember, in past days, how, when we talked of this matter, you have often said (wherein even then I scarce agreed with you,) that the love of man and woman should go before everything, before all friendship, all duty, all honour even? you thought so then; can you doubt now?" He ceased, and said no word for a little; then spoke doubtfully.

"And yet, and yet—are we not as men who reckon, as they say, without their host? What will Gertha say? ought we not to know before this great battle is fought, from which, perchance, neither of us will come alive? and we march to-morrow, and I may not leave the council and my work here: wherefore, dear Leuchnar, I pray you on your allegiance mount again and ride quickly away to that cottage, and ask her if she—loves you—and if—if—Leuchnar, we may be near to death; whatever happens we must be brothers—so God speed you on your wooing."

Leuchnar had risen while the king was speaking, and stood before him till he ceased with head sunk down on his breast; then raised his face, radiant now with a certain joy, to Olaf's; he spoke no word, as though that joy, or something else, confused and hurrying, that went with it, was too great for him; but, bending, kissed the king's hand and departed.

Then Olaf again leaned from the window and watched him go by again swiftly, till the sound of the horse-hoofs had died away: then he turned toward the council chamber, thinking:

"His face was not like the face of a man who is going to do what he thinks wrong: I fear lest he go as my ambassador— nay, do I *fear*? Yet surely that will be the best way to speed his own wooing—O Gertha! Gertha!—perhaps the sword will cut this knot so close wound up together now; yet I will not pray for that, only that Leuchnar may live."

Then presently he was in the midst of his lords. Oh what a weary ride that was of Leuchnar's! It was early morning when he started, high noon by the time he drew rein at the cottage door; and that joy which at first he had in his noble deed faded from off his face as the sun rose higher, even as the dew did from off the face of the meadows, and when he dismounted at that house of Sigurd's, his face was woful and ghastly to look on.

He knocked at the door, then entered when no one answered: he said out aloud, though he saw no one there, as if he distrusted his power to repeat that lesson got by heart with such pain: "I bear a message to the Lady Gertha."

Only the cool duskiness of the heavy-shadowed oak beams met his eye, only the echo of his own hollow voice, and the chirp of the sparrows, the scream of the swifts,—met his ear.

For Gertha was not within; but from the wood she had seen the glimmer of his arms in the hot noontide, and came down, stately and slow, unmoved to look on, but her heart of hearts wavering within her with hope and fear and ecstasy of love: perhaps (O poor heart, what wild hope!) it might be the king.

She met him just at the door from whence he had turned to seek her: he durst not meet her eyes, those grand fire-orbs that had pierced him through and through that other day; if he had looked up at her face he would have seen the disappointment, the sickness of hope deferred, showing somewhat there in spite of her efforts to keep the appearance of it back.

He, with his face turned away, said, in a hard voice as before, "I bear a message for the Lady Gertha." No blush coloured her pale cheeks, no start or trembling went through her grand form; she still held that flower in her hand, holding it with queenly sway, for it fitted in her hand like a sceptre: she said gently, "If you want *Lady* Gertha, you must go elsewhere, my lord; I am Sigurd the husbandman's daughter."

"But you are Gertha that we heard sing that day," he said fiercely, and turning his eager eyes suddenly on her.

"Yea," she said, trembling a little now, and turning even paler; for she saw how matters went with him, and feared, not any violence from him, for she soon read him through and through, but rather that he should fall down dead before her, his passion rent his heart so.

"Gertha, Olaf the king says, Will you be queen?" he said, still looking hungrily at her.

The crimson blood rushed up over her face, then went to her heart again, leaving her very lips grey. She paused a moment, with her arms stretched straight down, and her hands clenched: she said, without looking up:

"Tell him, 'No'; I am too lowly, not wise enough, I should shame him; I will not be queen— But——"

What wild passions rushed through poor Leuchnar's heart! how he fought with that Devil which had looked him steadily in the face so long, ever since he was born till now.

She stood there still before him, with arms stretched downward, hands clenched; he seized her by the wrist, and almost shrieked out; "But what?—Gertha! Gertha! before God, do you *love* him?"

Her colour came again as she looked him in the face, put very close to hers now, so close that she felt his breath upon it; she said calmly, almost proudly, "Yea, I love him; how could it be otherwise?"

"Some token then, for Christ's sake; quick, Gertha! and where will you be in the war time?"

"My father goes with me to-morrow to the city. I shall dwell at St. Agnes' convent of nuns till Borrace is defeated."

"Then some token!—here!" (and he tore down from the cottage eaves a bunch of golden stone-crop) "if you love him (think of God, Gertha), kiss this."

She bowed her head, and touched the yellow flowers with her lips; as she did so, he bent and kissed her forehead; then, with the flowers yet in his hand, he sprung impetuously to his saddle and galloped as if for his life. The Devil was conquered at last.

"Poor knight!" said Gertha, looking after him pityingly, "then he loves me too; it seems wrong to feel happy when such a noble knight is so miserable."

Yet she did feel very happy, and soon forgot poor Leuchnar

and his sorrows, who was riding meanwhile wildly through the forest; yet, as he drew further from her, the madness of his passion abated a little; he gave his horse rest at last, and, dismounting, lay down on the ferns by the side of the forest-path, and there, utterly worn out in mind and body, fell asleep; a dreamless sleep it was at first, as deep as death almost, yet, as it grew lighter, he fell to dreaming, and at last woke from a dream wherein Gertha had come to him, shrieked out that Olaf was slain, then thrown her arms about his neck; but, as he tried to kiss her, he awoke, and found himself under the beech-boughs, his horse standing over him, and the bridle, hanging loose from the bit, dangling about his face; for the horse doubted if he were dead.

He rose from that dream with a great wrench of his heart, and, mounting, rode on soberly. The moon shone down on him now, for he had slept far into the night. The stone-crop was fading fast, and as he looked at it, he doubted whether to curse it or bless it, but at last raised it to his mouth and kissed it, knowing whose lips had touched it before, looking half-fearfully over his shoulder as he did so; perhaps he thought a little also how Olaf's face would flush into perfect beauty for joy, when he saw it; for joy mixed with a certain regret for himself.

So, when he reached the palace, quite late at night, when the moon was already setting, he found Olaf standing in the great hall alone, looking pale and wearied.

Leuchnar came quite close to him, and said, taking his hand and smiling a sick smile: "Olaf, she sent you this, kissing it."

Olaf caught the faded flowers, kissed them a thousand times, knelt, and held them against his heart, against his forehead. He murmured—what words I know not, or, knowing, shall not say; while Leuchnar stood by with that old bitter smile on his lips. Poor fellow! he had expected sudden clasping of Olaf's arms about him, praise for his nobleness, consolation for his failure. Ah! did he not know himself what a passion love was? Then why did he expect from so true a man as Olaf protestation that he was the first when truly he was but the second? O! you all know what it is to be second in such a race; it is to be nowhere. Why he, too, if he had been successful, would have forgotten Olaf, and the way his sword flashed in the battle. It was only now in his disappointment that a certain natural instinct made him catch at all the love that came across him of whatsoever kind. That was why he thought so much of Olaf now. Yes, and in a little time he did think of all this, and smiled no more. "Poor Leuchnar!" he said to himself, "you must be very far in the background now, know that for certain. Then, did you not know all this when you knelt here some twelve hours back? O! foolish Leuchnar! yet, poor Leuchnar, too!"

And he was now so far from smiling that, but for his manhood, he would have wept for self-pity. Moreover, Olaf came to him and said, laying his hands on his shoulders, and leaning forward towards his face:

"You are the noblest of all men, and will in nowise lose your reward."

And Leuchnar knew that, or he might have gone mad; yet he prayed that his reward might be death presently, in the joyous battle.

So, on the morrow, they marched to meet King Borrace; and, on the evening of the third day, encamped but a little distance from his pirates.

And when, on the next morning, they stood in battle array, and the king rode up and down their line, Leuchnar saw in his helm the bunch of stone-crop, now quite withered.

Then that day, among the aspens, they joined battle.

CHAPTER III

THE LIGHT OF ISRAEL

THEN, in the midst of them, the old man rose up and spoke, while all the rest sat silent, some gazing fixedly on the ground, some on the fair dead king, that lay there before them.

For he had been slain with one wound that had gone right through his breast to the heart, and his body was not hacked or disfigured. They had taken his rent armour from off him, and washed his corpse, and spread out his long yellow hair to right and left of his face, along the samite cloth, purple, gold-starred, that he lay upon; and, behind him, at his head, they had laid his sword and armour, the helm yet having that stone-crop in it, the ends of the stalks at least; for all the rest had been shredded off in that fierce fight. Great waxen candles burned all about him; two priests sat at the head and two at the foot of the bier, clad in gorgeous robes of deep sorrowful purple, gold-embroidered; for these men reverenced man's body so, even when the soul was not so near to it as it had been, that, in those hours of doubt and danger, they thought the time well spent in making the body of their king, of him the best and most beautiful of all men, look as beautiful as God would ever have dead bodies look.

So, while some gazed on the ground, some on the fair dead king, none weeping, but all stern with thought; for they had to think of him as being present with them in their council, not *dead*—while they gazed earnestly, the old man, Barulf, arose and said,

"Sons of the men that go from east to west, and round again to the east! I advise you this day to do such a deed of valour as you have never done yet. Death in God's behalf, on the side of your friends, is not hard to bear, brothers, even when it comes slow and lingering; but how glorious to die in a great battle, borne down by over-many foes, to lie, never dead, but a living terror for all time to God's enemies and ours, a living hope to the sons of God. And to die altogether, beholding, between the sword-strokes, the faces of dear friends all a-light with intensest longing— is not that glorious!"

Their stern faces lighted up with flushing of cheek and flashing of eye as he spake; for in their hearts was fear of something far worse than dying on that field between the aspens with friends' eyes upon them. But Barulf went on.

"Yet, brothers, not this I bid you do. I give, as my counsel, that we depart this night, taking with us nothing but our arms, some small provision, and this dear dead thing here: turn our backs upon the foe, and depart, that we may reach the mother-city, where the women and children are; and I think I have good reasons for this."

"And how then shall we face the women and children?" said a young man moodily.

"Brother," said Barulf, "will you be a coward, indeed, from fear of being thought a coward? your heart does not counsel this, I know; and as for the women and children, are they mere beasts, so as not to understand this? will they not say rather? 'These men are warriors, they cannot fear death; then are they the braver to be so faithful, to be without fear of reproach for fear, so faithful to us above all things; we will love them all the more.'"

"But why should we not die here, fighting, Sir Barulf?" said another; "are there not men left when we are all dead?"

"Yea, dear knight, men, but not men *enough*. Think awhile—Adolf with his ten thousand men, and God's snow and storm that are tens and tens of thousands, guard the passes against the emperor. Good—they are enough as it is; but take away half for the defence of the cities, the mother-city above all, which is the weakest, the most beautiful, the fullest of women and children of all—and then would five thousand be enough to guard those passes? Even as it is, were not this summer a cold one and the snows deep, the emperor might drive his serf-soldiers, with whip and sword-point over our dead soldiers' bodies: but suppose they were lessened, our heroes would indeed die in their places, and would doubtless slay many of the enemy; but suppose they killed and wounded twice their own number, yet two days afterwards some 200,000 men would be marching over our land within fifty miles of the beautiful city.

"Again, Edwin and his 300 ships, diligently sailing into every nook and strait of the pirate island, and every day and night solemnly passing to and fro, with the white red-crossed banner at their mast-heads, guard the coast well; but let him land half, nay a third only of his men for the defence of the city, and in a week the sea-port towns and villages, safe from all scath now, would be blazing very high toward the heavens, and King Borrace's red and black ship-sides would gleam with the reflection of the Greek fire, as the dragons of it leapt toward the harbour-mouth.

"Moreover, the Lord Hugh, in his fortified camp, holds his own well enough now against the three Dukes; who prowl always like accursed cowardly wolves as they are, gnashing their teeth when they think that their provisions cannot last much longer, not more than another month; and, stamping on the ground, invoke the devil, their cousin-german, when they remember that not a blade of grass or ear of corn is left in the country behind them, laid waste as it was with fire, by the cruel fools as they marched: they, howling too for very rage when they see the wains in long lines entering Hugh's camp, and when they hear the merry sound of the trumpets, mingled often with the chaunting of the priests and the singing of men, singing about death that is no death. Ah! they howl, the wolves disappointed enough now; but suppose Hugh were to weaken his camp so as no longer to be able to send out his swarm of light-armed, who prevent the enemy from spoiling the yet unwasted country; then, also, no longer fearing an attack, the Dukes march nearer to him, get themselves corn and wine, cut off his supplies, march past him at last with their 50,000 men, not easy to destroy *then*. For cowards as the Dukes are, and imbecile drivellers, knowing nothing of war, yet have they along with them crafty captains, who, when their highnesses' passions master them not, give good advice which is listened to, and the commoner sort, though robbers by nature and nurture, have yet a certain kind of courage, and much strength in body and skill of arms."

In all the warriors' faces you might have seen a gloomy conviction that his counsel was good; but they sat silent, it seemed such a shame to turn and flee before this enemy they had just beaten.

Yet never for a moment did they doubt but that their people would in the end prevail over the enemies that hemmed them in, whatever became of those 20,000 left alive there on the plain; and Barulf spoke to the better part of all their hearts, when he said:

"Does it then seem so hard a thing to you, sons of the men that go westward, that we, having fought for three days such a battle as this, should have at last to turn and flee, carrying our dead king with us? Oh! it is hard, very bitter and cruel, brothers; yet is it God's will, and in his sight, doubtless, is as glorious as if we all died here in our places. And I am well assured that this and all things else only hasten us westward; it cannot be in any of your hearts that this people should fail. Nay, rather our sons' sons in the after-time will speak of these as glorious days in which the nations hedged us about, but in which we prevailed mightily against them.—

"But for another matter"—and as he spoke, the memory came across him bitterly that the king they had chosen but

two years since lay dead before them now: then his face
changed, and so it was with all of them, now that they were
free to think of that loss; for, but a little time back, he had
been with them; even just now, as they talked in their old
way of fresh battles, and thought of the swinging of the
swords, he had almost seemed to be there alive; but
now—

One of the priests who sat by him had fallen asleep,
wearied out with tending the wounded and dying, and his
head had fallen on his breast; another sat quite upright with
his hands laid on his knees, thinking dreadful things of what
was coming on the land; the third, a spare young man,
black-haired and sallow-faced, in his nervous anxiety twitched
at the border of his cope as he glanced about the tent, look-
ing uneasily on the face, first of one, then of another, of
those that sat there; the fourth, as he sat, sad-faced and
great-eyed, thinking of his mother and sisters whom he had
left in a castle of the lowland country, had taken one long
yellow tress of the dead man's hair, and was absently twining
it about his fingers.

Then arose Leuchnar with about as miserable a look on
his face as a good man can ever have, and said:

"Sir Barulf, I know what you were about to say, con-
cerning the king" (a shudder ran through them all), "I have
a message from the king to all of you. I was by him when
the spear pierced his true heart; I drew him a little out of
the fight; he said: 'I am wounded to death; but, alive or
dead, I must not leave this field, bury me just about where
the enemy makes his last stand before he turns.' For you
see, knights, our dead lord was sure of this, that the fair city
would be saved. Then the blood rising from his heart choked
him somewhat, yet he said gaspingly: 'Quick, Leuchnar,
bend to my mouth.' So I bent, and he said, faintly and
hurriedly: 'Undo my mail, and take the paper there, and
give it to the lords and knights in council.' So I took a
paper from his breast over his heart; the spear had pierced
it through, and had carried some of it into the wound, and
the trickling blood had stained it; I took it from off the
broken truncheon of the lance which was yet in the wound.
I showed it to him, he bowed his head in token that all was
well, when he had looked at it eagerly; then he said: 'I
wish to go, draw out the truncheon, faithful and true! poor

Leuchnar!' I drew it out; there was a great rush of blood; he smiled on me, and died."

Thereon Leuchnar stepped from his place, and, going up to Barulf, gave him the paper, very much stained and torn. Barulf read it.

"Good saints, how strange! do you know what is written in it, Sir Leuchnar?"

"Nay, I but guess, Sir Barulf; for I did not open it."

"Listen, knights!" said Barulf, and he read: "Knights and lords, if I die in this battle, as I think I shall, then (if so be it seem good to you) let Gertha, the daughter of Sigurd the husbandman, be queen in my stead; she lodges in the mother-city, with the abbess of St. Agnes' Abbey of nuns."

"Yes, I thought so," said Leuchnar, scarcely however speaking to them, for he was thinking to himself of himself; his sorrow seemed to have lessened much, even in the reading of that letter, for he thought: "Now she is queen, and has this sorrow on her, I can serve her much better, and my love will not trouble her now as it would have done, for it will seem only like the love of a good subject to his mistress; and I will lessen every grief of hers as it arises, loving her so, never vexing her in the least; O selfish Leuchnar, to be glad of her sorrow! yet I am glad, not of her sorrow, but of my service that will be."

These thoughts, and how many more, he thought in a single instant of time; how many pictures came up to be gazed on as it were for a long time, in that instant! pictures of his life before he saw her, and of the things which in his mind belonged to her; the white sandy shore that the low waves broke on; the feathering beech trees, with their tender green leaves in the early summer; king Borrace's burnt ships, great logs clomb over by the briony and clematis; the high-roofed cottage, whereon the loving golden-glowing stone-crop grew;—they came up before his eyes to be gazed at; and the heavy waxen candles burnt lower, the sleeping priest breathed heavily, the others sat in painful silence, nursing their grief; which things Leuchnar saw not because of those sweet pictures, even as they say that the drowning man, when the first fierce pain and struggle is over, sees no more the green, red-stained, swaying water-weeds, that lap his eyes and mouth, sees rather his old home, and all the things that have been, for memory is cruel-kind to men.

Still the candles flared and flickered in the gusts that stirred the tent, for the wind was rising with the moon ; and at last the one nearest the tent door was blown out by a long blast, and the priest who had been sleeping awoke, drew up his body with a start, trying to fix his blinded blinking eyes on Sir Barulf's face, as waked men use to do.

Thereat suddenly Barulf sprung to his feet, as if he too was waking from sleep, and cried out aloud :

"Rouse ye, lords and knights, that we may march to our queen ! for, for my part, our queen she shall be ; all he said and did was right and true when he was alive ; and he was, and is, the wisest of all men, and she too is a right noble woman ; was it never told you, knights, how she saved her father when king Borrace's men took him prisoner ? What say you, shall she be our queen ? "

And they all said " Yea."

Then again said Barulf : "Unless lords Edwin, Hugh, and Adolf gainsay it (as I have no doubt they will not), God save queen Gertha ! "

Then they all stood up and said : "God save queen Gertha ! "

And Barulf said : "Send a herald round about the army to proclaim Gertha queen, and to bid all to be ready to march some two hours before the setting of the moon. Cause also the knight who carries the great banner to be present, that we may bury the king."

So when all was ready, the noblest of the knights, Barulf and Leuchnar among them, lifted up the bier whereon the king lay, and they marched together towards the burial-place ; and the standard-bearer bore the great banner to flap above him, and the priests went before and after, chaunting ; and a great body of knights and soldiers went with them as they marched over the plain ; and the great moon, risen now, struck on their arms, threw the shadows of them weirdly on the dead that lay so thick among the trees, looked down on by the summer moon, rustled over by the full-leaved aspens.

They went a full mile, till they came to a place ringed about with aspen-trees, about which the enemy that past day had been finally broken.

Here they buried him, standing about in a ring, in as thick ranks as ever in the battle ; tearlessly and sternly they watched the incense smoke rising white in the moonlight, they listened to the chaunting, they lifted up their voices, and very musically their sorrow of heart was spoken.

"Listen!" said king Borrace's men, when they heard the singing; "Hark to the psalm-singing dogs! but by about this time to-morrow they will be beginning to leave off singing for good and all, for clearly the fools will wait to be killed, and we shall kill them all, and then hurrah for plunder!"

But the next day about noontide, when they, (not hurrying themselves, for they thought they were quite safe,) when they reached the camp, behold it was empty, for they all marched the night before, and were now still marching along the dusty road leagues and leagues from that battle-field.

Whereon king Borrace, instead of pursuing them, returned to his camp, where he gnashed his teeth for some half-hour or so, and held a great feast, he and his, and stayed on that field for three days,—"To give his army rest," he said.

————

CHAPTER IV

GERTHA THE QUEEN

AND meantime how did it fare with Gertha?

The time passed slowly between hope and fear, and all the time was weary with a sick longing that would have been no less had he but gone out on a hunting expedition. She had pity too for those who were sick with love and dread, and all those who looked on her loved her.

Then one evening about sunset-time, as the nuns were singing in their chapel and she with them, as the low sun struck through the western window, and smote upon the gold about the altar till it changed it to a wonderful crimson, upon which the pale painted angels that flecked the gold showed purer and paler than ever—there came, on that sunset evening, far off and faint at first, across, over the roofs of the houses up to the hill whereon the Abbey stood, a sound of shouting mingled with the wailing of women, and the still sadder and more awful wailing of the great trumpets, which seemed to be the gathered sorrow from the hearts of the men, who themselves could not wail because of their manhood.

Tremblingly the nuns heard it, and their hymns fainted
and died, as that awful sound of the indignant sorrow of a
whole people going up to heaven rose and deepened, and
swept onward: and Gertha turned pale even to the lips, and
trembled too, at first, like an aspen-leaf, her heart beating
so the while that she could hear the throbbings of it; but
with a mighty effort she put back the trembling fever; she
said low to herself: "He is dead, and I must not die yet."
Then she left her seat and walked, pale in her face like a
marble statue, up to the altar; she turned round and faced
the door and the sun, none hindering her, for they said,
"she waits for news about the battle."

The sun was on her forehead at first as she stood still,
but it sank lower till it touched her lips, and they seemed
to quiver (though she held them still) in that flood of light.

So she stood, when lo! the clash of arms in the vestibule,
and there entered armed knights without bowing to the altar
or crossing themselves, Leuchnar first, then Barulf and some
twenty lords following him; the others gazed about con-
fusedly at first, but Leuchnar going before them all, walked
swiftly up to the place where Gertha stood, and fell before
her feet, spreading his arms out towards her as he did so,
and his iron armour rattled with strange echo about the
vaulted roof; she did not look at him, her eyes beheld
rather the far off battle-field, and Olaf lying there some-
where under the earth.

"Queen Gertha," he began; but his voice failed him for
thronging memories; Sir Barulf and the others drew rever-
ently towards the two, and waited a little way off standing
in a half circle: he heaved a great sigh, then bent lower
yet, till his mail clinked against the step whereon she stood,
then suddenly raised his passionate eyes to hers, and gazed
till she was forced to look on him both with heart and eyes.

She beheld him pityingly: he said again: "Queen Gertha!"
(thereat she started) "Queen Gertha, he is dead."

"O Leuchnar, I heard the trumpets sing it so, therefore
I stayed here for his message; what is it?"

"That you must be Queen over us yet awhile, Lady
Gertha."

"Ah! and must I be; may I not go to him at once? for
do you know, Leuchnar," (and she stooped down low towards
him, and laid her hand on his head as he knelt) "do you

know, I saw him just now lying pale and cold, waiting for me, his arms stretched out this way towards me, his changed eyes looking longingly."

"O noblest," he said, "know you not with how many perils we are beset? Whose spirit but his can help us through, and with whom does it dwell but with you?"

She wept: "Leuchnar, though He call for me so, yet perhaps that is because he is sick and weak and scarce knows what he says: and I know that in his heart he desires above all things the safety of this people that goes westward; so I will be Queen till the last foe is vanquished —tell them so."

Then he took her hand; how strangely as he held it did the poor flesh of him quiver, how his heart melted in the midst of his body! he held her hand—and said, "I am Queen Gertha's liegeman." Then sprung to his feet and called out aloud: "Sir Barulf and Knights all, come and do homage to Gertha, our Queen!"

Then each man knelt before her, and took her hand, and said, "I am Queen Gertha's liegeman."

Afterwards all standing about her together, but lower than she, clashed their swords and axes across her that rang out joyfully, wildly, half madly in that quiet place; while the sun grew lower so that its light fell on her bosom, and her face above looked out sad and pale and calm from among the flashing steel.

So that day Gertha was made Queen. And then all throughout the city you might have heard the ringing of hammers on iron as the armourers did their work, and the clinking of the masons' trowels as they wrought at the walls, strengthening them; for the walls had grown somewhat weak, as it was very many years since any enemy had threatened the city with a land army.

And on the sixth day came King Borrace, having wasted the land far and wide as he marched. Now when he had sent a herald to demand the surrender of that city, who had not even been suffered to enter it, but had been answered scornfully from the walls, he gnashed his teeth, and mounting a great black horse and armed with a mace rode about, ordering his battle.

Then also Gertha, leaving her hall of Council, went round about the walls with a band of knights: over her robes of

purple and crimson her glorious hair flowed loose, and a gold
crown marked her, circling her head; while in her hand she
bore a slim white rod for a leader's staff.

Very faithful and true were all those in the town, both
soldiers and women, but when she drew near to any, their
faith grew so, that they seemed transported out of them-
selves; the women wept for very love, and the men shouted
"Gertha! Gertha!" till all the air rang; and King Borrace
muttered stupidly from between his teeth, "They are praying
to their gods, the fools." Then, turning about, he said to
one who was master of his artillery; "Gasgan, son of a dog,
bring up the catapults and shoot me down that woman there
—there she goes, poking her head over the battlements—
quick, O wretch begotten by the Devil's ram."

So Gasgan fixed his catapult and aimed the rugged stone
at Gertha as she leaned over the wall, thinking, forgetting
the fight and all, for him, just for a single instant.

He looked along the engine once, twice, thrice; once,
twice, thrice he started back without letting the catch slip.
"Dog," said Borrace, riding up, "why shootest not?"

The man looked up with drops of cold sweat hanging to
his brow, then stammered out,

"O my Lord, it is nothing,—that is, there is nothing there
now, nor was there when I fitted the levers; but when my
hand went to the bolt, each time I saw standing before me
that man, the King who was slain the other day, his sword
drawn in his hand, and frowning on me terribly; I cannot
shoot, my Lord—O Lord, save me!" he shrieked at last, for
Borrace, hitching up his great iron mace by its thong into
his hand, began to swing it, putting back his lips from his
teeth and setting his head forward.

"Son of a rotten sheep, can a ghost stop a stone from a
petraria? go and join King Olaf." So he struck him on the
uplifted face, between the eyes, and Gasgan fell dead without
a groan, not to be known any more by his wife or mother
even, for the mace had shattered his skull.

"Now then," said Borrace, "I will try the ghost of this
fellow whom I slew once, and whom I will slay again, God
being my help."

He leapt down from his horse, and let his hand fall to the
bolt, but just as he did so, before him, calm, but frowning,
stood Olaf with bright-gleaming sword and yellow hair blown

by the wind: "Art thou not dead, then?" shouted Borrace
furiously, and with a great curse he drew the bolt.

The stone flew fiercely enough, but not towards Gertha;
it went sideways, and struck down two of Borrace's own
lords, dashing the life out of the first and maiming the other
for life. Borrace flung on to his horse, howling out like a
mad dog, "Witch! Witch!" and like a man possessed
galloped toward the city as though he would leap wall and
ditch, screaming such mad blasphemy as cannot be written.

After him very swiftly galloped some fifty knights and
men-at-arms for his protection, and but just in time; for one
of the city gates swung open, the drawbridge fell with a heavy
thump, and out rode a single knight armed with a northern
axe instead of a spear, slim in figure, but seeming to be good
at war. He dashed through the first few of Borrace's horse-
men, who came up in scattered fashion because they had
been riding as in a race, unhorsing a man to right and left of
him as he passed through them, then made right at the
King; as they met, Borrace struck out blind with rage at the
knight, who putting aside the heavy mace smote him on the
side of the helm, that he tumbled clean out of the saddle.

"Gertha! Gertha!" shouted the knight, and he caught
Borrace's horse by the bridle, and dashed off towards the
gate again, where in the flanking towers the archers stood
ready to cover his retreat; for some twenty yards as they
galloped furiously on, Borrace dragged in the stirrup, then
the stirrup-leather broke, and his horsemen seeing him lie
still there, gave up the pursuit of the victorious knight, which
was the better advised, as the first flight of arrows from the
bowmen had already slain three outright, and wounded five,
and they were again getting their strings to their ears.

"Gertha! Leuchnar for Gertha!" rang from the knight
again, as he turned just before he crossed the drawbridge;
but the last of the enemies stood up in his stirrups and poised
his lance in act to throw; but before it left his hand an
arrow had leapt through his throat, and he fell dead.
"Gertha!" shouted the archer. And then again the draw-
bridge swayed up, letting little stones fall into the moat from
it, down rattled the portcullis, and the heavy gate swung to.

Then presently arose mightily the cry of "Gertha! Gertha
the Queen!"

But withal, when the pirates found that King Borrace was

not slain, but only very much bruised, they advanced their engines, and the catapults and balistæ and rams shook the wall, and made many sore cracks in the older parts, and the arrows flew like hail, and the "cats," great wooden towers covered with skins to protect them from fire, began to rise against the town.

Nevertheless, through all that weary day, though the defenders were so few for the great length of wall, they fought cheerfully and with good faith, like the men they were.

So that when they brought news to battered King Borrace, who lay tossing on his bed, concerning how little progress they had made, he gnashed his teeth, and cursed and was right mad.

And all the while through the thunder of the balistæ stones against the wall, through the howling of the catapult stones as they came among them into the city, through the gaunt uplifting of the misshapen rams, through the noise of the sledge-hammers clamping the iron bands of the cat-towers, through the whirr of arrows, through wounds and weariness, and death of friends, still rose the shout of "Gertha! Gertha the Queen! Gertha!"

Guess whether many people lay awake that night, or rather whether any slept at all, save those who were utterly wearied out by that day's fighting or by their own restless excitement. Many did not even try to sleep, but sat round about the cold hearth telling stories; brave stories, mostly of the good old times that were fathers to the good times now; or else they would go about the walls in an eager fever to see what was going on; and some there were who stood all that night by the bed of some sorely wounded friend; and some, mother, lover, friend, stood also by bedsides holding the cold hands with bitter thoughts that were hard to bear.

That night was dark, with much gusty wind and a drizzle of rain, therefore, though it was August and the days long, yet it was quite dark by nine o'clock, and a little after twilight the enemies' petrariæ left off playing, so that the besieged had rest: but before daybreak the drizzle had changed to steady rain, the wind having fallen.

Even before dawn the camp was a-stir, and two hours afterwards the cat-towers were again building, and the battering had begun again.

And so that day passed, through the rainy hours of it; and

about two hours after noon the enemy tried to scale the
lowest part of the wall near the harbour. Thereupon Gertha
came to that part and looked on the fighters from a tower
with a circle of knights round about.   Therefore her people
waxed so valiant, that though the pirates, fighting like mad-
men, fixed the ladders to the wall even through the storm of
arrows and stones, (for the tide was out and there was no
water now round about the wall,) they were nevertheless
driven back with great slaughter.

Also, on the other side of the town, one of the cat-towers
was fired, and many perished miserably therein.

That evening Gertha sat and took counsel with her lords
and knights; whereon Leuchnar arose and said, "Noble lady,
we must make a sortie, and collect every man, and every boy
too, to guard the walls meanwhile, for we are very few to
guard so great a city, and the enemy is very many; half our
men are utterly worn out with these two days' fighting,
coming so close upon their long march; the walls, either old
and crumbling, or new and still damp, are cracked in twenty
places: they are making a great raft for the crossing of the
moat; go to the open window, lady, and you will hear,
though it is night, the sound of their hammers busy on it.
When King Borrace can put on his armour again, (would that
I had slain him outright!) we shall be attacked in twenty
places at once, and then I fear it will go hard with the fair
city; we must make a night attack, and do all the burning
and slaying that we may."

"Dear knight," said Barulf, "you are young and wise, this
thing must be done: let some one get together two thousand
of our best men, and those that are least wearied; let them
be divided into two bands, and march out, the one by Gate
St. George, the other by the East Gate; you, Sir Leuchnar,
shall lead the one out of Gate St. George, and I will lead the
other."

He said this last quite eagerly, and the colour sprang up
to his face: Gertha looked at him half shyly, then spoke
to him.

"Nay, Sir Barulf, are you not then too old for blushing?
Except for the last word your speech was very wise, but that
spoilt it rather, for you must stay behind with us, some one
else must go."

She smiled serenely as she spoke; indeed she seemed quite

happy now, seeing prophetically perhaps that the end drew near.

"And I?" said Leuchnar, "may I not go?"

"Go, fair knight, and the Lord keep you from all harm."

But Barulf said, smiling also; "As for me, Queen Gertha, you know best, so I will stay behind, and hope to get a good drive at the three Dukes; they will keep, doubtless; may the Lord make their hands light! but who shall go in my stead?"

She looked round the noble assembly, and her eyes fixed on a young knight who sat over against her; their eyes met, and he seemed to Gertha to resemble somewhat her king, who was waiting for her near the poplar-trees. So she said:

"Sir knight, I know not your name; you I mean, with the blue surcoat and the golden Chevron on it; but will you take this service upon you?"

He had been gazing at her all the time they had sat there, and when he heard her speaking to him it must have seemed to him as if they two were alone together, for he looked this way and that, just as though he feared that some one might hear what they said one to the other; he rose and fell before her feet, not knowing if he were in Heaven or not, for his yearning was so strong that it almost satisfied itself. He muttered something almost inaudible about his unworthiness.

She gazed at him as he lay there with that inexpressible pity and tenderness in her face, which made all men love her so, trust in her.

"Wait, fair knight, and rise I pray you; have you Father or Mother alive yet?"

"No, Lady," he said, still kneeling, like a suppliant for dear life.

"Any sisters or brothers?"

"None, Lady Gertha, now."

"Have you a Lover?"

"Yea—one whom I love."

Oh how the look of pity deepened in her eyes! what wonder that every nerve trembled in his body?

"And would she give it to your charge to lead a desperate sortie, young as you are, with 'life all before you,' as men say?"

"Will she bid me go?" he said.

"Poor boy!—yet go—in the after-time we shall meet again,

whatever happens, and you and Olaf will be friends, and you will see all his glory. What is your name?"

"Richard."

"Farewell, Richard," and she gave him her hand to kiss; then he departed, saying no word, and sat outside for a minute or two, quite bewildered with his happiness.

Then came Leuchnar, and they went together to see concerning the men they wanted, and as they went they told each other that which was nearest their hearts: then said Richard:

"This is about the happiest time of my life, since I was a child; shall we not fight well, Sir Leuchnar?"

"Yes," he said, "we ought both to praise God, Sir Richard, that, things being so, he has shown us so clearly what to do; I remember now how often in the past days I used after my fashion to torment myself, with thinking how ever I should pass the time if it chanced that my love (when it came, for love of all kinds was long in coming to my dull heart) should fail me; and now God calls us merely to spend a few hours in glorious fight, and then doubtless he will give us forgetfulness till we see her again: and all this I have not at all deserved, for though men's lips formed themselves to speak my name often, praising it for my many good deeds, yet the heart knoweth its own bitterness, and I know wherefore I did such things, not for God's glory, but for my glory."

"Does not God then accept a man's deeds, even if he stumble up to do them through mixed motives, part bad and part good? is it not written, 'by their fruits ye shall know them'?—and your fruits—how often when I have heard men talking of you have I longed to be like you, so brave and wise and good!"

"Ah! the fruits, the fruits!" said Leuchnar, "when I think what the lawful fruits of my thoughts were, I shudder to see how near the Devil's House I have passed. Pray for me in the battle, Richard."

"You are very good and humble, Leuchnar," he said, "and I know not what good the prayers of such an one as I am could do you, but I will pray. Yet I myself have been careless about deeds at all; I have loved beauty so much that I fear if any crime had at any time stood between me and beauty I should have committed that crime to reach it; yet has God been so kind to me, and kindest of all in this, that

I who have done nothing all my life long yet, should do this and then die."

"And it is good to do one thing, and then die," said Leuchnar; "farewell."

So they departed each to his own band; and by this time the rain had ceased, the wind had risen, and was now blowing strong from the sea; the clouds were clearing off somewhat, but it was not quite bright; moreover the moon, though it had risen, was pretty much behind the clouds.

The two thousand horsemen went, each thousand in its own direction, very quietly along the streets; they opened Gate St. George quite quietly also, and Leuchnar passed out at the head of his men. Now on each side of that gate was a cat-tower; so a hundred men were sent to each of these to burn them first; they were then to follow the main body, doing such damage as they could to the petrariæ along their way: now this side of the camp happened to be very care-lessly guarded, scarcely guarded at all in fact; there was no one in the cats, and the guards about fifty in number, who ought to have been watching them, were asleep some twenty yards off; so both parties succeeded in firing the cats, taking care to put such store of tow and flax mingled with pitch into them that it should be impossible to drown the flames; moreover the guards awakened by the trampling of the horses and roar of the flames were put to the sword as they rose, sleepy, bewildered, unable to use their arms: then the two hundred men, burning as they went along the altogether unguarded petrariæ on their path, soon joined the main body, and they all rode on swiftly toward the camp, just beginning to stir because of the noise, and the flare of the burning cats. A few minutes' gallop brought Leuchnar to the foremost tents, which were fired, and then through the smoke and flame Leuchnar dashed into King Borrace's camp at the head of his thousand horsemen.

At first there was scarce any resistance, the men were cut down and speared as they ran half-armed from out of the burning tents, and the flames spread in the rising wind; but the alarm too spreading, and many bands coming up in good order, Leuchnar was surrounded almost before he knew it; so in a pause in the fight he looked about him to see how he and his could die most to the advantage of the People; he listened and looked towards the East Gate, there were no flames to be seen in that quarter where Richard was to have fired the great balistæ and the rams and the raft for the crossing of the moat; for, to leave Leuchnar about to do something desperate, some of King Borrace's men on that side had heard a stir in the town, and the bravest of them had gone to tell him : for at this time he was well nigh mad with his foil, and raged like the Devil himself, to whom indeed he must have been nearly related, and the service of telling him anything like bad news was indeed a desperate one.   However as I said, some brave men plucked up heart of grace to go and tell him that the townsmen seemed to be about to make a sally on that side of the camp.

He answered them first of all by throwing four javelins at them, one after another; for he had a sheaf of those weapons put by his bedside for that very purpose; one of them was wounded by this javelin-flight, the others by careful dodging managed to avoid him : then at last he listened to them, and being rather sobered ordered 5000 horsemen to fetch a compass and charge Richard's party in the rear when he was well drawn out towards the balistæ, which, as they were larger on this side, (for it was on this side that the enemy hoped most to make a breach,) were farther from the walls that they might be out of the range of the townsmen's engines.

So when Richard came out of the East Gate very softly, this band of 5000 men was quite close to him, and the balistæ were guarded by a great body of archers and slingers; and neither horsemen nor archers could be seen, because, the night being gusty, the moon was at that time behind the clouds : so then Rolf coming near to one of the great balistæ sent aside fifty men to fire it, who were straightway attacked in front and flank by arrow-flights, so that all those who were not armed in proof were either slain or too badly wounded to retreat; the rest rode back in haste to the main body, which had halted as soon as Richard saw how matters went : then indeed would Sir Richard and all his men have died without helping Gertha, or the People that went westward, much, as men count help : but the Captain of those 5000 thought he would not attack Richard from behind, lest he should ride down his own people in the darkness, who he saw had already had some contest with the townsmen; but thinking that he would turn at once toward the town meant to fall on him as he retreated without order.

But Richard, seeing well how things had really gone, turned round to his men, and called out, "Keep well together, and fight well for Gertha"—then, "Sound trumpets, and Richard for Gertha!" So they dashed right at the camp at the gallop, and entered it close to Borrace's tent, where it was not deep but straggling.

Now Borrace, thinking that nothing else could happen but that the townsmen should all be slain close to the walls, was standing near his tent, talking to some of his Captains, and armed all save his helm; for he was now well, or nearly well of his bruises, and intended to lead an attack the next day. So there he stood, and four Captains with him, he twirling his mace about in his nervous excitement, and sometimes looking uneasily at those that stood by, as if he thought they were getting something out of him. Judge of his astonishment when he heard Richard's shout of "Gertha," and then the thunder of the horse-hoofs.

"Curse that witch!" he ground out from between his teeth, "shall I never hear the last of her? only I think when I have seen her well burnt out of hand, after that——"

"For your life, my lord! for your life! they are coming this way, they will be over us in a minute!" and he turned and ran, and ran well too; and Borrace also began to run, and got clear out of the way of the main body, and would have escaped but that a certain knight, espying him, and knowing well the villainous wolf's face of the man, as he looked over his shoulder, under the clearing moon, turned off a little and rode at him while he ran like ten men, crying out with a great laugh as he knocked him over, "Twice, O King Borrace!"

And indeed King Borrace was not knocked over thrice, for this time the brains were fairly knocked out of his smashed head by the great horse-hoofs, the knight having disdained to use his sword on a runaway, and besides, being a genial sort of man, he had a kind of contemptuous pity for so stupid a brute, and thought to give him a chance.

However when the horsemen had ridden past, the Captains came back to see first of all what had become of their Lord and Master, for they had seen him go over, and with very mixed feelings. They found him as I said with his brains knocked out, and quite dead, whereat the first, Lord Robert, lifted his eyebrows and gave a long whistle in utter astonish-

ment that so slight a matter as a horse should have slain
him, for his head seemed to be solid and mostly of oak.
But Sebald, the second of them, lifted his foot and dug his
heel deep in the already fearfully lacerated face of the dead
tyrant, saying as he did so,

"Beast and devil, remember my sister! I told you then
I would do this one time or other," (and again he stamped,)
"said so openly, yet you took me into your service instead
of killing me as I hoped you would, madman that you were."

For in his madness of half-satisfied vengeance it seemed to
him that he had slain him with his own hands; but suddenly
it came across him how it was, and he said:

"Yet, O God! to think that I am disappointed in my
revenge: yet still it is pleasant to do this, though another
man slew him;" and again his heel came down on the dead
King's wretched face: then he stooped down and put his
hands to the warm blood that flowed from the wounds, and
raised them to his lips and drank, and the draught seemed
to please him.

Meanwhile Gherard, the third Captain, who had at first
stood still without saying a word and apparently in deep
thought, suddenly started, and catching hold of Sebald by the
shoulder said savagely: "Fool! can't you stop that play-
acting? Keep it till you are by yourself, for it is thrown
away upon us, I can tell you; and don't you see all of you
that this must not be known? quick! quick! help me to
carry him into the tent; here, Sebald, man, lift and quick—
ah!" he said, turning round and glancing about uneasily,
"where is Erwelt? but you carry him while I——"

And he darted off after the fourth Captain (Erwelt), who
had somehow disappeared, a man of mincing manners, very
elaborately dressed.

So Sebald and Robert, as they lifted the body, saw
Gherard as he ran in great bounds towards Erwelt; they
saw his hand slide down to his dagger, but there was no
weapon in the sheath; he ground his teeth with vexation,
but still went on till he had overtaken his man; then he
touched him on the shoulder and said: "Erwelt, I want to
speak to you." "Well," said the other, "what is it?"
But his heart sank and he felt as if Death stood before
him, dart and all, as indeed he did, for Gherard was a very
strong man, and, as he saw Erwelt's hand go down towards

the dagger-hilt, he felled him with a quick blow between the eyes, then before he could recover was kneeling on him; he dragged the broad double-edged dagger from its jewelled sheath, and buried it thrice in Erwelt's breast, then drew it across his throat from ear to ear; then, thrusting the dagger back again into its sheath, after he had carefully wiped it on the white and blue velvet of the dead man's dress, he sprang up and ran back towards the King's tent, leaving the body to lie piteously under the moon which was shining out from dark purple hollows between the clouds.

The light of it flashed on the poor fop's jewels, shone on his upturned face and gashed throat and feeble nerveless hands. How much more dreadful was that one corpse than all the many, lying now nearer to the walls; than those even who lay with ghastly breakings of the whole frame torn by great stones; or slain by wounds that struck them haphazard in strange unlikely places : or slain as they lay already wounded; or who lay with their bodies twisted into unimaginable writhings brought about by pain and fear. All these and many more, many, very many of each sort, they were altogether less horrible than this one corpse of a *murdered man.*

The murderer found the others already in the tent, for Robert had said : "Sebald, don't let us see that; you and I know nothing about it for the present; for we must hold together; and for my part I vote that we let Gherard work for us, he is such a clever fellow."

Sebald made no answer; his eyes were dry, his throat was dry, his heart was dry with intense thinking if by any means he could extend his vengeance beyond the present world. He thought of all the curses he had ever heard; how meaningless and uninventive they all seemed when set beside his hatred! he thought so that I know not into what uttermost hell he had dragged his own heart; he certainly did not feel as if he were on earth; his head grew dizzy, he could scarcely walk under his burden, but somehow between them they managed to get the body into the tent unperceived.

Then he thought : "I can bear this no longer, I must think of something else just now; but I will make it the work of my whole life hereafter."

So then Gherard burst in, muttering from between his teeth, " so much for one marplot:" and Sebald woke up and was in the world again.

So they began to talk, Robert sitting down and with his elbow on the table, stroking his cheek with his open hand; Sebald standing still, with knit brows, and blood-stained hands crossed over his breast; while Gherard walked up and down, twisting his fingers together behind his back, his cheek all a-flush and his eyes glistening—and Erwelt lay stiffening in the moonlight. So those three fell a-plotting.

Meanwhile such a hubbub and confusion had been going on before the walls as if the fiends were loose; for the archers, when Richard had passed beyond hope of pursuit, having sent a few arrows into the darkness at nothing, turned and looked about them.

Now they knew nothing at all concerning those horsemen who had been sent to take Richard in the rear, so, seeing some helmets glittering in the somewhat doubtful moonlight, they advanced a little towards them, and, thinking as a matter of course that they were from the town, sent two or three flights of arrows among them as an experiment, getting ready to run away in case they should be too many for them, doing all this before the horsemen could shout out that they were from the camp; and when they did so, the townsmen, seeing clearly that Richard and his men were away, opened a heavy fire on everything that they saw, and Borrace's archers believed that the horsemen lied, and still shot all they might.

Whereon the horsemen changed their minds, and settled that these were another band of men from the town whom they had not counted on, and so charged with a good will, especially as the long-bows and cross-bows and petrariæ were playing on them diligently from the city-walls.

Now the archers were more numerous than the horsemen, and, though not so well armed, fought stoutly, throwing away their bows and using their axes and swords, nor did they find out their mistake till many were slain both of horsemen and archers, and even then they were quite ready to go on with that work from sheer rage and vexation of heart; but restraining themselves, and being restrained by their leaders, they got separated somehow, and marched back to their own quarters, where one and all swore that they would stay, nor move again that night for man or Devil, whatever happened.

And so they fell to drinking all they might. But Sir Richard and all his, having won through the camp with but

little opposition (for the enemy were all drawn off other-where,)
crossed the river that lay beyond, by a broad shallow ford
that he knew well, (higher up it passed by that cottage,) then
took mere bridle-ways and waggon-roads through the woods
that lay beyond the river, after he had told his men that he
intended making a circuit and falling from behind on that
part of the camp where Leuchnar was. "For he is probably
hard pressed by this time," said he, "the sortie being from
the first somewhat desperate and wild, though necessary."
And he made this circuit lest he should be cut off before he
could reach Leuchnar; had he known that there would be
no pursuit, (there would have been but for Borrace's death,
and the happy clash between the horsemen and archers)—
had he known all this he would certainly not have gone so
far about, or gone through such intricate ways where the
men could not help straggling.

So the rain-drops fell in showers on their armour as they
passed, from the low tree-boughs brushed by their crests and
lowered spears; the moon flashed on the wet leaves that
danced in the rushing sea-wind; with whirr of swift wings
the wood-pigeon left the wood.

How often had Richard wandered here in the past days!
what thoughts were his in those old times, of the glory of his
coming manhood! what wonder at the stories of lovers that
he read, and their deeds! what brave purposes never to be
fulfilled! yet he meant them then honestly enough, yet he
was to do one deed at the last if only one, that was some-
thing; and as he thought this he straightway drove thoughts
of all other things from his mind, and thought of what he
should do now.

He called a halt, and listened; then perceiving clearly
that there was no pursuit at all, he led his men out of the
woods, by a way he knew well, round toward Gate St. George,
but cautiously and quietly for fear of an attack from the camp.

Then after a while they halted again, and he heard the
noise of the irregular *mêlée* I have told you about, and could
scarce account for it; he heard the noise of the fight about
where Leuchnar was; and he heard withal another sound
that made his heart beat with hope: it was a far-off sound
swelling and fainting in the rise and fall of the southwest
wind that blew from over the sea, the sound of triumphant
trumpets: he leaned forward from his saddle to listen better,

and many a soldier's eyes sparkled as he cried out suddenly, "Victory! it is Edwin—quick to Leuchnar!" So away they went toward Gate St. George at a smart pace.

They drew rein when they came within a few minutes' gallop from the camp that their horses might not go blown into the battle, then advanced with as little noise as possible, till they drew near and saw the enormous masses of the enemy surging round something which they knew well to be Leuchnar in a desperate case.

Then shouted their leader, "Richard! Richard for Gertha!" and with one mighty charge, which scattered the enemy to right and left, they were buried in the enormous multitude that was in vain striving to break Leuchnar's array.

For he, trying to win his way back to the city that he might sally out at the East Gate to the aid of Sir Richard, beset as he thought he was, as he was doing this he was first cut off from the city and driven back towards the camp, and then surrounded.

Whereupon the horsemen having dismounted formed a great square with closely planted shields, and long spears set out like the teeth of a great beast, and on this square King Borrace's horsemen, that were King Borrace's no more now, had wasted their strength for long : for howsoever many men of it were slain by the arrows and slings or by the hurling of the long lances, yet the living filled up the places of the dead, and the square, though lessening every moment, was not broken when Richard made that charge, and joined Leuchnar : having hewn his way through with most of his men to that square of serried spears, "Brother!" he shouted, "hold out yet awhile, for Edwin is coming in triumph over the sea, and we must live till then."

So they joined their two bands, and made a thicker and larger square than before, having cleared a space by one or two desperate charges, and soon the fight was fiercer than ever.

But the men fell fast before the arrow-flights and they grew utterly wearied with standing there on foot ; in pauses of the fight very anxiously did Richard and Leuchnar listen, and they heard a snatch now and then of the dear trumpet-music, and hoped, or tried to hope : yet it seemed that they must die before help came, the greater part at least.

Then an arrow whistled, and Leuchnar staggered and

bowed forward; he was wounded, not mortally indeed, but it dizzied and confused him. Almost at the same time the crowd opened, and there rose a shout of "Gherard! Gherard!" Forthwith a fresh band of horsemen charged, all armed in proof and splendidly mounted, with Gherard himself at the head of them.

How it all happened Richard scarce knew, but so it was that they broke the terrible hedge of spears, and presently each man found himself fighting separately or with one or two friends about him; tired men too against fresh ones, men on foot against horsemen, and all things seemed desperate.

Yet even then between all the clash of the battle Richard heard the roar of the bells from all the belfries and the shouting of the people. Edwin had landed. Then as he thought of this he grew half mad to think that they should die before the very eyes of their friends, and shouted out "Gertha! fight on, brave lads, and gather together all you may!" He with some half-dozen of his own men tried to gather others again, but, while he struggled desperately, his great sword flashing this way and that, but rising duller from every stroke because of the blood on it, he was suddenly borne away, and Leuchnar beheld him alone amidst a ring of foes, saw his sword still flashing for a little, then saw him fall with many wounds and lie dead, at peace at last.

He himself, though surrounded by a band of friends, was sorely wounded; and, sick with pain and loss of blood, he had nearly fainted; and the few around him were falling, falling fast under axe and sword and spear, when lo! the gates open, and the cry of "Edwin for Gertha!" rings all about, thousands pour out of the great gates, over the bridge, there is a sharp fight, and the bodies at least of Leuchnar and Richard are rescued.

For the pirates are driven back to their camp, not to stay quiet there for long; for even as they stand at bay about their tents the word goes that Borrace is slain; nor only so; the moon sinks, the east begins to redden, and within an hour after her setting many new spears fleck the clear light; the advanced guard of the Lord Hugh's victorious army who have marched night-long to come to the help of the fair city.

Close them all about, brave sons of the men that go westward! Borrace is dead, Gherard is dead, Erwelt is dead,

Sebald lies bleeding to death from four sore wounds, Robert
fled soon, but was drowned in crossing the river.

The cats are on fire, the petrariæ are in ashes, all the
camp is one blaze, everywhere the foe are throwing their arms
away and crying for quarter, soon they are all slain, wounded,
or prisoners.

Meanwhile a messenger, pale and worn out, is brought to
Gertha, and kneels down before her feet; he says, "Lady, I
have a message for you." (O Gertha! words spoken before.)

"Quick, good man," she says, "for these things draw to an
end;" and a smile of quiet triumph passes across her pale face.

"Three days ago," he says, "the Emperor strove to force
the passes; he and three of his captains were slain, and my
Lord Adolf will be here soon."

"Thank God!" she says, "but you, poor man, what
reward for you? ah! sleep has overmastered him:" for he
has fallen forward before her so that his head rests on her
feet; she touches him, takes his hand to raise him up; it is
stone-cold, he is dead.

"But for these men of King Borrace—let the wounded go
to our hospitals that they may learn there something of love
which they have not even dreamed about as yet; let the
slain be buried, and lie under the earth, under the grass
among the roots of the land they came to conquer: let the
prisoners depart unarmed, but with provisions for their
journey, let them cross the frontier, and never trouble the
good land more, lest a worse thing befall them."

CHAPTER V

WHAT EDITH THE HANDMAIDEN SAW FROM
THE WAR-SADDLE

AND in the fresh morning sat Gertha the Queen in the body,
while her spirit was a long way off, and round about her sat
the Lords and Knights with flushed joyful faces, she alone
pale though calm and serene, for she too was joyful.

Then into the midst of the great hall they bore Leuchnar
dying from his many wounds, not in great pain, for his spirit
was leaving his body gently, as if he were worn out merely.

And Gertha rose from her throne and went to meet them

that bore him, and there was a flutter along the tapestry that the hall was hung with, as the wind rushed through the opened door, and therewithal Gertha woke, her spirit came again as if Olaf had sent it.

So she gazed at him as he had hoped she might, as a Queen on her faithful subject: before this, often a certain uneasy feeling, not pity exactly, used to come across her when she saw him; it used to seem such a hard thing to her that it should be thus; it was just such a feeling as might have turned to love with one less constant than Gertha: but now even this was gone, and Leuchnar felt that it was so, even by the look of her eyes upon him.

And he, raising himself, hardly said to her, "Queen Gertha, I am come to say farewell for a little."

"Poor Leuchnar, who loved me so!"

"Nay," he said, "happy Leuchnar, who loves you still! in the time to come it may be that lovers, when they have not all they wish for, will say, 'Oh! that we might be as Leuchnar, who died for Queen Gertha in the old time!'"

"True," she said, "farewell, Sir Leuchnar."

Oh! how eagerly he took her hand! "Happy Leuchnar," he said faintly, then, "Domine, in manus tuas," and he fell asleep, his head falling back.

For a short time she stood, holding his dead hand; then gently disengaged it and laid it with the other one, crossing them downwards.

Then they carried him out again silently; and again ran that tremour through the gold wrought hangings, and her spirit had gone away again.

And within a while, as the great sun rose higher, came the sound of trumpets, and the roar of the bells from all the belfries: Adolf was come.

How near the end drew.

That noontide was windless, cloudless, and very bright, except that a soft haze had sprung up everywhere from the moist earth, into which all things far and fair melted.

She came from the midst of that knot of Lords that had clustered about her, and with her dark hair loose, stood in the balcony above the people, and through the hearts of all thrilled her clear speech.

"God has been very good to us, friends, and we have conquered, and now you must let me go as you promised.

And you may grieve that I must go, and wish me back often, but still I must go : it is not only because I wish to go that I must leave you, but I cannot help it : I think, nay am sure, that this also is best both for you and me. If I were Queen much longer you would be disappointed with me, yet would not say so, because you love me.

"Think now! I am but Gertha, the peasant's daughter, and I know it was only the spirit of your dead Lord working in me that made you love me so. But if I were Queen for long I should come to be only Gertha again ; so I must go. And if you will, let Barulf, who is old, but very wise, be King."

There was sad silence for a little when she had finished, then a confused sound of weeping, and sobs, and earnest wishes went up towards the balcony, where she stood with her arms lying down her side : already she looked as if she were a different kind of being from them : she said,

"Will you have Barulf for your King? if you will, say so to pleasure me ; then farewell."

They shouted, "Barulf! God save King Barulf!" and lo! even in that shout she had vanished, like an angel that comes from heaven when God lends him, and goes to heaven again when God calls him.

Gertha walked over the field of battle ; no meadow of sweet waving grass and lovely flowers, but something very horrible to gaze at, to pass over.

Yet she did not seem to take note of any of its horrors : her handmaiden was with her ; but when they came within fifty yards of the aspen circle where he lay, she charged her to stop, and watch all that came to pass there, that she might tell the people hereafter.

So the handmaiden sat down there on the mournful battle-field on some great war-saddle that had been thrown down there.

But Gertha, when she had kissed her, left her and walked toward those aspen-trees ; she was clad in her old peasants' raiment again, and was quite without ornament of gold or jewels ; only, her black hair hung braided on either side of her face and round about her head was a garland of yellow flowering stone-crop, such as he wore in his helmet that battle-day : but now when she entered the circle of aspens there seemed to be silence over all the earth, except that when she first stepped among the shadows of the trees, a faint breeze rose out of the south, and the lightly-hung leaves shivered, the golden haze trembled.

Now although all the rest of the battle-field was trodden into bloody mud, dry now again, but loaded with all dreadful things, this spot yet kept the summer flowers, neither was there any mark of his grave.

So there lay down Gertha, and the blue speedwell kissed her white cheek; there her breath left her, and she lay very still, while the wind passed over her now and then, with hands laid across her breast.

Nevertheless this was what Edith, her handmaiden, said to Barulf the King, and his Lords and Knights:

"And so I sat on the war-saddle and watched, and as my Lady stepped forward to enter that circle of trees, I saw my Lord Olaf, the King, as clearly as before he died, step forward to meet her, and he caught her in his arms, and kissed her on the mouth and on both cheeks.

"And they two were together there for hours (talking it seemed), sometimes sitting on the flowers and grass; (for that spot, my lords, is not trodden as the rest of the field is;) sometimes walking from tree to tree with fingers interlaced.

"But just about sunset time, I felt as if I must needs go and speak to my dear Lady once again, and hold her hand again: so I went up trembling; and lo! my Lord Olaf was not there any more, and I saw my Lady Gertha only, lying dead upon the flowers, with her hands crossed over her breast, and a soft wind that came from the place where the sun had set shook the aspen-leaves. So I came away."

Thereat the King and his Knights wondered.

And the People raised a mighty Church above the place where they lay, in memory of Olaf's deeds and Gertha's love: and soon about the Church there gathered a fair City, that was very famous in the after-time.

Yet it was strange that this Church, though the people wrought at it with such zeal and love, was never finished: something told them to stop by then they had reached the transepts of it: and to this day the mighty fragment, still unfinished, towering so high above the city roofs toward the sky, seems like a mountain cliff that went a-wandering once, and by earnest longing of the lowlanders was stayed among the poplar trees for ever.

SVEND AND HIS BRETHREN

A KING in the olden time ruled over a mighty nation: a proud man he must have been, any man who was king of that nation: hundreds of lords, each a prince over many people, sat about him in the council chamber, under the dim vault, that was blue like the vault of heaven, and shone with innumerable glistenings of golden stars.

North, south, east, and west, spread that land of his, the sea did not stop it; his empire clomb the high mountains, and spread abroad its arms over the valleys of them; all along the sea-line shone cities set with their crowns of towers in the midst of broad bays, each fit, it seemed, to be a harbour for the navies of all the world.

Inland the pastures and cornlands lay, chequered much with climbing, over-tumbling grape-vines, under the sun that crumbled their clods, and drew up the young wheat in the spring time, under the rain that made the long grass soft and fine, under all fair fertilising influences: the streams leapt down from the mountain tops, or cleft their way through the ridged ravines: they grew great rivers, like seas each one.

The mountains were cloven, and gave forth from their scarred sides wealth of ore and splendour of marble; all things this people that King Valdemar ruled over could do: they levelled mountains, that over the smooth roads the wains might go, laden with silk and spices from the sea: they drained lakes, that the land might yield more and more, as year by year the serfs, driven like cattle, but worse fed, worse housed, died slowly, scarce knowing that they had souls; they builded them huge ships, and said that they were masters of the sea too; only, I trow the sea was an unruly subject, and often sent them back their ships cut into more pieces than the pines of them were, when the adze first fell upon them; they raised towers, and bridges, and marble palaces with endless corridors rose-scented, and cooled with welling fountains.

They sent great armies and fleets to all the points of heaven that the wind blows from, who took and burned many happy cities, wasted many fields and valleys, blotted out from the memory of men the names of nations, made their men's lives a hopeless shame and misery to them, their women's lives a disgrace, and then—came home to have flowers thrown on them in showers, to be feasted and called heroes.

Should not then their king be proud of them? Moreover they could fashion stone and brass into the shapes of men; they could write books; they knew the names of the stars, and their number; they knew what moved the passions of men in the hearts of them, and could draw you up cunningly, catalogues of virtues and vices; their wise men could prove to you that any lie was true, that any truth was false, till your head grew dizzy, and your heart sick, and you almost doubted if there were a God.

Should not then their king be proud of them? Their men were strong in body, and moved about gracefully—like dancers; and the purple-black, scented hair of their gold-clothed knights seemed to shoot out rays under the blaze of light that shone like many suns in the king's halls. Their women's faces were very fair in red and white, their skins fair and half-transparent like the marble of their mountains, and their voices sounded like the rising of soft music from step to step of their own white palaces.

Should not then their king be proud of such a people, who seemed to help so in carrying on the world to its consummate perfection, which they even hoped their grandchildren would see?

Alas! alas! they were slaves—king and priest, noble and burgher, just as much as the meanest tasked serf, perhaps more even than he, for they were so willingly, but he unwillingly enough.

They could do everything but justice, and truth, and mercy; therefore God's judgments hung over their heads, not fallen yet, but surely to fall one time or other.

For ages past they had warred against one people only, whom they could not utterly subdue: a feeble people in numbers, dwelling in the very midst of them, among the mountains; yet now they were pressing them close; acre after acre, with seas of blood to purchase each acre, had been wrested from the free people, and their end seemed drawing near; and this time the king, Valdemar, had marched to their land with a great army, to make war on them, he boasted to himself, almost for the last time.

A walled town in the free land; in that town, a house built of rough, splintery stones; and in a great low-browed room of that house, a grey-haired man pacing to and fro impatiently: "Will she never come?" he says, "it is two hours since the sun set; news, too, of the enemy's being in the land; how dreadful if she is taken!" His great broad face is marked with many furrows made by the fierce restless energy of the man; but there is a wearied look on it, the look of a man who, having done his best, is yet beaten; he seemed to long to be gone and be at peace: he, the fighter in many battles, who often had seemed with his single arm to roll back the whole tide of fight, felt despairing enough now; this last invasion, he thought, must surely quite settle the matter; wave after wave, wave after wave, had broken on that dear land and been rolled back from it, and still the hungry sea pressed on; they must be finally drowned in that sea; how fearfully they had been tried for their sins. Back again to his anxiety concerning Cissela, his daughter, go his thoughts, and he still paces up and down wearily, stopping now and then to gaze intently on things which he had seen a hundred times; and the night has altogether come on.

At last the blast of a horn from outside, challenge and counter-challenge, and the wicket to the court-yard is swung open; for this house, being in a part of the city where the walls are somewhat weak, is a little fortress in itself, and is very carefully guarded. The old man's face brightened at the sound of the new comers, and he went toward the entrance of the house where he was met by two young knights fully armed, and a maiden. "Thank God you are come," he says; but stops when he sees her face, which is quite pale, almost wild with some sorrow. "The saints! Cissela, what is it?" he says, "Father, Eric will tell you." Then suddenly a clang, for Eric has thrown on the ground a richly-jewelled sword, sheathed, and sets his foot on it, crunching the pearls on the sheath; then says, flinging up his head,—"There, father, the enemy is in the land; may that happen to every one of them! but for my part I have accounted for two already." "Son Eric, son Eric, you talk

for ever about yourself; quick, tell me about Cissela in-
stead: if you go on boasting and talking always about
yourself, you will come to no good end, son, after all."
But as he says this, he smiles nevertheless, and his eyes
glisten.

"Well, father, listen—such a strange thing she tells us,
not to be believed, if she did not tell us herself; the
enemy has suddenly got generous, one of them at least,
which is something of a disappointment to me—ah! pardon,
about myself again; and that is about myself too. Well,
father, what am I to do?—But Cissela, she wandered some
way from her maidens, when—ah! but I never could tell a
story properly, let her tell it herself; here, Cissela!—well,
well, I see she is better employed, talking namely, how
should I know what! with Siur in the window-seat yonder—
but she told us that, as she wandered almost by herself, she
presently heard shouts and saw many of the enemy's knights
riding quickly towards her; whereat she knelt only and
prayed to God, who was very gracious to her; for when, as
she thought, something dreadful was about to happen, the
chief of the knights (a very noble-looking man, she said)
rescued her, and, after he had gazed earnestly into her face,
told her she might go back again to her own home, and her
maids with her, if only she would tell him where she dwelt
and her name; and withal he sent three knights to escort
her some way toward the city; then he turned and rode
away with all his knights but those three, who, when they
knew that he had quite gone, she says, began to talk
horribly, saying things whereof in her terror she under-
stood the import only: then, before worse came to pass
came I and slew two, as I said, and the other ran away
'lustily with a good courage;' and that is the sword of one
of the slain knights, or, as one might rather call them,
rascally caitiffs."

The old man's thoughts seemed to have gone wandering
after his son had finished; for he said nothing for some
time, but at last spoke dejectedly.

"Eric, brave son, when I was your age I too hoped,
and my hopes are come to this at last; you are blind in
your hopeful youth, Eric, and do not see that this king
(for the king it certainly was) will crush us, and not the
less surely because he is plainly not ungenerous, but rather

a good, courteous knight. Alas! poor old Gunnar, broken down now and ready to die, as your country is! How often, in the olden time, thou used'st to say to thyself, as thou didst ride at the head of our glorious house, 'this charge may finish this matter, this battle must.' They passed away, those gallant fights, and still the foe pressed on, and hope, too, slowly ebbed away, as the boundaries of our land grew less and less : behold this is the last wave but one or two, and then for a sad farewell to name and freedom. Yet, surely the end of the world must come when we are swept from off the face of the earth. God waits long, they say, before he avenges his own."

As he was speaking, Siur and Cissela came nearer to him, and Cissela, all traces of her late terror gone from her face now, raising her lips to his bended forehead, kissed him fondly, and said, with glowing face,

"Father, how can I help our people? Do they want deaths? I will die. Do they want happiness? I will live miserably through years and years, nor ever pray for death."

Some hope or other seemed growing up in his heart, and showing through his face ; and he spoke again, putting back the hair from off her face, and clasping it about with both his hands, while he stooped to kiss her.

"God remember your mother, Cissela! Then it was no dream after all, but true perhaps, as indeed it seemed at the time ; but it must come quickly, that woman's deliverance, or not at all. When was it that I heard that old tale, that sounded even then true to my ears? for we have not been punished for nought, my son ; that is not God's way. It comes across my memory somehow, mingled in a wonderful manner with the purple of the pines on the hill-side, with the fragrance of them borne from far towards me ; for know, my children, that in times past, long, long past now, we did an evil deed ; for our forefathers, who have been dead now, and forgiven so long ago, once mad with rage at some defeat from their enemies, fired a church, and burned therein many women who had fled thither for refuge ; and from that time a curse cleaves to us. Only they say, that at the last we may be saved from utter destruction by a woman; I know not. God grant it may be so."

Then she said, "Father, brother, and you, Siur, come

with me to the chapel; I wish you to witness me make
an oath."

Her face was pale, her lips were pale, her golden hair
was pale; but not pale, it seemed, from any sinking of
blood, but from gathering of intensest light from some-
where, her eyes perhaps, for they appeared to burn
inwardly.

They followed the sweeping of her purple robe in silence
through the low heavy-beamed passages: they entered the
little chapel, dimly lighted by the moon that night, as it
shone through one of the three arrow-slits of windows at
the east end.   There was little wealth of marble there, I
trow; little time had those fighting men for stone-smoothing.
Albeit, one noted many semblances of flowers even in the
dim half-light, and here and there the faces of BRAVE men,
roughly cut enough, but grand, because the hand of the
carver had followed his loving heart.   Neither was there
gold wanting to the altar and its canopy; and above the
low pillars of the nave hung banners, taken from the foe
by the men of that house, gallant with gold and jewels.

She walked up to the altar and took the blessed book of
the Gospels from the left side of it; then knelt in prayer
for a moment or two, while the three men stood behind
her reverently.   When she rose she made a sign to them,
and from their scabbards gleamed three swords in the
moonlight; then, while they held them aloft, and pointed
toward the altar, she opened the book at the page whereon
was painted Christ the Lord dying on the cross, pale against
the gleaming gold: she said, in a firm voice, " Christ God,
who diedst for all men, so help me, as I refuse not life,
happiness, even honour, for this people whom I love."

Then she kissed the face so pale against the gold, and
knelt again.

But when she had risen, and before she could leave the
space by the altar, Siur had stepped up to her, and seized
her hurriedly, folding both his arms about her; she let her-
self be held there, her bosom against his; then he held her
away from him a little space, holding her by the arms near
the shoulder; then he took her hands and laid them across
his shoulders, so that now she held him.

And they said nothing; what could they say? Do you
know any word for what they meant?

And the father and brother stood by, looking quite awe-struck, more so they seemed than by her solemn oath. Till Siur, raising his head from where it lay, cried out aloud: "May God forgive me as I am true to her! hear you, father and brother?"

Then said Cissela: "May God help me in my need, as I am true to Siur."

And the others went, and they two were left standing there alone, with no little awe over them, strange and shy as they had never yet been to each other. Cissela shuddered, and said in a quick whisper: "Siur, on your knees! and pray that these oaths may never clash."

"Can they, Cissela?" he said.

"O love," she cried, "you have loosed my hand; take it again, or I shall die, Siur!"

He took both her hands, he held them fast to his lips, to his forehead; he said: "No, God does not allow such things; truth does not lie; you are truth; this need not be prayed for."

She said; "Oh, forgive me! yet—yet this old chapel is damp and cold even in the burning summer weather. O knight Siur, something strikes through me; I pray you kneel and pray."

He looked steadily at her for a long time without answering, as if he were trying once for all to become indeed one with her; then said: "Yes, it is possible; in no other way could you give up everything."

Then he took from off his finger a thin golden ring, and broke it in two, and gave her the one half, saying: "When will they come together?"

Then within a while they left the chapel, and walked as in a dream between the dazzling lights of the hall, where the knights sat now, and between those lights sat down together, dreaming still the same dream each of them; while all the knights shouted for Siur and Cissela. Even if a man had spent all his life looking for sorrowful things, even if he sought for them with all his heart and soul, and even though he had grown grey in that quest, yet would he have found nothing in all the world, or perhaps in all the stars either, so sorrowful as Cissela.

They had accepted her sacrifice after long deliberation, they had arrayed her in purple and scarlet, they had crowned her with gold wrought about with jewels, they had spread abroad the veil of her golden hair; yet now, as they led her forth in the midst of the band of knights, her brother Eric holding fast her hand, each man felt like a murderer when he beheld her face, whereon was no tear, wherein was no writhing of muscle, twitching of nerve, wherein was no sorrow-mark of her own, but only the sorrow-mark which God sent her, and which she *must* perforce wear.

Yet they had not caught eagerly at her offer, they had said at first almost to a man: "Nay, this thing shall not be, let us die altogether rather than this." Yet as they sat, and said this, to each man of the council came floating dim memories of that curse of the burned women, and its remedy; to many it ran rhythmically, an old song better known by the music than the words, heard once and again, long ago, when the gusty wind overmastered the chestnut-boughs, and strewed the smooth sward with their star-leaves.

Withal came thoughts to each man, partly selfish, partly wise and just, concerning his own wife and children, concerning children yet unborn; thoughts too of the glory of the old name; all that had been suffered and done that the glorious free land might yet be a nation.

And the spirit of hope, never dead but sleeping only, woke up within their hearts: "We may yet be a people," they said to themselves, "if we can but get breathing time."

And as they thought these things, and doubted, Siur rose up in the midst of them and said: "You are right in what you think, countrymen, and she is right; she is altogether good and noble; send her forth."

Then, with one look of utter despair at her as she stood statue-like, he left the council, lest he should fall down and die in the midst of them, he said; yet he died not then, but lived for many years afterwards.

But they rose from their seats, and when they were armed, and she royally arrayed, they went with her, leading her through the dear streets, whence you always saw the great pine-shadowed mountains; she went away from all that was dear to her, to go and sit a crowned queen in the dreary marble palace, whose outer walls rose right up from the weary-hearted sea. She could not think, she durst not; she feared, if she did, that she would curse her beauty, almost curse the name of love, curse Siur, though she knew he was right, for not slaying her; she feared that she might curse God.

So she thought not at all, steeping her senses utterly in forgetfulness of the happy past, destroying all anticipation of the future: yet, as they left the city amid the tears of women, and fixed sorrowful gaze of men, she turned round once, and stretched her arms out involuntarily, like a dumb senseless thing, towards the place where she was born, and where her life grew happier day by day, and where his arms first crept round about her.

She turned away and thought, but in a cold speculative manner, how it was possible that she was bearing this sorrow; as she often before had wondered, when slight things vexed her overmuch, how people had such sorrows and lived, and almost doubted if the pain was so much greater in great sorrows than in small troubles, or whether the nobleness only was greater, the pain not sharper, but more lingering.

Halfway toward the camp the king's people met her; and over the trampled ground, where they had fought so fiercely but a little time before, they spread breadth of golden cloth, that her feet might not touch the arms of her dead country-men, or their brave bodies.

And so they came at last with many trumpet-blasts to the king's tent, who stood at the door of it, to welcome his bride that was to be: a noble man truly to look on, kindly, and genial-eyed; the red blood sprang up over his face when she came near; and she looked back no more, but bowed before him almost to the ground, and would have knelt, but that he caught her in his arms and kissed her; she was pale no more now; and the king, as he gazed delightedly at her, did not notice that sorrow-mark, which was plain enough to her own people.

So the trumpets sounded again one long peal that seemed to make all the air reel and quiver, and the soldiers and lords shouted: "Hurrah for the Peace-Queen, Cissela!"

.   .   .   .   .   .

"Come, Harald," said a beautiful golden-haired boy to one who was plainly his younger brother, "Come, and let us leave Robert here by the forge, and show our lady-mother this beautiful thing. Sweet master armourer, farewell."

"Are you going to the queen then?" said the armourer.

"Yea," said the boy, looking wonderingly at the strong craftsman's eager face.

" But, nay; let me look at you awhile longer, you remind me so much of one I loved long ago in my own land. Stay awhile till your other brother goes with you."

" Well, I will stay, and think of what you have been telling me; I do not feel as if I should ever think of anything else for long together, as long as I live."

So he sat down again on an old battered anvil, and seemed with his bright eyes to be beholding something in the land of dreams. A gallant dream it was he dreamed; for he saw himself with his brothers and friends about him, seated on a throne, the justest king in all the earth, his people the lovingest of all people : he saw the ambassadors of the restored nations, that had been unjustly dealt with long ago; everywhere love, and peace if possible, justice and truth at all events.

Alas! he knew not that vengeance, so long delayed, must fall at last in his life-time; he knew not that it takes longer to restore that whose growth has been through age and age, than the few years of a life-time; yet was the reality good, if not as good as the dream.

Presently his twin-brother Robert woke him from that dream, calling out: "Now, brother Svend, are we really ready; see here! but stop, kneel first; there, now am I the Bishop."

And he pulled his brother down on to his knees, and put on his head, where it fitted loosely enough now, hanging down from left to right, an iron crown fantastically wrought, which he himself, having just finished it, had taken out of the water, cool and dripping.

Robert and Harald laughed loud when they saw the crown hanging all askew, and the great drops rolling from it into Svend's eyes and down his cheeks, looking like tears : not so Svend; he rose, holding the crown level on his head, holding it back, so that it pressed against his brow hard, and, first dashing the drops to right and left, caught his brother by the hand, and said : " May I keep it, Robert? I shall wear it some day."

" Yea," said the other; "but it is a poor thing; better let Siur put it in the furnace again and make it into sword hilts."

Thereupon they began to go, Svend holding the crown in his hand : but as they were going, Siur called out : " Yet will I sell my dagger at a price, Prince Svend, even as you wished at first, rather than give it you for nothing."

"Well, for what?" said Svend, somewhat shortly, for he thought Siur was going back from his promise, which seemed ugly to him.

"Nay, be not angry prince," said the armourer, "only I pray you to satisfy this whim of mine; it is the first favour I have asked of you: will you ask the fair, noble lady, your mother, from Siur the smith, if she is happy now?"

"Willingly, sweet master Siur, if it pleases you; farewell."

And with happy young faces they went away; and when they were gone, Siur from a secret place drew out various weapons and armour, and began to work at them, having first drawn bolt and bar of his workshop carefully.

Svend, with Harald and Robert his two brethren, went their ways to the queen, and found her sitting alone in a fair court of the palace full of flowers, with a marble cloister round about it; and when she saw them coming, she rose up to meet them, her three fair sons.

Truly as that right royal woman bent over them lovingly, there seemed little need of Siur's question.

So Svend showed her his dagger, but not the crown; and she asked many questions concerning Siur the smith, about his way of talking and his face, the colour of his hair even, till the boys wondered, she questioned them so closely, with beaming eyes and glowing cheeks, so that Svend thought he had never before seen his mother look so beautiful.

Then Svend said: "And, mother, don't be angry with Siur, will you? because he sent a message to you by me."

"Angry!" and straightway her soul was wandering where her body could not come, and for a moment or two she was living as before, with him close by her, in the old mountain land.

"Well, mother, he wanted me to ask you if you were happy now."

"Did he, Svend, this man with brown hair, grizzled as you say it is now? Is his hair soft then, this Siur, going down on to his shoulders in waves? and his eyes, do they glow steadily, as if lighted up from his heart? and how does he speak? Did you not tell me that his words led you, whether you would or no, into dreamland? Ah well! tell him I am happy, but not so happy as we shall be, as we were. And so you, son Robert, are getting to be quite a cunning smith; but do you think you will ever beat Siur?"

"Ah, mother, no," he said, "there is something with him

that makes him seem quite infinitely beyond all other workmen I have ever heard of."

Some memory coming from that dreamland smote upon her heart more than the others; she blushed like a young girl, and said hesitatingly:

" Does he work with his left hand, son Robert; for I have heard that some men do so?" But in her heart she remembered how once, long ago in the old mountain country, in her father's house, some one had said that only men who were born so, could do cunningly with the left hand; and how Siur, then quite a boy, had said, "Well, I will try:" and how, in a month or two, he had come to her with an armlet of silver, very curiously wrought, which he had done with his own left hand.

So Robert said: " Yea, mother, he works with his left hand almost as much as with his right, and sometimes I have seen him change the hammer suddenly from his right hand to his left, with a kind of half smile, as one who would say, ' Cannot I then?' and this more when he does smith's work in metal than when he works in marble; and once I heard him say when he did so, ' I wonder where my first left hand work is; ah! I bide my time.' I wonder also, mother, what he meant by that."

She answered no word, but shook her arm free from its broad sleeve, and something glittered on it, near her wrist, something wrought out of silver set with quaint and uncouthly-cut stones of little value.

.   .   .   .

In the council chamber, among the lords, sat Svend and his six brethren; he chief of all in the wielding of sword or axe, in the government of people, in drawing the love of men and women to him; perfect in face and body, in wisdom and strength was Svend: next to him sat Robert, cunning in working of marble, or wood, or brass; all things could he make to look as if they lived, from the sweep of an angel's wings down to the slipping of a little field-mouse from under the sheaves in the harvest-time. Then there was Harald, who knew concerning all the stars of heaven and flowers of earth: Richard, who drew men's hearts from their bodies, with the words that swung to and fro in his glorious rhymes: William, to whom the air of heaven seemed a servant when the harp-strings quivered underneath his fingers: there were the two sailor-brothers, who the year before, young though they were, had come back from a long, perilous voyage, with news of an island they had found long and long away to the west, larger than any that this people knew of, but very fair and good, though uninhabited.

But now over all this noble brotherhood, with its various gifts hung one cloud of sorrow ; their mother, the Peace-Queen Cissela was dead, she who had taught them truth and nobleness so well ; she was never to see the beginning of the end that they would work ; truly it seemed sad.

There sat the seven brothers in the council chamber, waiting for the king, speaking no word, only thinking drearily ; and under the pavement of the great church Cissela lay, and by the side of her tomb stood two men, old men both, Valdemar the king, and Siur.

So the king, after that he had gazed awhile on the carven face of her he had loved well, said at last :

" And now, Sir Carver, must you carve me also to lie there." And he pointed to the vacant space by the side of the fair alabaster figure.

" O king," said Siur, " except for a very few strokes on steel, I have done work now, having carved the queen there ; I cannot do this thing for you."

What was it sent a sharp pang of bitterest suspicion through the very heart of the poor old man ? he looked steadfastly at him for a moment or two, as if he would know all secrets ; he could not, he had not strength of life enough to get to the bottom of things ; doubt vanished soon from his heart and his face under Siur's pitying gaze ; he said, " Then perhaps I shall be my own statue," and therewithal he sat down on the edge of the low marble tomb, and laid his right arm across her breast ; he fixed his eyes on the eastern belt of windows, and sat quite motionless and silent ; and he never knew that she loved him not.

But Siur, when he had gazed at him for awhile, stole away quietly, as we do when we fear to awaken a sleeper ; and the king never turned his head, but still sat there, never moving, scarce breathing, it seemed.

Siur stood in his own great hall (for his house was large), he stood before the daïs, and saw a fair sight, the work of his own hands.

For, fronting him, against the wall were seven thrones,

and behind them a cloth of samite of purple wrought with golden stars, and barred across from right to left with long bars of silver and crimson, and edged below with melancholy, fading green, like a September sunset; and opposite each throne was a glittering suit of armour wrought wonderfully in bright steel, except that on the breast of each suit was a face worked marvellously in enamel, the face of Cissela in a glory of golden hair; and the glory of that gold spread away from the breast on all sides, and ran cunningly along with the steel rings, in such a way as it is hard even to imagine: moreover, on the crest of each helm was wrought the phœnix, the never-dying bird, the only creature that knows the sun; and by each suit lay a gleaming sword terrible to look at, steel from pommel to point, but wrought along the blade in burnished gold that outflashed the gleam of the steel, was written in fantastic letters the word "Westward."

So Siur gazed till he heard footsteps coming; then he turned to meet them. And Svend and his brethren sat silent in the council chamber, till they heard a great noise and clamour of the people arise through all the streets; then they rose to see what it might be. Meanwhile on the low marble tomb, under the dim sweeping vault sat, or rather lay, the king; for, though his right arm still lay over her breast, his head had fallen forward, and rested now on the shoulder of the marble queen. There he lay, with strange confusion of his scarlet, gold-wrought robes; silent, motionless, and dead. The seven brethren stood together on a marble terrace of the royal palace, that was dotted about on the balusters of it with white statues: they were helmetted, and armed to the teeth, only over their armour great black cloaks were thrown.

Now the whole great terrace was a-sway with the crowd of nobles and princes, and others that were neither nobles or princes, but true men only; and these were helmetted and wrapped in black cloaks even as the princes were, only the crests of the princes' helms were wrought wonderfully with that bird, the phœnix, all flaming with new power, dying because its old body is not strong enough for its new-found power: and those on that terrace who were unarmed had anxious faces, some fearful, some stormy with Devil's rage at disappointment; but among the faces of those helmed ones, though here and there you might see a pale face, there was no fear or rage, scarcely even any anxiety, but calm, brave joy seemed to be on all.

Above the heads of all men on that terrace shone out Svend's brave face, the golden hair flowing from out of his helmet: a smile of quiet confidence overflowing from his mighty heart, in the depths of which it was dwelling, just showed a very little on his eyes and lips.

While all the vast square, and all the windows and roofs even of the houses over against the palace, were alive with an innumerable sea of troubled raging faces, showing white, upturned from the undersea of their many-coloured raiment; the murmur from them was like the sough of the first tempest-wind among the pines; and the gleam of spears here and there like the last few gleams of the sun through the woods when the black thunder-clouds come up over all, soon to be shone through, those woods, by the gleam of the deep lightning.

Also sometimes the murmur would swell, and from the heart of it would come a fierce, hoarse, tearing, shattering roar, strangely discordant, of "War! War! give us war, O king!"

Then Svend stepping forward, his arms hidden under his long cloak as they hung down quietly, the smile on his face broadening somewhat, sent from his chest a mighty, effortless voice over all the raging:

"Hear, O ye people! War with all that is ugly and base; peace with all that is fair and good.—NO WAR with my brother's people."

Just then one of those unhelmetted, creeping round about stealthily to the place where Svend stood, lifted his arm and smote at him with a dagger; whereupon Svend clearing his right arm from his cloak with his left, lifted up his glittering right hand, and the traitor fell to the earth groaning with a broken jaw, for Svend had smitten him on the mouth a backward blow with his open hand.

One shouted from the crowd, "Ay, murderer Svend, slay our good nobles, as you poisoned the king your father, that you and your false brethren might oppress us with the memory of that Devil's witch, your mother!"

The smile left Svend's face and heart now, he looked very stern as he said:

"Hear, O ye people! In years past when I was a boy my dream of dreams was ever this, how I should make you good, and because good, happy, when I should become king over you; but as year by year passed I saw my dream flitting;

the deep colours of it changed, faded, grew grey in the light of coming manhood; nevertheless, God be my witness, that I have ever striven to make you just and true, hoping against hope continually; and I had even determined to bear every-thing and stay with you, even though you should remain unjust and liars, for the sake of the few who really love me: but now, seeing that God has made you mad, and that his vengeance will speedily fall, take heed how you cast out from you all that is good and true-hearted! Once more—which choose you, Peace or War?"

Between the good and the base, in the midst of the passionate faces and changing colours stood the great terrace, cold, and calm, and white, with its changeless statues; and for awhile there was silence.

Broken through at last by a yell, and the sharp whirr of arrows, and the cling, clang, from the armour of the terrace as Prince Harald staggered through unhurt, struck by the broad point on the helmet.

"What! War?" shouted Svend wrathfully, and his voice sounded like a clap of thunder following the lightning flash when a tower is struck. "What! war? swords for Svend! round about the king, good men and true! Sons of the golden-haired, show these men WAR."

As he spoke he let his black cloak fall, and up from their sheaths sprang seven swords, steel from pommel to point only; on the blades of them in fantastic letters of gold, shone the word WESTWARD.

Then all the terrace gleamed with steel, and amid the hurt-ling of stones and whizz of arrows they began to go westward.

. . . .

The streets ran with blood, the air was filled with groans and curses, the low waves nearest the granite pier were edged with blood, because they first caught the drippings of the blood.

Then those of the people who durst stay on the pier saw the ships of Svend's little fleet leaving one by one; for he had taken aboard those ten ships whosoever had prayed to go, even at the last moment, wounded, or dying even; better so, for in their last moments came thoughts of good things to many of them, and it was good to be among the true.

But those haughty ones left behind, sullen and untamed, but with a horrible indefinable dread on them that was worse than death, or mere pain, howsoever fierce—these saw all the ships go out of the harbour merrily with swelling sail and dashing oar, and with joyous singing of those aboard; and Svend's was the last of all.

Whom they saw kneel down on the deck unhelmed, then all sheathed their swords that were about him; and the Prince Robert took from Svend's hand an iron crown fantastically wrought, and placed it on his head as he knelt; then he continued kneeling still, till, as the ship drew further and further away from the harbour, all things aboard of her became indistinct.

And they never saw Svend and his brethren again.

Here ends what William the Englishman wrote; but afterwards (in the night-time) he found the book of a certain chronicler which saith:

"In the spring-time, in May, the 550th year from the death of Svend the wonderful king, the good knights, sailing due eastward, came to a harbour of a land they knew not: wherein they saw many goodly ships, but of a strange fashion like the ships of the ancients, and destitute of any mariners: besides they saw no beacons for the guidance of seamen, nor was there any sound of bells or singing, though the city was vast, with many goodly towers and palaces. So when they landed they found that which is hardly to be believed, but which is nevertheless true: for about the quays and about the streets lay many people dead, or stood, but quite without motion, and they were all white or about the colour of new-hewn freestone, yet were they not statues but real men, for they had, some of them, ghastly wounds which showed their entrails, and the structure of their flesh, and veins, and bones.

"Moreover the streets were red and wet with blood, and the harbour waves were red with it, because it dripped in great drops slowly from the quays.

"Then when the good knights saw this, they doubted not but that it was a fearful punishment on this people for sins of theirs; thereupon they entered into a church of that city and prayed God to pardon them; afterwards, going back to their ships, sailed away marvelling.

"And I John who wrote this history saw all this with mine own eyes."

THE HOLLOW LAND

A TALE

" We find in ancient story wonders many told,
Of heroes in great glory, with spirit free and bold;
Of joyances and high-tides, of weeping and of woe,
Of noble recken striving, mote ye now wonders know."
Niebelungen Lied (see Carlyle's Miscellanies).

CHAPTER I

STRUGGLING IN THE WORLD

Do you know where it is—the Hollow Land?

I have been looking for it now so long, trying to find it again—the Hollow Land—for there I saw my love first.

I wish to tell you how I found it first of all; but I am old, my memory fails me: you must wait and let me think if I perchance can tell you how it happened.

Yea, in my ears is a confused noise of trumpet-blasts singing over desolate moors, in my ears and eyes a clashing and clanging of horse-hoofs, a ringing and glittering of steel; drawn-back lips, set teeth, shouts, shrieks, and curses.

How was it that no one of us ever found it till that day? for it is near our country: but what time have we to look for it, or any good thing; with such biting carking cares hemming us in on every side—cares about great things— mighty things: mighty things, O my brothers! or rather little things enough, if we only knew it.

Lives past in turmoil, in making one another unhappy; in bitterest misunderstanding of our brothers' hearts, making those sad whom God has not made sad,—alas, alas! what chance for any of us to find the Hollow Land? what time even to look for it?

Yet who has not dreamed of it? Who, half miserable yet the while, for that he knows it is but a dream, has not felt

235

the cool waves round his feet, the roses crowning him, and through the leaves of beech and lime the many whispering winds of the Hollow Land?

Now, my name was Florian, and my house was the house of the Lilies; and of that house was my father Lord, and after him my eldest brother Arnald: and me they called Florian de Liliis.

Moreover, when my father was dead, there arose a feud between the Lilies' house and Red Harald; and this that follows is the history of it.

Lady Swanhilda, Red Harald's mother, was a widow, with one son, Red Harald; and when she had been in widow-hood two years, being of princely blood, and besides comely and fierce, King Urrayne sent to demand her in marriage. And I remember seeing the procession leaving the town, when I was quite a child; and many young knights and squires attended the Lady Swanhilda as pages, and amongst them, Arnald, my eldest brother.

And as I gazed out of the window, I saw him walking by the side of her horse, dressed in white and gold very deli-cately; but as he went it chanced that he stumbled. Now he was one of those that held a golden canopy over the lady's head, so that it now sunk into wrinkles, and the lady had to bow her head full low, and even then the gold brocade caught in one of the long slim gold flowers that were wrought round about the crown she wore. She flushed up in her rage, and her smooth face went suddenly into the carven wrinkles of a wooden water-spout, and she caught at the brocade with her left hand, and pulled it away furiously, so that the warp and woof were twisted out of their places, and many gold threads were left dangling about the crown; but Swanhilda stared about when she rose, then smote my brother across the mouth with her gilded sceptre, and the red blood flowed all about his garments; yet he only turned exceeding pale, and dared say no word, though he was heir to the house of the Lilies: but my small heart swelled with rage, and I vowed revenge, and, as it seems, he did too.

So when Swanhilda had been queen three years, she suborned many of King Urrayne's knights and lords, and slew her husband as he slept, and reigned in his stead. And her son, Harald, grew up to manhood, and was counted a strong knight, and well spoken of, by then I first put on my armour.

Then, one night, as I lay dreaming, I felt a hand laid on my face, and starting up saw Arnald before me fully armed. He said, "Florian, rise and arm." I did so, all but my helm, as he was.

He kissed me on the forehead; his lips felt hot and dry; and when they brought torches, and I could see his face plainly, I saw he was very pale. He said:

"Do you remember, Florian, this day sixteen years ago? It is a long time, but I shall never forget it unless this night blots out its memory."

I knew what he meant, and because my heart was wicked, I rejoiced exceedingly at the thought of vengeance, so that I could not speak, but only laid my palm across his lips.

"Good; you have a good memory, Florian. See now, I waited long and long: I said at first, I forgive her; but when the news came concerning the death of the king, and how that she was shameless, I said I will take it as a sign, if God does not punish her within certain years, that he means me to do so; and I have been watching and watching now these two years for an opportunity, and behold it is come at last; and I think God has certainly given her into our hands, for she rests this night, this very Christmas Eve, at a small walled town on the frontier, not two hours' gallop from this; they keep little ward there, and the night is wild: moreover, the prior of a certain house of monks, just without the walls, is my fast friend in this matter, for she has done him some great injury. In the courtyard below, a hundred and fifty knights and squires, all faithful and true, are waiting for us: one moment and we shall be gone."

Then we both knelt down, and prayed God to give her into our hands: we put on our helms, and went down into the courtyard.

It was the first time I expected to use a sharp sword in anger, and I was full of joy as the muffled thunder of our horse-hoofs rolled through the bitter winter night.

In about an hour and a half we had crossed the frontier, and in half an hour more the greater part had halted in a wood near the Abbey, while I and a few others went up to the Abbey gates, and knocked loudly four times with my sword-hilt, stamping on the ground meantime. A long, low whistle answered me from within, which I in my turn answered : then the wicket opened, and a monk came out, holding a lantern. He seemed yet in the prime of life, and was a tall, powerful man. He held the lantern to my face, then smiled, and said, " The banners hang low." I gave the countersign, " The crest is lopped off." " Good my son," said he ; " the ladders are within here. I dare not trust any of the brethren to carry them for you, though they love not the witch either, but are timorsome."

" No matter," I said, " I have men here." So they entered and began to shoulder the tall ladders : the prior was very busy. " You will find them just the right length, my son, trust me for that." He seemed quite a jolly, pleasant man, I could not understand his nursing furious revenge ; but his face darkened strangely whenever he happened to mention her name.

As we were starting he came and stood outside the gate, and putting his lantern down that the light of it might not confuse his sight, looked earnestly into the night, then said : " The wind has fallen, the snow flakes get thinner and smaller every moment, in an hour it will be freezing hard, and will be quite clear ; everything depends upon the surprise being complete ; stop a few minutes yet, my son." He went away chuckling, and returned presently with two more sturdy monks carrying something : they threw their burdens down before my feet, they consisted of all the white albs in the abbey : " There, trust an old man, who has seen more than one stricken fight in his carnal days ; let the men who scale the walls put these over their arms, and they will not be seen in the least. God make your sword sharp, my son."

So we departed, and when I met Arnald again, he said, that what the prior had done was well thought of ; so we agreed that I should take thirty men, an old squire of our house, well skilled in war, along with them, scale the walls as quietly as possible, and open the gates to the rest.

I set off accordingly, after that with low laughing we had put the albs all over us, wrapping the ladders also in white. Then we crept very warily and slowly up the wall ; the moat was frozen over, and on the ice the snow lay quite thick ; we all thought that the guards must be careless enough, when they did not even take the trouble to break the ice in the moat. So we listened—there was no sound at all, the Christmas midnight mass had long ago been over, it was nearly three o'clock, and the moon began to clear, there was scarce any snow falling now, only a flake or two from some low hurrying cloud or other: the wind sighed gently about the round towers there, but it was bitter cold, for it had begun to freeze again: we listened for some minutes, about a quarter of an hour I think, then at a sign from me, they raised the ladders carefully, muffled as they were at the top with swathings of wool. I mounted first, old Squire Hugh followed last; noiselessly we ascended, and soon stood altogether on the walls; then we carefully lowered the ladders again with long ropes; we got our swords and axes from out of the folds of our priests' raiments, and set forward, till we reached the first tower along the wall; the door was open, in the chamber at the top there was a fire slowly smouldering, nothing else; we passed through it, and began to go down the spiral staircase, I first, with my axe shortened in my hand.— "What if we were surprised there," I thought, and I longed to be out in the air again;—"What if the door were fast at the bottom."

As we passed the second chamber, we heard some one within snoring loudly: I looked in quietly, and saw a big man with long black hair, that fell off his pillow and swept the ground, lying snoring, with his nose turned up and his mouth open, but he seemed so sound asleep that we did not stop to slay him.—Praise be !—the door was open, without even a whispered word, without a pause, we went on along the streets, on the side that the drift had been on, because our garments were white, for the wind being very strong all that day, the houses on that side had caught in their cornices and carvings, and on the rough stone and wood of them, so much snow, that except here and there where the black walls grinned out, they were quite white ; no man saw us as we stole along, noiselessly because of the snow, till we stood within 100 yards of the gates and their house of guard. And we stood because we heard the voice of some one singing :

" Queen Mary's crown was gold,
    King Joseph's crown was red,
  But Jesus' crown was diamond
    That lit up all the bed
        Mariæ Virginis."

So they had some guards after all; this was clearly the sentinel that sung to keep the ghosts off.—Now for a fight.—We drew nearer, a few yards nearer, then stopped to free ourselves from our monks' clothes.

> "Ships sail through the Heaven
> With red banners dress'd,
> Carrying the planets seven
> To see the white breast
> *Mariæ Virginis.*"

Thereat he must have seen the waving of some alb or other as it shivered down to the ground, for his spear fell with a thud, and he seemed to be standing open-mouthed, thinking something about ghosts; then, plucking up heart of grace, he roared out like ten bull-calves, and dashed into the guard-house.

We followed smartly, but without hurry, and came up to the door of it just as some dozen half-armed men came tumbling out under our axes: thereupon, while our men slew them, I blew a great blast upon my horn, and Hugh with some others drew bolt and bar and swung the gates wide open.

Then the men in the guard-house understood they were taken in a trap, and began to stir with great confusion; so lest they should get quite waked and armed, I left Hugh at the gates with ten men, and myself led the rest into that house. There while we slew all those that yielded not, came Arnald with the others, bringing our horses with them: then all the enemy threw their arms down. And we counted our prisoners and found them over fourscore; therefore, not knowing what to do with them (for they were too many to guard, and it seemed unknightly to slay them all), we sent up some bowmen to the walls, and turning our prisoners out of gates, bid them run for their lives, which they did fast enough, not knowing our numbers, and our men sent a few flights of arrows among them that they might not be undeceived.

Then the one or two prisoners that we had left, told us, when we had crossed our axes over their heads, that the people of the good town would not willingly fight us, in that they hated the Queen; that she was guarded at the palace by some fifty knights, and that beside, there were no others to oppose us in the town: so we set out for the palace, spear in hand.

We had not gone far, before we heard some knights coming, and soon, in a turn of the long street, we saw them riding towards us; when they caught sight of us they seemed astonished, drew rein, and stood in some confusion.

We did not slacken our pace for an instant, but rode right at them with a yell, to which I lent myself with all my heart.

After all they did not run away, but waited for us with their spears held out; I missed the man I had marked, or hit him rather just on the top of the helm; he bent back, and the spear slipped over his head, but my horse still kept on, and I felt presently such a crash that I reeled in my saddle, and felt mad. He had lashed out at me with his sword as I came on, hitting me in the ribs (for my arm was raised), but only flatlings.

I was quite wild with rage, I turned, almost fell upon him, caught him by the neck with both hands, and threw him under the horse-hoofs, sighing with fury: I heard Arnald's voice close to me, " Well fought, Florian ": and I saw his great stern face bare among the iron, for he had made a vow in remembrance of that blow always to fight unhelmed; I saw his great sword swinging, in wide gyres, and hissing as it started up, just as if it were alive and liked it.

So joy filled all my soul, and I fought with my heart, till the big axe I swung felt like nothing but a little hammer in my hand, except for its bitterness : and as for the enemy, they went down like grass, so that we destroyed them utterly, for those knights would neither yield nor fly, but died as they stood, so that some fifteen of our men also died there.

Then at last we came to the palace, where some grooms and such like kept the gates armed, but some ran, and some we took prisoners, one of whom died for sheer terror in our hands, being stricken by no wound: for he thought we would eat him.

These prisoners we questioned concerning the queen, and so entered the great hall.

There Arnald sat down in the throne on the dais, and laid his naked sword before him on the table : and on each side of him sat such knights as there was room for, and the others stood round about, while I took ten men, and went to look for Swanhilda.

I found her soon, sitting by herself in a gorgeous chamber. I almost pitied her when I saw her looking so utterly desolate and despairing; her beauty too had faded, deep lines cut through her face. But when I entered she knew who I was, and her look of intense hatred was so fiend-like, that it changed my pity into horror of her.

"Knight," she said, "who are you, and what do you want, thus discourteously entering my chamber?"

"I am Florian de Liliis, and I am to conduct you to judgment."

She sprung up, "Curse you and your whole house,— you I hate worse than any,—girl's face,—guards! guards!" and she stamped on the ground, her veins on the forehead swelled, her eyes grew round and flamed out, as she kept crying for her guards, stamping the while, for she seemed quite mad.

Then at last she remembered that she was in the power of her enemies, she sat down, and lay with her face between her hands, and wept passionately.

"Witch,"—I said between my closed teeth, "will you come, or must we carry you down to the great hall?"

Neither would she come, but sat there, clutching at her dress and tearing her hair.

Then I said, "Bind her, and carry her down." And they did so.

I watched Arnald as we came in, there was no triumph on his stern white face, but resolution enough, he had made up his mind.

They placed her on a seat in the midst of the hall over against the dais. He said, "Unbind her, Florian." They did so, she raised her face, and glared defiance at us all, as though she would die queenly after all.

Then rose up Arnald and said, "Queen Swanhilda, we judge you guilty of death, and because you are a queen and of a noble house, you shall be slain by my knightly sword, and I will even take the reproach of slaying a woman, for no other hand than mine shall deal the blow."

Then she said, "O false knight, show your warrant from God, man, or devil."

"This warrant from God, Swanhilda," he said, holding up

his sword, "listen !—fifteen years ago, when I was just winning my spurs, you struck me, disgracing me before all the people ; you cursed me, and meant that curse well enough. Men of the house of the Lilies, what sentence for that ? "

" Death ! " they said.

" Listen !—afterwards you slew my cousin, your husband, treacherously, in the most cursed way, stabbing him in the throat, as the stars in the canopy above him looked down on the shut eyes of him. Men of the house of the Lily, what sentence for that ? "

" Death ! " they said.

" Do you hear them, Queen ? there is warrant from man; for the devil, I do not reverence him enough to take warrant from him, but, as I look at that face of yours, I think that even he has left you."

And indeed just then all her pride seemed to leave her, she fell from the chair, and wallowed on the ground moaning, she wept like a child, so that the tears lay on the oak floor; she prayed for another month of life; she came to me and kneeled, and kissed my feet, and prayed piteously, so that water ran out of her mouth.

But I shuddered, and drew away; it was like having an adder about one; I could have pitied her had she died bravely, but for one like her to whine and whine !—pah !—

Then from the dais rang Arnald's voice terrible, much changed. "Let there be an end of all this." And he took his sword and strode through the hall towards her ; she rose from the ground and stood up, stooping a little, her head sunk between her shoulders, her black eyes turned up and gleaming, like a tigress about to spring. When he came within some six paces of her something in his eye daunted her, or perhaps the flashing of his terrible sword in the torch-light ; she threw her arms up with a great shriek, and dashed screaming about the hall. Arnald's lip never once curled with any scorn, no line in his face changed : he said, "Bring her here and bind her."

But when one came up to her to lay hold on her she first of all ran at him, hitting with her head in the belly. Then while he stood doubled up for want of breath, and staring with his head up, she caught his sword from the girdle, and cut him across the shoulders, and many others she wounded sorely before they took her.

Then Arnald stood by the chair to which she was bound, and poised his sword, and there was a great silence.

Then he said, " Men of the House of the Lilies, do you justify me in this, shall she die ? " Straightway rang a great shout through the hall, but before it died away the sword had swept round, and therewithal was there no such thing as Swanhilda left upon the earth, for in no battle-field had Arnald struck truer blow. Then he turned to the few servants of the palace and said, " Go now, bury this accursed woman, for she is a king's daughter." Then to us all, " Now knights, to horse and away, that we may reach the good town by about dawn." So we mounted and rode off.

What a strange Christmas-day that was, for there, about nine o'clock in the morning, rode Red Harald into the good town to demand vengeance ; he went at once to the king, and the king promised that before nightfall that very day the matter should be judged ; albeit the king feared somewhat, because every third man you met in the streets had a blue cross on his shoulder, and some likeness of a lily, cut out or painted, stuck in his hat ; and this blue cross and lily were the bearings of our house, called " De Liliis." Now we had seen Red Harald pass through the streets, with a white banner borne before him, to show that he came peaceably as for this time ; but I trow he was thinking of other things than peace.

And he was called Red Harald first at this time, because over all his arms he wore a great scarlet cloth, that fell in heavy folds about his horse and all about him. Then, as he passed our house, some one pointed it out to him, rising there with its carving and its barred marble, but stronger than many a castle on the hill-tops, and its great overhanging battlement cast a mighty shadow down the wall and across the street ; and above all rose the great tower, our banner floating proudly from the top, whereon was emblazoned on a white ground a blue cross, and on a blue ground four white lilies. And now faces were gazing from all the windows, and all the battlements were thronged ; so Harald turned, and rising in his stirrups, shook his clenched fist at our house ; natheless, as he did so, the east wind, coming down the street, caught up the corner of that scarlet cloth and drove it over his face, and therewithal disordering his long black hair, well nigh choked him, so that he bit both his hair and that cloth.

So from base to cope rose a mighty shout of triumph and defiance, and he passed on.

Then Arnald caused it to be cried, that all those who loved the good House of the Lilies should go to mass that morning in Saint Mary's Church, hard by our house. Now this church belonged to us, and the abbey that served it, and always we appointed the abbot of it on condition that our trumpets should sound all together when on high masses they sing the "Gloria in Excelsis." It was the largest and most beautiful of all the churches in the town, and had two exceeding high towers, which you could see from far off, even when you saw not the town or any of its other towers : and in one of these towers were twelve great bells, named after the twelve Apostles, one name being written on each one of them ; as Peter, Matthew, and so on ; and in the other tower was one great bell only, much larger than any of the others, and which was called Mary. Now this bell was never rung but when our house was in great danger, and it had this legend on it, "When Mary rings the earth shakes ;" and indeed from this we took our war cry, which was, "Mary rings ;" somewhat justifiably indeed, for the last time that Mary rung, on that day before nightfall there were four thousand bodies to be buried, which bodies wore neither cross nor lily.

So Arnald gave me in charge to tell the abbot to cause Mary to be tolled for an hour before mass that day.

The abbot leaned on my shoulder as I stood within the tower and looked at the twelve monks laying their hands to the ropes. Far up in the dimness I saw the wheel before it began to swing round about ; then it moved a little ; the twelve men bent down to the earth and a roar rose that shook the tower from base to spire-vane : backwards and forwards swept the wheel, as Mary now looked downwards towards earth, now looked up at the shadowy cone of the spire, shot across by bars of light from the dormers.

And the thunder of Mary was caught up by the wind and carried through all the country ; and when the good man heard it, he said goodbye to wife and child, slung his shield behind his back, and set forward with his spear sloped over his shoulder, and many a time, as he walked toward the good town, he tightened the belt that went about his waist, that he might stride the faster, so long and furiously did Mary toll.

And before the great bell, Mary, had ceased ringing, all the ways were full of armed men.

But at each door of the church of Saint Mary stood a row of men armed with axes, and when any came, meaning to go into the church, the two first of these would hold their axes (whose helves were about four feet long) over his head, and would ask him, "Who went over the moon last night?" then if he answered nothing or at random they would bid him turn back, which he for the more part would be ready enough to do; but some, striving to get through that row of men, were slain outright; but if he were one of those that were friends to the House of the Lilies he would answer to that question, "Mary and John."

By the time the mass began the whole church was full, and in the nave and transept thereof were three thousand men, all of our house and all armed. But Arnald and myself, and Squire Hugh, and some others sat under a gold-fringed canopy near the choir; and the abbot said mass, having his mitre on his head. Yet, as I watched him, it seemed to me that he must have something on beneath his priest's vestments, for he looked much fatter than usual, being really a tall lithe man.

Now, as they sung the "Kyrie," some one shouted from the other end of the church, "My lord Arnald, they are slaying our people without;" for, indeed, all the square about the church was full of our people, who for the press had not been able to enter, and were standing there in no small dread of what might come to pass.

Then the abbot turned round from the altar, and began to fidget with the fastenings of his rich robes.

And they made a lane for us up to the west door; then I put on my helm and we began to go up the nave, then suddenly the singing of the monks and all stopped. I heard a clinking and a buzz of voices in the choir; I turned, and saw that the bright noon sun was shining on the gold of the priest's vestments, as they lay on the floor, and on the mail that the priests carried.

So we stopped, the choir gates swung open, and the abbot marched out at the head of *his* men, all fully armed, and began to strike up the psalm "Exsurgat Deus."

When we got to the west door, there was indeed a tumult, but as yet no slaying; the square was all a-flicker with steel, and we beheld a great body of knights, at the head of them Red Harald and the king, standing over against us; but our people, pressed against the houses, and into the corners of the square, were, some striving to enter the doors, some beside themselves with rage, shouting out to the others to charge; withal, some were pale and some were red with the blood that had gathered to the wrathful faces of them.

Then said Arnald to those about him, "Lift me up." So they laid a great shield on two lances, and these four men carried, and thereon stood Arnald, and gazed about him.

Now the king was unhelmed, and his white hair (for he was an old man) flowed down behind him on to his saddle; but Arnald's hair was cut short, and was red.

And all the bells rang.

Then the king said, "O Arnald of the Lilies, will you settle this quarrel by the judgment of God?" And Arnald thrust up his chin, and said, "Yea." "How then," said the king, "and where?" "Will it please you try now?" said Arnald.

Then the king understood what he meant, and took in his hand from behind tresses of his long white hair, twisting them round his hand in his wrath, but yet said no word, till I suppose his hair put him in mind of something, and he raised it in both his hands above his head, and shouted out aloud, "O knights, hearken to this traitor." Whereat, indeed, the lances began to move ominously. But Arnald spoke.

"O you king and lords, what have we to do with you? were we not free in the old time, up among the hills there? Wherefore give way, and we will go to the hills again; and if any man try to stop us, his blood be on his own head; wherefore now," (and he turned) "all you House of the Lily, both soldiers and monks, let us go forth together fearing nothing, for I think there is not bone enough or muscle enough in these fellows here that have a king that they should stop us withal, but only skin and fat."

And truly, no man dared to stop us, and we went.

CHAPTER II

FAILING IN THE WORLD

Now at that time we drove cattle in Red Harald's land.

And we took no hoof but from the Lords and rich men, but of these we had a mighty drove, both oxen and sheep, and horses, and besides, even hawks and hounds, and a huntsman or two to take care of them.

And, about noon, we drew away from the corn-lands that lay beyond the pastures, and mingled with them, and reached a wide moor, which was called "Goliah's Land." I scarce know why, except that it belonged neither to Red Harald or us, but was debatable.

And the cattle began to go slowly, and our horses were tired, and the sun struck down very hot upon us, for there was no shadow, and the day was cloudless.

All about the edge of the moor, except on the side from which we had come was a rim of hills, not very high, but very rocky and steep, otherwise the moor itself was flat ; and through these hills was one pass, guarded by our men, which pass led to the Hill castle of the Lilies.

It was not wonderful, that of this moor many wild stories were told, being such a strange lonely place, some of them one knew, alas! to be over true. In the old time, before we went to the good town, this moor had been the mustering place of our people, and our house had done deeds enough of blood and horror to turn our white lilies red, and our blue cross to a fiery one. But some of those wild tales I never believed ; they had to do mostly with men losing their way without any apparent cause, (for there were plenty of landmarks,) finding some well-known spot, and then, just beyond it, a place they had never even dreamed of.

"Florian! Florian!" said Arnald, "for God's sake stop! as every one else is stopping to look at the hills yonder; I always thought there was a curse upon us. What does God mean by shutting us up here? Look at the cattle; O Christ, they have found it out too! See, some of them are turning to run back again towards Harald's land. Oh! unhappy, unhappy, from that day forward!"

He leaned forward, rested his head on his horse's neck, and wept like a child.

I felt so irritated with him, that I could almost have slain him then and there. Was he mad? had these wild doings of ours turned his strong wise head?

"Are you my brother Arnald, that I used to think such a grand man when I was a boy?" I said, "or are you changed too, like everybody, and everything else? What do *you* mean?"

"Look! look!" he said, grinding his teeth in agony.

I raised my eyes: where was the one pass between the rim of stern rocks? Nothing: the enemy behind us—that grim wall in front: what wonder that each man looked in his fellow's face for help, and found it not. Yet I refused to believe that there was any truth either in the wild stories that I had heard when I was a boy, or in this story told me so clearly by my eyes now.

I called out cheerily, "Hugh, come here!" He came. "What do you think of this? Some mere dodge on Harald's part? Are we cut off?"

"Think! Sir Florian? God forgive me for ever thinking at all; I have given up that long and long ago, because thirty years ago I thought this, that the House of Lilies would deserve anything in the way of bad fortune that God would send them: so I gave up thinking, and took to fighting. But if you think that Harald had anything to do with this, why—why—in God's name, I wish *I* could think so!"

I felt a dull weight on my heart. Had our house been the devil's servants all along? I thought we were God's servants.

The day was very still, but what little wind there was, was at our backs. I watched Hugh's face, not being able to answer him. He was the cleverest man at war that I have known, either before or since that day: sharper than any hound in ear and scent, clearer sighted than any eagle; he was listening now intently. I saw a slight smile cross his face; heard him mutter, "Yes! I think so: verily that is better, a great deal better." Then he stood up in his stirrups, and shouted, "Hurrah for the Lilies! Mary rings!" "Mary rings!" I shouted, though I did not know the reason for his exultation: my brother lifted his head, and smiled too,

grimly. Then as I listened I heard clearly the sound of a
trumpet, and enemy's trumpet too.

"After all, it was only mist, or some such thing," I said,
for the pass between the hills was clear enough now.

"Hurrah! only mist," said Arnald, quite elated; "Mary
rings!" and we all began to think of fighting: for after
all what joy is equal to that?

There were five hundred of us; two hundred spears,
the rest archers; and both archers and men at arms were
picked men.

"How many of them are we to expect?" said I.

"Not under a thousand, certainly, probably more, Sir
Florian." (My brother Arnald, by the way, had knighted
me before we left the good town, and Hugh liked to give
me the handle to my name. How was it, by the way, that
no one had ever made *him* a knight?)

"Let every one look to his arms and horse, and come
away from these silly cows' sons!" shouted Arnald.

Hugh said, "They will be here in an hour, fair Sir."

So we got clear of the cattle, and dismounted, and both
ourselves took food and drink, and our horses; afterwards
we tightened our saddle-girths, shook our great pots of
helmets on, except Arnald, whose rusty-red hair had been
his only head-piece in battle for years and years, and stood
with our spears close by our horses, leaving room for the
archers to retreat between our ranks; and they got their
arrows ready, and planted their stakes before a little peat
moss: and there we waited, and saw their pennons at last
floating high above the corn of the fertile land, then heard
their many horse-hoofs ring upon the hard-parched moor,
and the archers began to shoot.

.   .   .   .

IT had been a strange battle; we had never fought better,
and yet withal it had ended in a retreat; indeed all along
every man but Arnald and myself, even Hugh, had been
trying at least to get the enemy between him and the way
toward the pass; and now we were all drifting that way,
the enemy trying to cut us off, but never able to stop us,
because he could only throw small bodies of men in our
way, whom we scattered and put to flight in their turn.

I never cared less for my life than then; indeed, in spite
of all my boasting and hardness of belief, I should have

been happy to have died, such a strange weight of apprehension was on me; and yet I got no scratch even. I had soon put off my great helm, and was fighting in my mail-coif only: and here I swear that three knights together charged me, aiming at my bare face, yet never touched me; for, as for one, I put his lance aside with my sword, and the other two in some most wonderful manner got their spears locked in each other's armour, and so had to submit to be knocked off their horses.

And we still neared the pass, and began to see distinctly the ferns that grew on the rocks, and the fair country between the rift in them, spreading out there, blue-shadowed.

Whereupon came a great rush of men of both sides, striking side blows at each other, spitting, cursing, and shrieking, as they tore away like a herd of wild hogs. So, being careless of life, as I said, I drew rein, and turning my horse, waited quietly for them; and I knotted the reins, and laid them on the horse's neck, and stroked him, that he whinnied; then got both my hands to my sword.

Then, as they came on, I noted hurriedly that the first man was one of Arnald's men, and one of our men behind him leaned forward to prod him with his spear, but could not reach so far, till he himself was run through the eye with a spear, and throwing his arms up fell dead with a shriek. Also I noted concerning this first man that the laces of his helmet were loose, and when he saw me he lifted his *left* hand to his head, took off his helm and cast it at me, and still tore on; the helmet flew over my head, and I sitting still there, swung out, hitting him on the neck; his head flew right off, for the mail no more held than a piece of silk.

" Mary rings," and my horse whinnied again, and we both of us went at it, and fairly stopped that rout, so that there was a knot of quite close and desperate fighting, wherein we had the best of that fight and slew most of them, albeit my horse was slain and my mail-coif cut through. Then I bade a squire fetch me another horse, and began meanwhile to upbraid those knights for running in such a strange disorderly race, instead of standing and fighting cleverly.

Moreover we had drifted even in this successful fight still nearer to the pass, so that the conies who dwelt there were beginning to consider whether they should not run into their holes.

But one of those knights said: " Be not angry with me, Sir Florian, but do you think you will go to Heaven ? "

" The saints ! I hope so," I said, but one who stood near him whispered to him to hold his peace, so I cried out :

" O friend ! I hold this world and all therein so cheap now, that I see not anything in it but shame which can any longer anger me ; wherefore speak out."

" Then, Sir Florian, men say that at your christening some fiend took on him the likeness of a priest and strove to baptize you in the Devil's name, but God had mercy on you so that the fiend could not choose but baptize you in the name of the most holy Trinity : and yet men say that you hardly believe any doctrine such as other men do, and will at the end only go to Heaven round about as it were, not at all by the intercession of our Lady ; they say too that you can see no ghosts or other wonders, whatever happens to other Christian men."

I smiled.—" Well, friend, I scarcely call this a disadvantage, moreover what has it to do with the matter in hand ? "

How was this in Heaven's name ? we had been quite still, resting, while this talk was going on, but we could hear the hawks chattering from the rocks, we were so close now.

And my heart sunk within me, there was no reason why this should not be true ; there was no reason why anything should not be true.

" This, Sir Florian," said the knight again, " how would you feel inclined to fight if you thought that everything about you was mere glamour ; this earth here, the rocks, the sun, the sky ? I do not know where I am for certain, I do not know that it is not midnight instead of undern : I do not know if I have been fighting men or only *simulacra*— but I think, we all think, that we have been led into some devil's trap or other, and—and—may God forgive me my sins !—I wish I had never been born."

There now ! he was weeping—they all wept—how strange it was to see those rough, bearded men blubbering there, and snivelling till the tears ran over their armour and mingled with the blood, so that it dropped down to the earth in a dim, dull, red rain.

My eyes indeed were dry, but then so was my heart ; I

felt far worse than weeping came to, but nevertheless I spoke cheerily.

"Dear friends, where are your old men's hearts gone to now? See now! this is a punishment for our sins, is it? well, for our forefathers' sins or our own? if the first, O brothers, be very sure that if we bear it manfully God will have something very good in store for us hereafter; but if for our sins, is it not certain that He cares for us yet, for note that He suffers the wicked to go their own ways pretty much; moreover brave men, brothers, ought to be the masters of *simulacra*—come, is it so hard to die once for all?"

Still no answer came from them, they sighed heavily only. I heard the sound of more than one or two swords as they rattled back to the scabbards: nay, one knight, stripping himself of surcoat and hauberk, and drawing his dagger, looked at me with a grim smile, and said, "Sir Florian, do so!" then he drew the dagger across his throat and he fell back dead.

They shuddered, those brave men, and crossed themselves. And I had no heart to say a word more, but mounted the horse which had been brought to me and rode away slowly for a few yards; then I became aware that there was a great silence over the whole field.

So I lifted my eyes and looked, and behold no man struck at another.

Then from out of a band of horsemen came Harald, and he was covered all over with a great scarlet cloth as before, put on over the head, and flowing all about his horse, but rent with the fight. He put off his helm and drew back his mail-coif, then took a trumpet from the hand of a herald and blew strongly.

And in the midst of his blast I heard a voice call out: "O Florian! come and speak to me for the last time!"

So when I turned I beheld Arnald standing by himself, but near him stood Hugh and ten others with drawn swords.

Then I wept, and so went to him weeping; and he said, "Thou seest, brother, that we must die, and I think by some horrible and unheard-of death, and the House of the Lilies is just dying too; and now I repent me of Swanhilda's death; now I know that it was a poor cowardly piece of revenge, instead of a brave act of justice; thus has God shown us the right.

"O Florian! curse me! So will it be straighter; truly thy mother when she bore thee did not think of this; rather saw thee in the tourney at this time, in her fond hopes, glittering with gold and doing knightly; or else mingling thy brown locks with the golden hair of some maiden weeping for the love of thee. God forgive me! God forgive me!"

"What harm, brother?" I said, 'this is only failing in the world; what if we had not failed, in a little while it would have made no difference; truly just now I felt very miserable, but now it has passed away, and I am happy."

"O brave heart!" he said, "yet we shall part just now, Florian, farewell."

"The road is long," I said, "farewell."

Then we kissed each other, and Hugh and the others wept.

Now all this time the trumpets had been ringing, ringing, great doleful peals, then they ceased, and above all sounded Red Harald's voice.

(So I looked round towards that pass, and when I looked I no longer doubted any of those wild tales of glamour concerning Goliah's Land; for though the rocks were the same, and though the conies still stood gazing at the doors of their dwellings, though the hawks still cried out shrilly, though the fern still shook in the wind, yet beyond, oh such a land! not to be described by any because of its great beauty, lying, a great *hollow* land, the rocks going down on this side in precipices, then reaches and reaches of loveliest country, trees and flowers, and corn, then the hills, green and blue, and purple, till their ledges reached the white snowy mountains at last. Then with all manner of strange feelings, " my heart in the midst of my body was even like melting wax.")

"O you House of the Lily! you are conquered—yet I will take vengeance only on a few, therefore let all those who wish to live come and pile their swords, and shields, and helms behind me in three great heaps, and swear fealty afterwards to me; yes, all but the false knights Arnald and Florian."

We were holding each other's hands and gazing, and we saw all our knights, yea, all but Squire Hugh and his ten heroes, pass over the field singly, or in groups of three or four, with their heads hanging down in shame, and they cast down their notched swords and dinted, lilied shields, and brave-crested helms into three great heaps, behind Red Harald, then stood behind, no man speaking to his fellow, or touching him.

Then dolefully the great trumpets sang over the dying House of the Lily, and Red Harald led his men forward, but slowly : on they came, spear and mail glittering in the sunlight; and I turned and looked at that good land, and a shuddering delight seized my soul.

But I felt my brother's hand leave mine, and saw him turn his horse's head and ride swiftly toward the pass ; that was a strange pass now.

And at the edge he stopped, turned round and called out aloud, " I pray thee, Harald, forgive me ! now farewell all ! "

Then the horse gave one bound forward, and we heard the poor creature's scream when he felt that he must die, and we heard afterwards (for we were near enough for that even) a clang and a crash.

So I turned me about to Hugh, and he understood me though I could not speak.

We shouted all together, " Mary rings," then laid our bridles on the necks of our horses, spurred forward, and—in five minutes they were all slain, and I was down among the horse-hoofs.

Not slain though, not wounded. Red Harald smiled grimly when he saw me rise and lash out again ; he and some ten others dismounted, and holding their long spears out, I went back—back, back,—I saw what it meant, and sheathed my sword, and their laughter rolled all about me, and I too smiled.

Presently they all stopped, and I felt the last foot of turf giving under my feet ; I looked down and saw the crack there widening ; then in a moment I fell, and a cloud of dust and earth rolled after me ; then again their mirth rose into thunder-peals of laughter. But through it all I heard Red Harald shout, " Silence ! evil dogs ! "

For as I fell I stretched out my arms, and caught a tuft of yellow broom some three feet from the brow, and hung there by the hands, my feet being loose in the air.

Then Red Harald came and stood on the precipice above me, his great axe over his shoulder ; and he looked down on me not ferociously, almost kindly, while the wind from the

Hollow Land blew about his red raiment, tattered and dusty now.

And I felt happy, though it pained me to hold straining by the broom, yet I said, "I will hold out to the last."

It was not long, the plant itself gave way and I fell, and as I fell I fainted.

CHAPTER III

LEAVING THE WORLD.—FYTTE THE FIRST

I HAD thought when I fell that I should never wake again; but I woke at last: for a long time I was quite dizzied and could see nothing at all: horrible doubts came creeping over me; I half expected to see presently great half-formed shapes come rolling up to me to crush me; some thing fiery, not strange, too utterly horrible to be strange, but utterly vile and ugly, the sight of which would have killed me when I was upon the earth, come rolling up to torment me. In fact I doubted if I were in hell.

I knew I deserved to be, but I prayed, and then it came into my mind that I could not pray if I were in hell.

Also there seemed to be a cool green light all about me, which was sweet.

Then presently I heard a glorious voice ring out clear, close to me—

"Christ keep the Hollow Land
Through the sweet spring-tide,
When the apple-blossoms bless
The lowly bent hill side."

Thereat my eyes were slowly unsealed, and I saw the blessedest sight I have ever seen before or since: for I saw my Love.

She sat about five yards from me on a great grey stone that had much moss on it, one of the many scattered along the side of the stream by which I lay; she was clad in loose white raiment close to her hands and throat; her feet were bare, her hair hung loose a long way down, but some of it lay on her knees: I said "white" raiment, but long spikes of light scarlet went down from the throat, lost here and there in the shadows of the folds, and growing smaller and smaller, died before they reached her feet.

I was lying with my head resting on soft moss that some one had gathered and placed under me. She, when she saw me moving and awake, came and stood over me with a gracious smile.—She was so lovely and tender to look at, and so kind, yet withal no one, man or woman, had ever frightened me half so much.

She was not fair in white and red, like many beautiful women are, being rather pale, but like ivory for smoothness, and her hair was quite golden, not light yellow, but dusky golden.

I tried to get up on my feet, but was too weak, and sunk back again. She said:

"No, not just yet, do not trouble yourself or try to remember anything just at present."

There withal she kneeled down, and hung over me closer.

" To-morrow you may, perhaps, have something hard to do or bear, I know, but now you must be as happy as you can be, quietly happy. Why did you start and turn pale when I came to you? Do you not know who I am? Nay, but you do, I see; and I have been waiting here so long for you; so you must have expected to see me.—You cannot be frightened of me, are you? "

But I could not answer a word, but all the time strange knowledge, strange feelings were filling my brain and my heart, she said:

" You are tired; rest, and dream happily."

So she sat by me, and sung to lull me to sleep, while I turned on my elbow, and watched the waving of her throat: and the singing of all the poets I had ever heard, and of many others too, not born till years long after I was dead, floated all about me as she sung, and I did indeed dream happily.

When I awoke it was the time of the cold dawn, and the colours were gathering themselves together, whereat in fatherly approving fashion the sun sent all across the east long bars of scarlet and orange that after faded through yellow to green and blue.

And she sat by me still; I think she had been sitting there and singing all the time; all through hot yesterday, for I had been sleeping day-long and night-long, all through the falling evening under moonlight and starlight the night through.

And now it was dawn, and I think too that neither of us had moved at all ; for the last thing I remembered before I went to sleep was the tips of her fingers brushing my cheek, as she knelt over me with down-drooping arm, and still now I felt them there. Moreover she was just finishing some fainting measure that died before it had time to get painful in its passion.

Dear Lord ! how I loved her ! yet did I not dare to touch her, or even speak to her. She smiled with delight when she saw I was awake again, and slid down her hand on to mine, but some shuddering dread made me draw it away again hurriedly ; then I saw the smile leave her face : what would I not have given for courage to hold her body quite tight to mine ? but I was so weak. She said :

" Have you been very happy ? "

" Yea," I said.

It was the first word I had spoken there, and my voice sounded strange.

" Ah ! " she said, " you will talk more when you get used to the air of the Hollow Land. Have you been thinking of your past life at all ? If not, try to think of it. What thing in Heaven or Earth do you wish for most ? "

Still I said no word ; but she said in a wearied way :

" Well now, I think you will be strong enough to get to your feet and walk ; take my hand and try."

Therewith she held it out : I strove hard to be brave enough to take it, but could not ; I only turned away shuddering, sick, and grieved to the heart's core of me ; then struggling hard with hand and knee and elbow, I scarce rose, and stood up totteringly ; while she watched me sadly, still holding out her hand.

But as I rose, in my swinging to and fro the steel sheath of my sword struck her on the hand so that the blood flowed from it, which she stood looking at for a while, then dropped it downwards, and turned to look at me, for I was going.

Then as I walked she followed me, so I stopped and turned and said almost fiercely :

" I am going alone to look for my brother."

The vehemence with which I spoke, or something else, burst some blood-vessel within my throat, and we both stood there with the blood running from us on to the grass and summer flowers.

She said: "If you find him, wait with him till I come."

"Yea," and I turned and left her, following the course of the stream upwards, and as I went I heard her low singing that almost broke my heart for its sadness.

And I went painfully because of my weakness, and because also of the great stones; and sometimes I went along a spot of earth where the river had been used to flow in flood-time, and which was now bare of everything but stones; and the sun, now risen high, poured down on everything a great flood of fierce light and scorching heat, and burnt me sorely, so that I almost fainted.

But about noontide I entered a wood close by the stream, a beech-wood, intending to rest myself; the herbage was thin and scattered there, sprouting up from amid the leaf-sheaths and nuts of the beeches, which had fallen year after year on that same spot; the outside boughs swept low down, the air itself seemed green when you entered within the shadow of the branches, they over-roofed the place so with tender green, only here and there showing spots of blue.

But what lay at the foot of a great beech tree but some dead knight in armour, only the helmet off? A wolf was prowling round about it, who ran away snarling when he saw me coming.

So I went up to that dead knight, and fell on my knees before him, laying my head on his breast, for it was Arnald.

He was quite cold, but had not been dead for very long; I would not believe him dead, but went down to the stream and brought him water, tried to make him drink—what would you? He was as dead as Swanhilda: neither came there any answer to my cries that afternoon but the moaning of the wood-doves in the beeches.

So then I sat down and took his head on my knees, and closed the eyes, and wept quietly while the sun sunk lower.

But a little after sunset I heard a rustle through the leaves, that was not the wind, and looking up my eyes met the pitying eyes of that maiden.

Something stirred rebelliously within me; I ceased weeping, and said:

"It is unjust, unfair: What right had Swanhilda to live?

did not God give her up to us? How much better was he than ten Swanhildas? and look you—See!—he is DEAD."

Now this I shrieked out, being mad; and though I trembled when I saw some stormy wrath that vexed her very heart and loving lips, gathering on her face, I yet sat there looking at her and screaming, screaming, till all the place rang.

But when growing hoarse and breathless I ceased; she said, with straightened brow and scornful mouth:

"So! bravely done! must I then, though I am a woman, call you a liar, for saying God is unjust? You to punish her, had not God then punished her already? How many times when she woke in the dead night do you suppose she missed seeing King Urrayne's pale face and hacked head lying on the pillow by her side? Whether by night or day, what things but screams did she hear when the wind blew loud round about the Palace corners? And did not that face too, often come before her, pale and bleeding as it was long ago, and gaze at her from unhappy eyes! poor eyes! with changed purpose in them—no more hope of converting the world when that blow was once struck, truly it was very wicked — no more dreams, but only fierce struggles with the Devil for very life, no more dreams but failure at last, and death, happier so in the Hollow Land."

She grew so pitying as she gazed at his dead face that I began to weep again unreasonably, while she saw not that I was weeping, but looked only on Arnald's face, but after turned on me frowning.

"Unjust! yes truly unjust enough to take away life and all hope from her; you have done a base cowardly act, you and your brother here, disguise it as you may; you deserve all God's judgments—you——"

But I turned my eyes and wet face to her, and said:

"Do not curse me—there—do not look like Swanhilda: for see now, you said at first that you had been waiting long for me, give me your hand now, for I love you so."

Then she came and knelt by where I sat, and I caught her in my arms, and she prayed to be forgiven.

"O, Florian! I have indeed waited long for you, and when I saw you my heart was filled with joy, but you would neither touch me or speak to me, so that I became almost mad,—forgive me, we will be so happy now. O! do you know this is what I have been waiting for all these years ; it made me glad I know, when I was a little baby in my mother's arms to think I was born for this ; and afterwards, as I grew up, I used to watch every breath of wind through the beech-boughs, every turn of the silver poplar leaves, thinking it might be you or some news of you."

Then I rose and drew her up with me ; but she knelt again by my brother's side, and kissed him, and said :

"O brother ! the Hollow Land is only second best of the places God has made, for Heaven also is the work of His hand."

Afterwards we dug a deep grave among the beech-roots and there we buried Arnald de Liliis.

And I have never seen him since, scarcely even in dreams ; surely God has had mercy on him, for he was very leal and true and brave; he loved many men, and was kind and gentle to his friends, neither did he hate any but Swanhilda.

But as for us two, Margaret and me, I cannot tell you concerning our happiness, such things cannot be told ; only this I know, that we abode continually in the Hollow Land until I lost it.

Moreover this I can tell you.   Margaret was walking with me, as she often walked near the place where I had first seen her; presently we came upon a woman sitting, dressed in scarlet and gold raiment, with her head laid down on her knees ; likewise we heard her sobbing.

"Margaret, who is she ?" I said : "I knew not that any dwelt in the Hollow Land but us two only."

She said, "I know not who she is, only sometimes, these many years, I have seen her scarlet robe flaming from far away, amid the quiet green grass : but I was never so near her as this.   Florian, I am afraid : let us come away."

FYTTE THE SECOND.

Such a horrible grey November day it was, the fog-smell all about, the fog creeping into our very bones.

And I sat there, trying to recollect, at any rate some-thing, under those fir-trees that I ought to have known so well.

Just think now ; I had lost my best years somewhere ; for I was past the prime of life, my hair and beard were scattered with white, my body was growing weaker, my memory of all things was very faint.

My raiment, purple and scarlet and blue once, was so stained that you could scarce call it any colour, was so tattered that it scarce covered my body, though it seemed once to have fallen in heavy folds to my feet, and still, when I rose to walk, though the miserable November mist lay in great drops upon my bare breast, yet was I obliged to wind my raiment over my arm, it draggled so (wretched, slimy, textureless thing!) in the brown mud.

On my head was a light morion, which pressed on my brow and pained me; so I put my hand up to take it off; but when I touched it I stood still in my walk shuddering; I nearly fell to the earth with shame and sick horror; for I laid my hand on a lump of slimy earth with worms coiled up in it. I could scarce forbear from shrieking, but breathing such a prayer as I could think of, I raised my hand again and seized it firmly. Worse horror still! the rust had eaten it into holes, and I gripped my own hair as well as the rotting steel, the sharp edge of which cut into my fingers; but setting my teeth, gave a great wrench, for I knew that if I let go of it then, no power on the earth or under it could make me touch it again. God be praised! I tore it off and cast it far from me; I saw the earth, and the worms and green weeds and sun-begotten slime, whirling out from it radiatingly, as it spun round about.

I was girt with a sword too, the leathern belt of which had shrunk and squeezed my waist: dead leaves had gathered in knots about the buckles of it, the gilded handle was encrusted with clay in many parts, the velvet sheath miserably worn.

But, verily, when I took hold of the hilt, and dreaded lest instead of a sword I should find a serpent in my hand; lo! then, I drew out my own true blade and shook it flawless from hilt to point, gleaming white in that mist.

Therefore it sent a thrill of joy to my heart, to know that there was one friend left me yet: I sheathed it again carefully, and undoing it from my waist, hung it about my neck.

Then catching up my rags in my arms, I drew them up till my legs and feet were altogether clear from them, afterwards folded my arms over my breast, gave a long leap and ran, looking downward, but not giving heed to my way.

Once or twice I fell over stumps of trees, and such-like, for it was a cut-down wood that I was in, but I rose always, though bleeding and confused, and went on still; sometimes tearing madly through briars and forse bushes, so that my blood dropped on the dead leaves as I went.

I ran in this way for about an hour; then I heard a gurgling and splashing of waters; I gave a great shout and leapt strongly, with shut eyes, and the black water closed over me.

When I rose again, I saw near me a boat with a man in it; but the shore was far off; I struck out toward the boat, but my clothes which I had knotted and folded about me, weighed me down terribly.

The man looked at me, and began to paddle toward me with the oar he held in his left hand, having in his right a long, slender spear, barbed like a fish-hook; perhaps, I thought, it is some fishing spear; moreover his raiment was of scarlet, with upright stripes of yellow and black all over it.

When my eye caught his, a smile widened his mouth as if some one had made a joke; but I was beginning to sink, and indeed my head was almost under water just as he came and stood above me, but before it went quite under, I saw his spear gleam, then *felt* it in my shoulder, and for the present, felt nothing else.

When I woke I was on the bank of that river; the flooded waters went hurrying past me; no boat on them now; from the river the ground went up in gentle slopes till it grew a great hill, and there, on that hill-top,—Yes, I might forget many things, almost everything, but not that, not the old castle of my fathers up among the hills, its towers blackened now and shattered, yet still no enemy's banner waved from it.

So I said I would go and die there; and at this thought I drew my sword, which yet hung about my neck, and shook it in the air till the true steel quivered; then began to pace towards the castle. I was quite naked, no rag about me; I took no heed of that, only thanking God that my sword was left, and so toiled up the hill. I entered the castle soon by the outer court; I knew the way so well, that I did not lift my eyes from the ground, but walked on over the lowered drawbridge through the unguarded gates, and stood in the great hall at last—my father's hall—as bare of everything but

my sword as when I came into the world fifty years before :
I had as little clothes, as little wealth, less memory and
thought, I verily believe, than then.

So I lifted up my eyes and gazed ; no glass in the windows,
no hangings on the walls ; the vaulting yet held good
throughout, but seemed to be going ; the mortar had fallen
out from between the stones, and grass and fern grew in the
joints ; the marble pavement was in some places gone, and
water stood about in puddles, though one scarce knew how it
had got there.

No hangings on the walls—no ; yet, strange to say, in-
stead of them, the walls blazed from end to end with scarlet
paintings, only striped across with green damp-marks in
many places, some falling bodily from the wall, the plaster
hanging down with the fading colour on it.

In all of them, except for the shadows and the faces of the
figures, there was scarce any colour but scarlet and yellow ;
here and there it seemed the painter, whoever it was, had
tried to make his trees or his grass green, but it would not
do ; some ghastly thoughts must have filled his head, for all
the green went presently into yellow, out-sweeping through
the picture dismally. But the faces were painted to the very
life, or it seemed so ;—there were only five of them, however,
that were very marked or came much in the foreground ; and
four of these I knew well, though I did not then remember
the names of those that had borne them. They were Red
Harald, Swanhilda, Arnald, and myself. The fifth I did not
know ; it was a woman's, and very beautiful.

Then I saw that in some parts a small penthouse roof had
been built over the paintings, to keep them from the weather.
Near one of these stood a man painting, clothed in red, with
stripes of yellow and black : then I knew that it was the
same man who had saved me from drowning by spearing me
through the shoulder ; so I went up to him, and saw further-
more that he was girt with a heavy sword.

He turned round when he saw me coming, and asked me
fiercely what I did there.

I asked why he was painting in my castle.

Thereupon, with that same grim smile widening his mouth
as heretofore, he said, " I paint God's judgments."

And as he spoke, he rattled the sword in his scabbard ; but
I said,

"Well, then, you paint them very badly. Listen; I know God's judgments much better than you do. See now; I will teach you God's judgments, and you shall teach me painting."

While I spoke he still rattled his sword, and when I had done, shut his right eye tight, screwing his nose on one side; then said:

"You have got no clothes on, and may go to the devil! What do *you* know about God's judgments?"

"Well, they are not all yellow and red, at all events; you ought to know better."

He screamed out, "O you fool! yellow and red! Gold and blood, what do they make?"

"Well," I said; "what?"

"HELL!" And, coming close up to me, he struck me with his open hand in the face, so that the colour with which his hand was smeared was dabbed about my face. The blow almost threw me down; and, while I staggered, he rushed at me furiously with his sword. Perhaps it was good for me that I had got no clothes on; for, being utterly unencumbered, I leapt this way and that, and avoided his fierce, eager strokes till I could collect myself somewhat; while he had a heavy scarlet cloak on that trailed on the ground, and which he often trod on, so that he stumbled.

He very nearly slew me during the first few minutes, for it was not strange that, together with other matters, I should have forgotten the art of fence: but yet, as I went on, and sometimes bounded about the hall under the whizzing of his sword, as he rested sometimes, leaning on it, as the point sometimes touched my bare flesh, nay, once as the whole sword fell flatlings on my head and made my eyes start out, I remembered the old joy that I used to have, and the *swy, swy,* of the sharp edge, as one gazed between one's horse's ears; moreover, at last, one fierce swift stroke, just touching me below the throat, tore up the skin all down my body, and fell heavy on my thigh, so that I drew my breath in and turned white; then first, as I swung my sword round my head, our blades met, oh! to hear that *tchink* again! and I felt the notch my sword made in his, and swung out at him; but he guarded it and returned on me; I guarded right and left, and grew warm, and opened my mouth to shout, but knew not what to say; and our sword points fell on the floor together: then, when we had panted awhile, I wiped from my face the blood that had been dashed over it, shook my sword and cut at him, then we spun round and round in a mad waltz to the measured music of our meeting swords, and sometimes either wounded the other somewhat, but not much, till I beat down his sword on to his head, that he fell grovelling, but not cut through. Verily, thereupon my lips opened mightily with " Mary rings."

Then, when he had gotten to his feet, I went at him again, he staggering back, guarding wildly; I cut at his head; he put his sword up confusedly, so I fitted both hands to my hilt, and smote him mightily under the arm: then his shriek mingled with my shout, made a strange sound together; he rolled over and over, dead, as I thought.

I walked about the hall in great exultation at first, striking my sword point on the floor every now and then, till I grew faint with loss of blood; then I went to my enemy and stripped off some of his clothes to bind up my wounds withal; afterwards I found in a corner bread and wine, and I eat and drank thereof.

Then I went back to him, and looked, and a thought struck me, and I took some of his paints and brushes, and kneeling down, painted his face thus, with stripes of yellow and red, crossing each other at right angles; and in each of the squares so made I put a spot of black, after the manner of the painted letters in the prayer-books and romances when they are ornamented.

So I stood back as painters use, folded my arms, and admired my own handiwork. Yet there struck me as being something so utterly doleful in the man's white face, and the blood running all about him, and washing off the stains of paint from his face and hands, and splashed clothes, that my heart misgave me, and I hoped that he was not dead; I took some water from a vessel he had been using for his painting, and, kneeling, washed his face.

Was it some resemblance to my father's dead face, which I had seen when I was young, that made me pity him? I laid my hand upon his heart, and felt it beating feebly; so I lifted him up gently, and carried him towards a heap of straw that he seemed used to lie upon; there I stripped him and looked to his wounds, and used leech-craft, the memory of which God gave me for this purpose, I suppose, and within seven days I found that he would not die.

Afterwards, as I wandered about the castle, I came to a room in one of the upper stories, that had still the roof on, and windows in it with painted glass, and there I found green raiment and swords and armour, and I clothed myself.

So when he got well I asked him what his name was, and he me, and we both of us said, "truly I know not." Then said I, " but we must call each other some name, even as men call days."

"Call me Swerker," he said, "some priest I knew once had that name."

"And me Wulf," said I, "though wherefore I know not."

Then he said:

"Wulf, I will teach you painting now, come and learn."

Then I tried to learn painting till I thought I should die, but at last learned it through very much pain and grief.

And, as the years went on and we grew old and grey, we painted purple pictures and green ones instead of the scarlet and yellow, so that the walls looked altered, and always we painted God's judgments.

And we would sit in the sunset and watch them with the golden light changing them, as we yet hoped God would change both us and our works.

Often too we would sit outside the walls and look at the trees and sky, and the ways of the few men and women we saw ; therefrom sometimes befell adventures.

Once there went past a great funeral of some king going to his own country, not as he had hoped to go, but stiff and colourless, spices filling up the place of his heart.

And first went by very many knights, with long bright hauberks on, that fell down before their knees as they rode, and they all had tilting-helms on with the same crest, so that their faces were quite hidden : and this crest was two hands clasped together tightly as though they were the hands of one praying forgiveness from the one he loves best ; and the crest was wrought in gold.

Moreover, they had on over their hauberks surcoats which were half scarlet and half purple, strewn about with golden stars.

Also long lances, that had forked knights'-pennons, half purple and half scarlet, strewn with golden stars.

And these went by with no sound but the fall of their horse-hoofs.

And they went slowly, so slowly that we counted them all, five thousand five hundred and fifty-five.

Then went by many fair maidens whose hair was loose and yellow, and who were all clad in green raiment ungirded, and shod with golden shoes.

These also we counted, being five hundred; moreover some of the outermost of them, viz., one maiden to every twenty, had long silver trumpets, which they swung out to right and left, blowing them, and their sound was very sad.

Then many priests, and bishops, and abbots, who wore white albs and golden copes over them ; and they all sang together mournfully, " *Propter amnen Babylonis ;* " and these were three hundred.

After that came a great knot of the Lords, who wore tilting helmets and surcoats emblazoned with each one his own device; only each had in his hand a small staff two feet long whereon was a pennon of scarlet and purple. These also were three hundred.

And in the midst of these was a great car hung down to the ground with purple, drawn by grey horses whose trappings were half scarlet, half purple.

And on this car lay the King, whose head and hands were bare ; and he had on him a surcoat, half purple and half scarlet, strewn with golden stars.

And his head rested on a tilting helmet, whose crest was the hands of one praying passionately for forgiveness.

But his own hands lay by his side as if he had just fallen asleep.

And all about the car were little banners, half purple and half scarlet, strewn with golden stars.

Then the King, who counted but as one, went by also.

And after him came again many maidens clad in ungirt white raiment strewn with scarlet flowers, and their hair was loose and yellow and their feet bare: and, except for the falling of their feet and the rustle of the wind through their raiment, they went past quite silently. These also were five hundred.

Then lastly came many young knights with long bright

hauberks falling over their knees as they rode, and surcoats, half scarlet and half purple, strewn with golden stars; they bore long lances with forked pennons which were half purple, half scarlet, strewn with golden stars; their heads and their hands were bare, but they bore shields, each one of them, which were of bright steel wrought cunningly in the midst with that bearing of the two hands of one who prays for forgiveness; which was done in gold. These were but five hundred.

Then they all went by winding up and up the hill roads, and, when the last of them had departed out of our sight, we put down our heads and wept, and I said, "Sing us one of the songs of the Hollow Land."

Then he whom I had called Swerker put his hand into his bosom, and slowly drew out a long, long tress of black hair, and laid it on his knee and smoothed it, weeping on it: So then I left him there and went and armed myself, and brought armour for him.

And then came back to him and threw the armour down so that it clanged, and said:

"O! Harald, let us go!"

He did not seem surprised that I called him by the right name, but rose and armed himself, and then he looked a good knight; so we set forth.

And in a turn of the long road we came suddenly upon a most fair woman, clothed in scarlet, who sat and sobbed, holding her face between her hands, and her hair was very black.

And when Harald saw her, he stood and gazed at her for long through the bars of his helmet, then suddenly turned, and said:

"Florian, I must stop here; do you go on to the Hollow Land. Farewell."

"Farewell." And then I went on, never turning back, and him I never saw more.

And so I went on, quite lonely, but happy, till I had reached the Hollow Land.

Into which I let myself down most carefully, by the jutting rocks and bushes and strange trailing flowers, and there lay down and fell asleep.

FYTTE THE THIRD.

And I was waked by some one singing; I felt very happy; I felt young again; I had fair delicate raiment on, my sword was gone, and my armour; I tried to think where I was, and could not for my happiness; I tried to listen to the words of the song. Nothing, only an old echo in my ears, only all manner of strange scenes from my wretched past life before my eyes in a dim, far-off manner: then at last, slowly, without effort, I heard what she sang.

> " Christ keep the Hollow Land
>   All the summer-tide ;
> Still we cannot understand
>   Where the waters glide ;
>
> Only dimly seeing them
>   Coldly slipping through
> Many green-lipp'd cavern mouths,
>   Where the hills are blue."

"Then," she said, "come now and look for it, love, a hollow city in the Hollow Land."

I kissed Margaret, and we went.

.   .   .   .

Through the golden streets under the purple shadows of the houses we went, and the slow fanning backward and forward of the many-coloured banners cooled us : we two alone ; there was no one with us, no soul will ever be able to tell what we said, how we looked.

At last we came to a fair palace, cloistered off in the old time, before the city grew golden from the din and hubbub of traffic ; those who dwelt there in the old ungolden times had had their own joys, their own sorrows, apart from the joys and sorrows of the multitude : so, in like manner, was it now cloistered off from the eager leaning and brotherhood of the golden dwellings : so now it had its own gaiety, its own solemnity, apart from theirs ; unchanged, unchangeable, were its marble walls, whatever else changed about it.

We stopped before the gates and trembled, and clasped each other closer ; for there among the marble leafage and tendrils that were round and under and over the archway that held the golden valves, were wrought two figures of a man and woman, winged and garlanded, whose raiment flashed with stars; and their faces were like faces we had seen or half seen in some dream long and long and long ago, so that we trembled with awe and delight; and I turned, and seeing Margaret, saw that her face was that face seen or half seen long and long and long ago; and in the shining of her eyes I saw that other face, seen in that way and no other long and long and long ago—my face.

And then we walked together toward the golden gates, and opened them, and no man gainsaid us.

And before us lay a great space of flowers.

GOLDEN WINGS

" Lyf lythes to mee,
Twa wordes or three,
Of one who was fair and free,
And fell in his fight."
Sir Percival.

I SUPPOSE my birth was somewhat after the birth of Sir
Percival of Galles, for I never saw my father, and my
mother brought me up quaintly; not like a poor man's son,
though, indeed, we had little money, and lived in a lone
place: it was on a bit of waste land near a river; moist,
and without trees; on the drier parts of it folks had built
cottages—see, I can count them on my fingers—six cottages,
of which ours was one.

Likewise, there was a little chapel, with a yew tree and
graves in the church-yard—graves—yes, a great many graves,
more than in the yards of many Minsters I have seen,
because people fought a battle once near us, and buried
many bodies in deep pits, to the east of the chapel; but
this was before I was born.

I have talked to old knights since who fought in that
battle, and who told me that it was all about an old lady that
they fought; indeed, this lady, who was a queen, was after-
wards, by her own wish, buried in the aforesaid chapel in a
most fair tomb; her image was of latoun gilt, and with a
colour on it; her hands and face were of silver, and her
hair, gilded and most curiously wrought, flowed down from
her head over the marble.

It was a strange thing to see that gold and brass and
marble inside that rough chapel which stood on the marshy
common, near the river.

Now, every St. Peter's day, when the sun was at its
hottest, in the midsummer noontide, my mother (though at
other times she only wore such clothes as the folk about us)
would dress herself most richly, and shut the shutters

against all the windows, and light great candles, and sit as though she were a queen, till the evening : sitting and working at a frame, and singing as she worked.

And what she worked at was two wings, wrought in gold, on a blue ground.

And as for what she sung, I could never understand it, though I know now it was not in Latin.

And she used to charge me straightly never to let any man into the house on St. Peter's day; therefore, I and our dog, which was a great old bloodhound, always kept the door together.

But one St. Peter's day, when I was nearly twenty, I sat in the house watching the door with the bloodhound, and I was sleepy, because of the shut-up heat and my mother's singing, so I began to nod, and at last, though the dog often shook me by the hair to keep me awake, went fast asleep, and began to dream a foolish dream without hearing, as men sometimes do : for I thought that my mother and I were walking to mass through the snow on a Christmas day, but my mother carried a live goose in her hand, holding it by the neck, instead of her rosary, and that I went along by her side, not walking, but turning somersaults like a mountebank, my head never touching the ground; when we got to the chapel-door, the old priest met us, and said to my mother, "Why dame alive, your head is turned green! Ah! never mind, I will go and say mass, but don't let little Mary there go," and he pointed to the goose, and went.

Then mass begun, but in the midst of it, the priest said out loud, "Oh I forgot," and turning round to us began to wag his grey head and white beard, throwing his head right back, and sinking his chin on his breast alternately; and when we saw him do this, we presently began also to knock our heads against the wall, keeping time with him and with each other, till the priest said, "Peter! it's dragon-time now," whereat the roof flew off, and a great yellow dragon came down on the chapel-floor with a flop, and danced about clumsily, wriggling his fat tail, and saying to a sort of tune, "O the Devil, the Devil, the Devil, O the Devil," so I went up to him, and put my hand on his breast, meaning to slay him, and so awoke, and found myself standing up with my hand on the breast of an armed knight; the door lay flat on the ground, and under it lay Hector, our dog, whining and dying.

For eight hours I had been asleep; on awaking, the blood rushed up into my face, I heard my mother's low mysterious song behind me, and knew not what harm might happen to her and me, if that knight's coming made her cease in it; so I struck him with my left hand, where his face was bare under his mail coif, and getting my sword in my right, drove its point under his hawberk, so that it came out behind, and he fell, turned over on his face, and died.

Then, because my mother still went on working and singing, I said no word, but let him lie there, and put the door up again, and found Hector dead.

I then sat down again and polished my sword with a piece of leather after I had wiped the blood from it; and in an hour my mother arose from her work, and raising me from where I was sitting, kissed my brow, saying, " Well done, Lionel, you have slain your greatest foe, and now the people will know you for what you are before you die—Ah God! though not before *I* die."

So I said, " Who is he, mother? he seems to be some Lord; am I a Lord then?"

" A King, if the people will but know it," she said.

Then she knelt down by the dead body, turned it round again, so that it lay face uppermost, as before, then said:

" And so it has all come to this, has it? To think that you should run on my son's sword-point at last, after all the wrong you have done me and mine; now must I work carefully, lest when you are dead you should still do me harm, for that you are a King—Lionel!"

" Yea, Mother."

" Come here and see; this is what I have wrought these many Peter's days by day, and often other times by night."

" It is a surcoat, Mother; for me?"

" Yea, but take a spade, and come into the wood."

So we went, and my mother gazed about her for a while as if she were looking for something, but then suddenly went forward with her eyes on the ground, and she said to me:

" Is it not strange, that I who know the very place I am going to take you to, as well as our own garden, should have a sudden fear come over me that I should not find it after all; though for these nineteen years I have watched the trees change and change all about it—ah! here, stop now."

We stopped before a great oak ; a beech tree was behind us—she said, " Dig, Lionel, hereabouts."

So I dug and for an hour found nothing but beech roots, while my mother seemed as if she were going mad, sometimes running about muttering to herself, sometimes stooping into the hole and howling, sometimes throwing herself on the grass and twisting her hands together above her head ; she went once down the hill to a pool that had filled an old gravel pit, and came back dripping and with wild eyes ; " I am too hot," she said, " far too hot this St. Peter's day."

Clink just then from my spade against iron ; my mother screamed, and I dug with all my might for another hour, and then beheld a chest of heavy wood bound with iron ready to be heaved out of the hole ; " Now, Lionel, weigh it out—hard for your life ! "

And with some trouble I got the chest out ; she gave me a key, I unlocked the chest, and took out another wrapped in lead, which also I unlocked with a silver key that my mother gave me, and behold therein lay armour—mail for the whole body, made of very small rings wrought most wonderfully, for every ring was fashioned like a serpent, and though they were so small yet could you see their scales and their eyes, and of some even the forked tongue was on it, and lay on the rivet, and the rings were gilded here and there into patterns and flowers so that the gleam of it was most glorious.—And the mail coif was all gilded and had red and blue stones at the rivets; and the tilting helms (inside which the mail lay when I saw it first) was gilded also, and had flowers pricked out on it; and the chain of it was silver, and the crest was two gold wings. And there was a shield of blue set with red stones, which had two gold wings for a cognizance ; and the hilt of the sword was gold, with angels wrought in green and blue all up it, and the eyes in their wings were of pearls and red stones, and the sheath was of silver with green flowers on it.

Now when I saw this armour and understood that my mother would have me put it on, and ride out without fear, leaving her alone, I cast myself down on the grass so that I might not see its beauty (for it made me mad), and strove to think ; but what thoughts soever came to me were only of the things that would be, glory in the midst of ladies, battle-joy among knights, honour from all kings and princes and people —these things.

But my mother wept softly above me, till I arose with a great shudder of delight and drew the edges of the hawberk over my cheek, I liked so to feel the rings slipping, slipping, till they fell off altogether; then I said:

"O Lord God that made the world, if I might only die in this armour!"

Then my mother helped me to put it on, and I felt strange and new in it, and yet I had neither lance nor horse.

So when we reached the cottage again she said: "See now, Lionel, you must take this knight's horse and his lance, and ride away, or else the people will come here to kill another king; and when you are gone, you will never see me any more in life."

I wept thereat, but she said:

"Nay, but see here."

And taking the dead knight's lance from among the garden lilies, she rent from it the pennon (which had a sword on a red ground for bearing), and cast it carelessly on the ground, then she bound about it a pennon with my bearing, gold wings on a blue ground; she bid me bear the Knight's body, all armed as he was, to put on him his helm and lay him on the floor at her bed's foot, also to break his sword and cast it on our hearthstone; all which things I did.

Afterwards she put the surcoat on me, and then lying down in her gorgeous raiment on her bed, she spread her arms out in the form of a cross, shut her eyes, and said:

"Kiss me, Lionel, for I am tired."

And after I had kissed her she died.

And I mounted my dead foe's horse and rode away; neither did I ever know what wrong that was which he had done me, not while I was in the body at least.

And do not blame me for not burying my mother; I left her there because, though she did not say so to me, yet I knew the thoughts of her heart, and that the thing she had wished so earnestly for these years, and years, and years, had been but to lie dead with him lying dead close to her.

So I rode all that night, for I could not stop because of the thoughts that were in me, and, stopping at this place and that, in three days came to the city.

And there the King held his court with great pomp.

And so I went to the palace, and asked to see the King; whereupon they brought me into the great hall where he was with all his knights, and my heart swelled within me to think that I too was a King.

So I prayed him to make me a knight, and he spake graciously and asked me my name; so when I had told it him, and said that I was a king's son, he pondered, not knowing what to do, for I could not tell him whose son I was.

Whereupon one of the knights came near me and shaded his eyes with his hand as one does in a bright sun, meaning to mock at me for my shining armour, and he drew nearer and nearer till his long stiff beard just touched me, and then I smote him on the face, and he fell on the floor.

So the King being in a rage, roared out from the door, "Slay him!" but I put my shield before me and drew my sword, and the women drew together aside and whispered fearfully, and while some of the knights took spears and stood about me, others got their armour on.

And as we stood thus we heard a horn blow, and then an armed knight came into the hall and drew near to the King; and one of the maidens behind me, came and laid her hand on my shoulder; so I turned and saw that she was very fair, and then I was glad, but she whispered to me:

"Sir Squire, for a love I have for your face and gold armour, I will give you good counsel; go presently to the King and say to him: 'In the name of Alys des Roses and Sir Guy le bon amant I pray you three boons,'—do this, and you will be alive, and a knight by to-morrow, otherwise I think hardly the one or the other."

"The Lord reward you damozel," I said. Then I saw that the King had left talking with that knight and was just going to stand up and say something out loud, so I went quickly and called out with a loud voice:

"O King Gilbert of the rose-land, I, Lionel of the golden wings, pray of you three boons in the name of Alys des roses and Sir Guy le bon amant."

Then the King gnashed his teeth, because he had promised if ever his daughter Alys des roses came back safe again, he would on that day grant any three boons to the first man who asked them, even if he were his greatest foe. He said, "Well, then, take them, what are they?"

"First, my life; then, that you should make me a knight; and thirdly, that you should take me into your service."

He said, "I will do this, and moreover, I forgive you freely if you will be my true man."

Then we heard shouting arise through all the city because they were bringing the Lady Alys from the ship up to the palace, and the people came to the windows, and the houses were hung with cloths and banners of silk and gold, that swung down right from the eaves to the ground; likewise the bells all rang: and within a while they entered the palace, and the trumpets rang and men shouted, so that my head whirled; and they entered the hall, and the King went down from the daïs to meet them.

Now a band of knights and of damozels went before and behind, and in the midst Sir Guy led the Lady Alys by the hand, and he was a most stately knight, strong and fair.

And I indeed noted the first band of knights and damozels well, and wondered at the noble presence of the knights, and was filled with joy when I beheld the maids, because of their great beauty; the second band I did not see, for when they passed I was leaning back against the wall, wishing to die with my hands before my face.

But when I could see, she was hanging about her father's neck, weeping, and she never left him all that night, but held his hand in feast and dance, and even when I was made knight, while the King with his right hand laid his sword over my shoulder, she held his left hand and was close to me.

And the next day they held a grand tourney, that I might be proven; and I had never fought with knights before, yet I did not doubt. And Alys sat under a green canopy, that she might give the degree to the best knight, and by her sat the good knight Sir Guy, in a long robe, for he did not mean to joust that day; and indeed at first none but young knights jousted, for they thought that I should do much.

But I, looking up to the green canopy, overthrew so many of them, that the elder knights began to arm, and I grew most joyful as I met them, and no man unhorsed me; and always I broke my spear fairly, or else overthrew my adversary.

Now that maiden who counselled me in the hall, told me afterwards that as I fought, the Lady Alys held fast to the rail before her, and leaned forward and was most pale, never answering any word that any one might say to her, till the Knight Guy said to her in anger: "Alys! what ails you? you would have been glad enough to speak to me when

King Wadrayns carried you off shrieking, or that other time when the chain went round about you, and the faggots began to smoke in the Brown City: do you not love me any longer? O Alys, Alys! just think a little, and do not break your faith with me; God hates nothing so much as this. Sweet, try to love me, even for your own sake! See, am I not kind to you?"

That maiden said that she turned round to him wonderingly, as if she had not caught his meaning, and that just for one second, then stretched out over the lists again.

Now till about this time I had made no cry as I jousted. But there came against me a very tall knight, on a great horse, and when we met our spears both shivered, and he howled with vexation, for he wished to slay me, being the brother of that knight I had struck down in the hall the day before.

And they say that when Alys heard his howl sounding faintly through the bars of his great helm, she trembled; but I know not, for I was stronger than that knight, and when we fought with swords, I struck him right out of his saddle, and near slew him with that stroke.

Whereupon I shouted "Alys," out loud, and she blushed red for pleasure, and Sir Guy took note of it, and rose up in a rage and ran down and armed.

Then presently I saw a great knight come riding in with three black chevrons on a gold shield: and so he began to ride at me, and at first we only broke both our spears, but then he drew his sword, and fought quite in another way to what the other knights had, so that I saw at once that I had no chance against him: nevertheless, for a long time he availed nothing, though he wounded me here and there, but at last drove his sword right through mine, through my shield and my helm, and I fell, and lay like one dead.

And thereat the King cried out to cease, and the degree was given to Sir Guy, because I had overthrown forty knights and he had overthrown me.

Then they told me, I was carried out of the lists and laid in a hostelry near the palace, and Guy went up to the pavilion where Alys was and she crowned him, both of them being very pale, for she doubted if I were slain, and he knew that she did not love him, thinking before that she did; for he was good and true, and had saved her life and

honour, and she (poor maid!) wished to please her father,
and strove to think that all was right.

But I was by no means slain, for the sword had only
cleft my helm, and when I came to myself again I felt
despair of all things, because I knew not that she loved me,
for how should she, knowing nothing of me? likewise dust
had been cast on my gold wings, and she saw it done.

Then I heard a great crying in the street, that sounded
strangely in the quiet night, so I sent to ask what it might
be: and there came presently into my chamber a man in
gilded armour; he was an old man, and his hair and beard
were gray, and behind him came six men armed, who carried
a dead body of a young man between them, and I said,
"What is it? who is he?" Then the old man, whose head
was heavy for grief, said: "Oh, sir! this is my son; for as
we went yesterday with our merchandize some twenty miles
from this fair town, we passed by a certain hold, and there-
from came a knight and men-at-arms, who when my son
would have fought with them, overthrew him and bound
him, and me and all our men they said they would slay if
we did ought; so then they cut out my son's eyes, and cut
off his hands, and then said, 'The Knight of High Gard
takes these for tribute.' Therewithal they departed, taking
with them my son's eyes and his hands on a platter; and
when they were gone I would have followed them, and slain
some of them at least, but my own people would not suffer
me, and for grief and pain my son's heart burst, and he died,
and behold I am here."

Then I thought I could win glory, and I was much re-
joiced thereat, and said to the old man,

"Would you love to be revenged?"

But he set his teeth, and pulled at the skirt of his sur-
coat, as hardly for his passion he said, "Yes."

"Then," I said, "I will go and try to slay this knight, if
you will show me the way to La Haute Garde."

And he, taking my hand, said, "O glorious knight, let us
go now!" And he did not ask who I was, or whether I
was a good knight, but began to go down the stairs at once,
so I put on my armour and followed him.

And we two set forth alone to La Haute Garde, for no
man else dared follow us, and I rejoiced in thinking that
while Guy was sitting at the King's table feasting, I was

riding out to slay the King's enemies, for it never once seemed possible to me that I should be worsted.

It was getting light again by then we came in sight of High Gard; we wound up the hill on foot, for it was very steep; I blew at the gates a great blast which was even as though the stag should blow his own mort, or like the blast that Balen heard.

For in a very short while the gates opened and a great band of armed men, more than thirty I think, and a knight on horseback among them, who was armed in red, stood before us, and on one side of him was a serving-man with a silver dish, on the other, one with a butcher's cleaver, a knife, and pincers.

So when the knight saw us he said, " What, are you come to pay tribute in person, old man, and is this another fair son? Good sir, how is your lady?"

So I said grimly, being in a rage, "I have a will to slay you."

But I could scarce say so before the old merchant rushed at the red knight with a yell, who without moving slew his horse with an axe, and then the men-at-arms speared the old man, slaying him as one would an otter or a rat.

Afterwards they were going to set on me, but the red knight held them back, saying: "Nay, I am enough," and we spurred our horses.

As we met, I felt just as if some one had thrown a dull brown cloth over my eyes, and I felt the wretched spear-point slip off his helm; then I felt a great pain somewhere, that did not seem to be in my body, but in the world, or the sky, or something of that sort.

And I know not how long that pain seemed to last now, but I think years, though really I grew well and sane again in a few weeks.

And when I woke, scarce knowing whether I was in the world or heaven or hell, I heard some one singing.

I tried to listen but could not, because I did not know where I was, and was thinking of that; I missed verse after verse of the song, this song, till at last I saw I must be in the King's palace.

There was a window by my bed, I looked out at it, and saw that I was high up; down in the street the people were going to and fro, and there was a knot of folks gathered about a minstrel, who sat on the edge of a fountain, with his head laid sideways on his shoulder, and nursing one leg on the other ; he was singing only, having no instrument, and he sang the song I had tried to listen to, I heard some of it now :

> " He was fair and free,
> At every tourney
> He wan the degree,
>   Sir Guy the good knight.
>
> He wan Alys the fair,
> The king's own daughtere,
> With all her gold hair,
>   That shone well bright.
>
> He saved a good knight,
> Who also was wight,
> And had wingès bright
>   On a blue shield.
>
> And he slew the Knight,
> Of the High Gard in fight,
> In red weed that was dight
>   In the open field."

I fell back in my bed and wept, for I was weak with my illness ; to think of this ! truly this man was a perfect knight, and deserved to win Alys. Ah ! well ! but was this the glory I was to have, and no one believed that I was a King's son.

And so I passed days and nights, thinking of my dishonour and misery, and my utter loneliness ; no one cared for me ; verily, I think, if any one had spoken to me lovingly, I should have fallen on his neck and died, while I was so weak.

But I grew strong at last, and began to walk about, and in the Palace Pleasaunce, one day, I met Sir Guy walking by himself.

So I told him how that I thanked him with all my heart for my life, but he said it was only what a good knight ought to do ; for that hearing the mad enterprise I had ridden on, he had followed me swiftly with a few knights, and so saved me.

He looked stately and grand as he spoke, yet I did not love him, nay, rather hated him, though I tried hard not to do so, for there was some air of pitiless triumph and coldness of heart in him that froze me ; so scornfully, too, he said that about "my mad enterprise," as though I *must* be wrong in everything I did. Yet afterwards, as I came to know more, I pitied him instead of hating ; but at that time I thought his life was without a shadow, for I did not know that the Lady Alys loved him not.

And now I turned from him, and walked slowly up and down the garden-paths, not exactly thinking, but with some ghosts of former thoughts passing through my mind. The day, too, was most lovely, as it grew towards evening, and I had all the joy of a man lately sick in the flowers and all things; if any bells at that time had begun to chime, I think I should have lain down on the grass and wept; but now there was but the noise of the bees in the yellow musk, and that had not music enough to bring me sorrow.

And as I walked I stooped and picked a great orange lily, and held it in my hand, and lo! down the garden-walk, the same fair damozel that had before this given me good counsel in the hall.

Thereat I was very glad, and walked to meet her smiling, but she was very grave, and said:

"Fair sir, the Lady Alys des roses wishes to see you in her chamber."

I could not answer a word, but turned, and went with her while she walked slowly beside me, thinking deeply, and picking a rose to pieces as she went; and I, too, thought much, what could she want me for? surely, but for one thing; and yet—and yet.

But when we came to the lady's chamber, behold! before the door stood a tall knight, fair and strong, and in armour, save his head, who seemed to be guarding the door, though not so as to seem so to all men.

He kissed the damozel eagerly, and then she said to me, "This is Sir William de la Fosse, my true knight;" so the knight took my hand and seemed to have such joy of me, that all the blood came up to my face for pure delight.

But then the damozel Blanche opened the door and bade me go in while she abode still without; so I entered, when I had put aside the heavy silken hanging that filled the doorway.

And there sat Alys; she arose when she saw me, and stood pale, and with her lips apart, and her hands hanging loose by her side.

And then all doubt and sorrow went quite away from me; I did not even feel drunk with joy, but rather felt that I could take it all in, lose no least fragment of it; then at once I felt that I was beautiful, and brave and true; I had no doubt as to what I should do now.

I went up to her, and first kissed her on the forehead, and then on the feet, and then drew her to me, and with my arms round about her, and her arms hanging loose, and her lips dropped, we held our lips together so long that my eyes failed me, and I could not see her, till I looked at her green raiment.

And she had never spoken to me yet; she seemed just then as if she were going to, for she lifted her eyes to mine, and opened her mouth; but she only said, "Dear Lionel," and fell forward as though she were faint; and again I held her, and kissed her all over; and then she loosed her hair that it fell to her feet, and when I clipped her next, she threw it over me, that it fell all over my scarlet robes like the trickling of some golden well in Paradise.

Then, within a while, we called in the Lady Blanche and Sir William de la Fosse, and while they talked about what we should do, we sat together and kissed; and what they said, I know not.

But I remember, that that night, quite late, Alys and I rode out side by side from the good city in the midst of a great band of knights and men-at-arms, and other bands drew to us as we went, and in three days we reached Sir William's castle, which was called " La Garde des Chevaliers."

And straightway he caused toll the great bell, and to hang out from the highest tower a great banner of red and gold, cut into so many points that it seemed as if it were tattered; for this was the custom of his house when they wanted their vassals together.

And Alys and I stood up in the tower by the great bell as they tolled it; I remember now that I had passed my hand underneath her hair, so that the fingers of it folded over and just lay on her cheek; she gazed down on the bell, and at every deafening stroke she drew in her breath and opened her eyes to a wide stare downwards.

But on the very day that we came, they arrayed her in gold and flowers (and there were angels and knights and ladies wrought on her gold raiment), and I waited for an hour in the chapel till she came, listening to the swallows outside, and gazing with parted lips at the pictures on the golden walls; but when she came, I knelt down before the alter, and she knelt down and kissed my lips; and then the priest came in, and the singers and the censer-boys; and that chapel was soon confusedly full of golden raiment, and incense, and ladies and singing; in the midst of which I wedded Alys.

And men came into knights' gard till we had two thousand men in it, and great store of munitions of war and provisions.

But Alys and I lived happily together in the painted hall and in the fair water-meadows, and as yet no one came against us.

And still her talk was of deeds of arms, and she was never tired of letting the serpent rings of my mail slip off her wrist and long hand, and she would kiss my shield and helm and the gold wings on my surcoat, my mother's work, and would talk of the ineffable joy that would be when we had fought through all the evil that was coming on us.

Also she would take my sword and lay it on her knees and talk to it, telling it how much she loved me.

Yea in all things, O Lord God, Thou knowest that my love was a very child, like thy angels. Oh! my wise soft-handed love! endless passion! endless longing always satisfied!

Think you that the shouting curses of the trumpet broke off our love, or in any way lessened it? no, most certainly, but from the time the siege began, her cheeks grew thinner, and her passionate face seemed more and more a part of me; now too, whenever I happened to see her between the grim fighting she would do nothing but kiss me all the time, or wring my hands, or take my head on her breast, being so eagerly passionate that sometimes a pang shot through me that she might die.

Till one day they made a breach in the wall, and when I heard of it for the first time, I sickened, and could not call on God; but Alys cut me a tress of her yellow hair and tied it in my helm, and armed me, and saying no word, led me down to the breach by the hand, and then went back most ghastly pale.

So there on the one side of the breach were the spears of William de la Fosse and Lionel of the gold wings, and on the other the spears of King Gilbert and Sir Guy le bon amant, but the King himself was not there; Sir Guy was.

Well,—what would you have? in this world never yet could two thousand men stand against twenty thousand; we were almost pushed back with their spear-points, they were so close together:—slay six of them and the spears were as thick as ever; but if two of our men fell there was straightway a hole.

Yet just at the end of this we drove them back in one charge two yards beyond the breach, and behold in the front rank, Sir Guy, utterly fearless, cool, and collected; nevertheless, with one stroke I broke his helm, and he fell to the ground before the two armies, even as I fell that day in the lists; and we drove them twenty feet farther, yet they saved Sir Guy.

Well, again,—what would you have? They drove us back again, and they drove us into our inner castle-walls. And I was the last to go in, and just as I was entering, the boldest and nearest of the enemy clutched at my love's hair in my helm, shouting out quite loud, "Whore's hair for John the goldsmith!"

At the hearing of which blasphemy, the Lord gave me such strength, that I turned and caught him by the ribs with my left hand, and with my right, by sheer strength, I tore off his helm and part of his nose with it, and then swinging him round about, dashed his brains out against the castle-walls.

Yet thereby was I nearly slain, for they surrounded me, only Sir William and the others charged out and rescued me, but hardly.

May the Lord help all true men! In an hour we were all fighting pell mell on the walls of the castle itself, and some were slain outright, and some were wounded, and some yielded themselves and received mercy; but I had scarce the heart to fight any more, because I thought of Alys lying with her face upon the floor and her agonized hands outspread, trying to clutch something, trying to hold to the cracks of the boarding. So when I had seen William de la Fosse slain by many men, I cast my shield and helm over the battlements, and gazed about for a second, and lo! on one of the flanking towers, my gold wings still floated by the side of William's white lion, and in the other one I knew my poor Love, whom they had left quite alone, was lying.

So then I turned into a dark passage and ran till I reached the tower stairs, up that too I sprang as though a ghost were after me, I did so long to kiss her again before I died, to soothe her too, so that she should not feel this day, when in the aftertimes she thought of it as wholly miserable to her. For I knew they would neither slay her nor treat her cruelly, for in sooth all loved her, only they would make her marry Sir Guy le bon amant.

In the topmost room I found her, alas! alas! lying on the floor, as I said; I came to her and kissed her head as she lay, then raised her up; and I took all my armour off and broke my sword over my knee.

And then I led her to the window away from the fighting, from whence we only saw the quiet country, and kissed her lips till she wept and looked no longer sad and wretched; then I said to her:

"Now, O Love, we must part for a little, it is time for me to go and die."

"Why should you go away?" she said, "they will come here quick enough, no doubt, and I shall have you longer with me if you stay; I do not turn sick at the sight of blood."

"O my poor Love!" And I could not go because of her praying face; surely God would grant anything to such a face as that.

"Oh!" she said, "you will let me have you yet a little longer, I see; also let me kiss your feet."

She threw herself down and kissed them, and then did not get up again at once, but lay there holding my feet.

And while she lay there, behold a sudden tramping that she did not hear, and over the green hangings the gleam of helmets that she did not see, and then one pushed aside the hangings with his spear, and there stood the armed men.

"Will not somebody weep for my darling?"

She sprung up from my feet with a low, bitter moan, most terrible to hear, she kissed me once on the lips, and then stood aside, with her dear head thrown back, and holding her lovely loose hair strained over her outspread arms, as though she were wearied of all things that had been or that might be.

Then one thrust me through the breast with a spear, and another with his sword, which was three inches broad, gave me a stroke across the thighs that hit to the bone; and as I fell forward one cleft me to the teeth with his axe.

And then I heard my darling shriek.

NOTES

The Defence of Guenevere. A form of the story is related by Malory
in the *Morte D'Arthur*, Bks XVIII–XX, but there Agravaine
rather than Gauwaine is the accuser of Guenevere. There is a
good expository essay by Laurence Perrine, 'Morris's Guene-
vere—An Interpretation', in *Philological Quarterly* XXXIX,
2 (April, 1960), 234–41.

p. 5. *as if one should slip slowly down:* this elaborate simile is
psychologically effective as well as pictorial, giving a strong
sense of the desire to abandon the effort of will.

p. 7. *your mother:* Gauwaine's mother was Morgause, wife of
King Lot and sister of Arthur, who was killed while adulterously
in bed with Lamorak.

p. 8. *La Fausse Garde:* the False Castle, belonging to Mellya-
graunce.

p. 9. *stake and pen:* enclosure.
caitiff: wretch.

p. 10. *See my breast rise:* the effect of Guenevere's speech here
is to make the scene pictorially vivid rather than dramatic.
woof: weaving, blend.

King Arthur's Tomb. The scene is described in Malory XXI, 9–10,
but the meeting takes place at Almesbury.

p. 13. *Sir Gareth:* Gauwaine's brother.
Dinadan: a sportive knight.
God . . . took Enoch: a rabbinical and Moslem tale.
Maiden Margaret: Margaret of Antioch, the virgin martyr.

p. 15. *St Joseph:* (of Arimathea) was believed to have come to
Glastonbury.

p. 16. *Grew into lumps of sin:* a striking instance of Morris's
ability to make abstractions concrete and substantial.
rood: cross.
jennet: a small horse.

p. 17. *If even I go hell:* Morris added 'to' in the Kelmscott
edition.

p. 18. *mark'd with V:* believed to be the sign of a poisonous snake.
Lucius: the King or Emperor of Italy, killed by Launcelot for
impugning Guenevere's honour; in Malory he is killed by Arthur.

p. 19. *Breuse even:* the Knight without pity; Rossetti made a
painting of 'The Death of Breuse Sans Pitié' in 1857.
back-toll'd bells: employing a vigorous method of bell-ringing.

Notes

p. 20. *two spots on earth:* the place where he was, and the place where she was, conscious of the separation.

Iseult from the West . . . Iseult of Brittany: both beautiful and both loved by Tristram.

p. 21. *Palomydes:* the unsuccessful rival of Tristram, who bore the device of the beast Gratislaunt on his shield.

p. 22. *Kay:* the seneschal.

crease: kris, a Malayan knife.

p. 23. *myself, much better so,/Never:* the punctuation of this stanza is defective.

Sir Galahad, a Christmas Mystery. Galahad, the son of Launcelot, was the purest of the Arthurian knights, and therefore permitted the vision of the Grail. In this poem he begins with doubts of his celibate vocation, which are resolved by a vision. Malory, XVII, gives some elements of the story.

p. 25. *still:* always.

Candlemas: February 2nd, the Feast of the Purification of the Virgin Mary.

Palace-pleasaunce: pleasure gardens of the Palace.

minster: church.

p. 26. *Sangreal:* The Holy Grail.

Mador de la porte: a Knight of the Round Table.

raiment half blood-red, half white as snow: suggesting Christ's passion and his purity.

destrier: charger.

p. 27. *whose sword first made him knight:* Arthur.

p. 28. *Miserere:* 'Have mercy'; the opening of Psalm LI (Vulgate L) and the other penitential Psalms.

the wondrous ship: of Faith and Belief; see Malory, XVII, 7.

spindles of King Solomon: cut from the tree grown by Eve after the Fall from the bough on which the apple hung; see Malory, XVII, 5.

sister of Perceval: she became a nun and saw the Grail.

Sir Bors: de Ganis, cousin of Launcelot.

Sir Perceval: de Gales, a knight of the Grail.

p. 29. *First Lady:* the ladies who aid Galahad are all virgin martyrs; Margaret of Antioch, Cecilia, Lucy of Syracuse, and Katherine of Alexandria.

hauberke: coat of mail.

basnet: light helmet.

God's body: the Grail.

p. 30. *Lionel:* nephew of Launcelot.

Lauvaine: brother of Elaine of Astolat.

The Chapel in Lyoness. The poem was originally published in the *Magazine* in September 1856. Its events do not occur in Malory; Curtis Dahl in 'Morris's *Chapel in Lyoness*' in *Studies in Philology* LI, 3 (July, 1954), 482–91, argues strongly that the poem is a 'symbolic drama of salvation by grace', but there are elements of decorative romance too.

p. 31. *truncheon:* broken end.

parclose: screen.

samite: rich silk.

p. 34. *No long time hence:* the last six lines replace two in the first published version of 1856:

> Her hair against the jasper sea
> Wondrously does shine.

jasper: a green precious stone; appropriate therefore to the heavenly sea.

Sir Peter Harpdon's End. The first and most elaborate poem in the volume dealing with the period described by Froissart; much of the fighting took place in the Poictou region. Gascony belonged to the King of England as Duke of Aquitaine; hence Sir Peter's allegiance. Morris's free handling of his source is well described by F. J. J. Davies in 'William Morris's *Sir Peter Harpdon's End*', *Philological Quarterly XI*, 3 (July, 1932), 314–317.

p. 36. *villaynes:* serfs.

Clisson: Sir Oliver de Clisson, a famous Breton knight and Constable of France from 1380.

Sanzerre: Louis de Sancerre, Marechal of France from 1369.

p. 37. *Lusac:* Lussac-les-Châteaux on the Vienne. Froissart describes the fight in Book II of the *Chronicles*.

Chandos: Sir John Chandos, a famous English knight who died in 1370.

Pembroke: John Hastings, Earl of Pembroke, Lieutenant in Aquitaine from 1372.

Phelton: Thomas de Felton, Seneschal of Aquitaine from 1372.

Manny: Sir Walter de Manny, Hainaulter squire to Queen Philippa and a famous English commander, died in 1372, and was buried in the house of the Carthusian monks he had founded the previous year.

Oliver Clisson: see above; Clisson was brought up at the court of Edward III, but went over to the French in 1367.

The Captal: captain, chief.

Edward the prince: Edward, Prince of Wales, famed as the Black Prince, died in 1376.

Edward the King: Edward III died in 1377.

Guesclin: Bertrand du Guesclin, Breton gentleman and Constable of France who died in 1380.

petrariae: stone-throwing machines.

p. 38. *glaives:* blades fixed to the end of poles.

basnet: helmet.

Now this is hard: Sir Peter's reflections give the romantic background of his love for Alice and Sir Lambert's jealousy, which explains the subsequent events in the poem. The exclamatory and conversational manner is like Browning's.

burs, and clumsily carven puppets: misleading and derogatory ideas.

Notes

p. 39. *I am like Balen:* Sir Balen le Savage was always unlucky, and finally killed his brother Balan by accident.

Bergerath: Bergerac, on the Dordogne, an area much contested by the French and English.

marish: marsh.

She . . . started a little: Sir Peter is imagining the scene he would have liked to take place, but at its climax here describes it to himself as if it had actually occurred. In the next lines, however, he returns to the less romantic reality.

p. 40. *gard:* castle.

archgays: spears.

postern: back way.

p. 43. *Richards:* Richard had become King of England in 1377.

St. Dennis: patron saint of France, invoked as a war-cry.

St. Lambert: invoked as Sir Lambert's patron saint.

p. 44. *flatlings:* with the side.

St. George Guienne: the English war-cry; Guienne being an area claimed by England in Bordeaux.

p. 46. *righteous Job would give up skin for skin:* see Job, II, 4.

p. 47. *cousin Lambert's ears:* cut off at Sir Peter's orders in the previous scene.

Do you care altogether more than France: corrected to 'for France' in the Kelmscott edition.

p. 48. *Clement:* the French anti-pope; the Cistercian grey monks generally supported the English cause.

Laurence being grilled: referring to the martyrdom of the saint on the gridiron.

p. 50. *For I am Alice:* this scene of Lambert teasing his victim has an unpleasant power and certainly went beyond Victorian ideas of good taste. Clisson interrupts to express, somewhat crudely, the reader's feelings of disgust and impatience.

p. 52. *Hotel de la Barde:* the home of the Lady Alice, Sir Peter's lady.

p. 53. *Avalon:* the mysterious island to which Arthur went to heal his wounds after the last battle with Mordred, as beautifully evoked by Tennyson in his *Morte D'Arthur* (1842).

p. 54. *lombards:* military engines, canons.

base-court: lower, outer court.

p. 57. *Let us go, You and I:* the extravagant wishes of Alice express the depth of her feelings.

dustiness is altered to 'duskness' in the Kelmscott edition.

Eh Guesclin!: knowing only the messenger's account, Alice blames Guesclin rather than Lambert for Sir Peter's death.

Countess Mountford: Sir Walter de Manny rode into Britanny to rescue her from the French.

wight: brave.

p. 58. *Wade:* mythical Teutonic hero.

p. 59. *Therefore be it believed:* this song is not one of Morris's best, but it serves to suggest that heroes survive in song long after their deaths and even though their lives are not—like Launcelot's and Peter's—completely blameless.

Omnes homines benedicite!: 'All men give praise!'
fitte: part (of a song).

Rapunzel. This poem, based on a well-known fairytale, is placed
incongruously among the Froissartian poems, presumably
because of its length. (Morris placed more of the shorter poems
later in the volume, not always grouping them according to
their subject matter.)
p. 65. *wem:* blemish; the phrase as applied to Mary is thor-
oughly medieval.
gold Michael . . . Rouen town: a weather-vane.
p. 66. *crayfish:* seen in her nightmare.
p. 67. *speed-walk:* (the flower) speedwell in Kelmscott Press
edition.
p. 69. *'Twixt the sunlight and the shade:* this song was originally
published separately in the *Magazine* as 'Hands'.
p. 70. *kirtle:* gown, tunic.

Concerning Geffray Teste Noire. A Froissartian poem about a
different kind of English supporter from Sir Peter Harpdon,
written in rhyming quatrains. There is complication, which
some early reviewers disliked, in the setting of a story within
the story. Froissart records this Breton freebooter and his
defence of the castle of Ventadour.
p. 72. *The Canon of Chimay:* Froissart himself, who died in the
small town in Hainault.
Ortaise: Orthez, on the Gave de Pau near the Pyrenees.
The Duke of Berry: third son of John II of France (1340–1416).
bastides: besieging-huts.
Ventadour: in the Commune of Moustier-Ventadour, with a
castle on a rock.
Auvergne: area of southern France.
camaille: chain-mail for the neck.
p. 73. *Carcassoune:* city in Languedoc.
damned blackhead: Teste Noire himself.
hap: luck.
sumpter: pack, carrier.
like the horse in Job: see Job, XXXIX, 24.
p. 74. *What have we lying here?:* the discovery of the two skele-
tons with armour gives rise to the most interesting part of the
poem, the story of the dead lovers.
no plate: no plate-armour (all mail).
rowels: small spiked wheel or disc at the end of a spur.
ceinture: girdle.
coif: skull-cap.
The Jacquerie: the rebellious peasantry.
p. 75. *Beauvais:* town in the Oise district attacked by the
Jacquerie. The narrator's recollections of the brutalities he
had known from an early age give poignancy to the story of
chivalric love.

p. 76. *O most pale face:* these lines must be addressed to the narrator's Lady, whom he is led to think of by the skeleton.
like an overwinded harp: on the point of breaking (from joy into sorrow).
I kiss their soft lips there: the italics perhaps express the narrator's longings as distinct from recollections.

p. 77. *Cry out St. Peter now:* the poem here comes back to the dramatic present.
Months after that he died: a clumsiness in these two stanzas makes 'blackhead' and Teste Noire sound like two different people.
Jaques Picard: an imaginary sculptor.

A Good Knight in Prison. A poem with Arthurian associations, while the Pagan castle in which the knight is imprisoned suggests the campaigns against the Crusaders. The form is irregular octosyllabic couplets.
p. 79. *castellan:* keeper.
barbican: outer fortification or entrance-tower.
p. 80. *Laus Deo!:* 'Praise be to God!'
Mahound: Mahommed.
p. 81. *la perriere:* the ballistic stone-throwing machine.
. . . Because today we have been wed: these three lines give the poem a very sudden and awkward finish.

Old Love. A disillusioned romantic poem written in octosyllabic quatrains.
p. 82. *basnet:* light steel headpiece terminating in a point.
salade: light globular headpiece.
no Venice flag: the great maritime power of Venice had to come to terms with the increasing power of the Turks in the fifteenth century.
Constantine must fall this year: Constantinople was eventually stormed by the Turks in 1453.
p. 83. *I said:* The punctuation in this section of the poem is imperfect; probably the first words of the stanza are spoken, whereas the previous stanza contains Sir John's thoughts.
p. 84. *smutch:* stain, blacken.

The Gilliflower of Gold. A chivalric poem in octosyllabic triplets, with an effective refrain in medieval French. The yellow gilliflower is the wallflower.
p. 85. *Honneur aux fils des preux:* 'Honour to the sons of the valiant'; the herald's cry at a tournament.
p. 86. *tabard:* emblazoned surcoat.
The yellow flowers stained with red: the knight has stimulated himself by imagining what might happen to his lady if he failed—the idea being expressed by a visual impression—and even after winning he cannot rid himself of the vision of her death.

Shameful Death. This poem of death and vengeance has some of the feeling of a ballad in its simplicity and forcefulness.
p. 87. *hornbeams:* Morris's imagination places these events into the landscape he knew best himself.

The Eve of Crecy. A heroic romance, in triplets, with an effective refrain which catches the note of the early French romances.
p. 89. *the arriere-ban:* king's call of his subjects to military service.
Six basnets: only six men.
Philip of France: King Philip VI (1328–50).
p. 90. *banneret:* knight, especially one who has performed valiantly in the presence of the king.
St. Ives: Sir Lambert's war-cry.

The Judgment of God. A dramatic poem in quatrains, of the Froissartian period, dealing (in a less than clear way) with a single combat, the attempt to resolve a wrong committed earlier, and the narrator's love for Ellayne. The title was an old name for trial by single combat.
p. 91. *Lord Roger:* the narrator himself, 'son Roger', presumably responsible for the cutting off of an enemy's hands and head. Sir Oliver is now seeking revenge for 'that wrong'.
bore his face: his decapitated head.
the Hainault Knights: famous for their chivalry and courage.
He sat: the dead man, at a previous contest.
pall: cloth, the whiteness suggests the purity of his cause.
p. 92. *Now these say:* the present onlookers, who once favoured Roger.
p. 93. *the fire crept:* Ellayne was being burnt as a witch until rescued by Roger.
this mere grin: at the moment the onlookers are merely smiling, but they might turn dangerous.

The Little Tower. The energetic couplets give this heroic romance great vitality.
p. 95. *glaive-strokes:* lance-strokes.

The Sailing of the Sword. This is a well-managed ballad, with an effective refrain.
p. 97. *leads:* roofing (of lead).

Spell-Bound. The octosyllabic quatrains move slowly to give an impression of the knight's enchantment in this poem of magic, with its effective pathos.
p. 99. *broken ivory wands:* perhaps stays in the rich dresses now discarded and neglected.
samite: rich silk cloth.

The Wind. This is the first of the poems usually classified as fantastic or purely imaginative (see Introduction, p. xv).
p. 102. *flambeau:* torch.

p. 104. *vest:* robe.

p. 105. *Olaf, king and saint:* Olaf Haraldson (c. 995–1030), King of Norway and that country's saint.

The **Blue Closet.** Rossetti painted a beautiful water-colour of this name in 1857, which was bought by Morris together with four others, 'The Damsel of the Sanc Grael', 'The Death of Breuse Sans Pitié', 'The Chapel before the Lists' and 'The Tune of Seven Towers'. 'The Blue Closet' shows two queenly figures playing upon opposite sides of a dulcimer, while two other ladies stand singing behind them. The wall and floor are tiled in blue. The whole effect is solemn and elevated. Morris was fond of the picture, but his poem is by no means derived from it, except perhaps in atmosphere.

p. 106. *Laudate, pueri:* 'Praise, O ye servants of the Lord'; the opening of Psalm CXIII (Vulgate CXII); the Latin phrase gives an appropriate sense of religious ritual.

The **Tune of Seven Towers.** Rossetti's painting with this title, owned by Morris, shows a strange scene. A lady is sitting in a chair, playing a musical instrument; a man is sitting nearby, watching her, while a second lady stands behind. A maid is reaching through a little window at the back to place an orange branch on a bed. A banner-pole divides the picture diagonally. Again, Morris's poem does no more than take the picture as its starting point.

p. 109. *arow:* in a row.

Golden Wings. This narrative poem in the 'In Memoriam' quatrain takes place in the French chivalric past. The opening evocation of happiness, with its Pre-Raphaelite vividness of detail and colour, is well known; but the movement of the poem is towards tragedy, both personal (in the suicide of Jehane) and social (in the war that desolates the castle). Each beautiful detail of the opening is recapitulated, in a sombre form, at the end. The title refers to the device of the absent knight and lover of Jehane; the prose story of the same name (pp. 272–87) is not directly related to the poem.

p. 113. *Undern:* afternoon.

The **Haystack in the Floods.** The vigorous octosyllabic couplets of this Froissartian narrative poem have made it probably the best-known of the volume. It tells a grim story in a direct and dramatic manner. The anonymity of the characters in the opening scene is particularly effective.

p. 118. *kilted:* tucked up.

p. 119. *thirty heads:* Morris does not exaggerate the scale in search of excitement.

The gratings of the Chatelet: an ancient fortress in Paris where Jehane will be imprisoned.

296 Notes

> *The swift Seine:* into which she will be thrown as a witch, according to Godmar's threat, unless she will marry him.
> *St. George for Marny:* but none of the men responds to Robert's war-cry.

Two Red Roses Across the Moon. Another chivalric poem, of which the title refers to a Knight's device. Difficulty occurs because the battle in the poem is between 'the scarlet and the blue' (who are defeated) and 'the gold' (for whom the victorious Knight fights). Presumably the lady is singing of her own love, real or imagined.

Welland River. A successful poem in the ballad metre, with an appropriate vocabulary.
> p. 125. *Welland, Stamford:* the river Welland flows through Stamford in Lincolnshire.
> *the Easterlings:* people of the east.
> p. 126. *bascinet:* basnet, helmet.
> *Collayne:* from Cologne, famous for its metalwork. In the ballads 'swords of fyne Collayne' are often referred to.
> *jennet:* small horse.
> *burd:* maiden.
> *fell:* coat.
> p. 127. *one gift:* the child she is carrying.

Riding Together. This poem, originally published in the *Magazine* in May 1856, is a narrative in quatrains. It celebrates knightly fellowship in one of the campaigns against the Saracens in the eighth century.
> p. 129. *mazed:* looked stupefied.

Father John's War-Song. This short, jerky poem belongs to the Froissartian world of medieval fighting. It has a more assertative ending than many of the poems.

Sir Giles' War-Song. A brief addition to the Froissartian group.
> p. 132. *leopards and lilies:* devices of the English and French, which the Kings of England quartered for their device.
> *St. George Guienne:* the English war-cry.
> *the barrier:* a fence down the centre of the lists.
> *Clisson:* see Note to *Sir Peter Harpdon's End* (p. 290).
> *basnet:* helmet.

Near Avalon. A mysterious poem in rhyming quatrains, with vivid, dream-like details.
> p. 133. *Avalon:* see Note to p. 53.
> *heaumes:* helmets.

Praise of My Lady. This romantic poem in rhyming triplets with a Latin refrain expresses Morris's elevated, quasi-religious feelings about Jane Burden, whom he had recently met in Oxford.

Notes 297

Summer Dawn. This sonnet, which appeared in the *Magazine* in October 1856, is the only poem in the volume without historical adjuncts.

In Prison. This evocative little poem appeared in the *Magazine* in April 1856, in a story called 'Frank's Sealed Letter': a first-person narrative of Hugh's unhappy love for Mabel, and the advice, in a letter from his dead friend Frank, to admit the reality of the rejected love. The story is over-emotional and gives no scope for Morris's historical imagination, though it contains a vivid Pre-Raphaelite scene with the boy Hugh reading to the proud Mabel; see May Morris (ed.), *Collected Works*, I, 309–25.

The Story of the Unknown Church. Appeared in the first number of the *Magazine*, in January 1856; apart from the pathos of its romantic story, it shows Morris's profound feeling for medieval architecture.

Lindenborg Pool. In the September number of the *Magazine*. Benjamin Thorpe's three volumes of *Northern Mythology* appeared in 1851; among the Danish traditions recorded is one entitled 'The Sunken Mansion' (vol. ii, pp. 214–15), from which the bare bones of Morris's story are derived.
p. 151. *segs:* sedge.
ten years ago I slew him: introduced by Morris to give psychological continuity.
p. 153. *Dixit insipiens:* 'The fool hath said in his heart, There is no God'; Psalm XIV, 1; the priest uses the Latin of the Vulgate, Psalm XIII.
p. 153–4. "*The Duke went to Treves*": Morris had considerable facility in inventing songs when he wanted to introduce them into his narrative.
p. 154. *the pyx:* vessel in which the sacrament is reserved.
the alb: white surplice.

A Dream. Originally published in the *Magazine* in March, this story is the most overt romantic dream of the group; its setting is unspecifically medieval.
p. 158. *pike:* peak.
p. 166. *Laus Deo:* 'Thanks be to God'; a conventional expression of relief.

Gertha's Lovers. The first three chapters appeared in the July number of the *Magazine*, the last two in August. The story, told in the third person, is a heroic romance with an early Nordic-medieval setting.
p. 173. "*All thoughts, all passions, all delights*": the opening stanza of Coleridge's poem 'Love' (1799), in which the poet wins his 'bright and beauteous Bride', Genevieve, by singing a sad romantic lay of a knight and his lady.
p. 174. *think of the desperate fights:* Morris had throughout his

life a profound feeling for freedom and respect for those who heroically defended it; see also 'Svend and His Brethren'.

p. 176. "*The King rode out in the morning early*": another of the songs in which Morris successfully conveyed the spirit of an earlier age.

p. 177. *Leuchnar:* in Leuchnar Morris tries to create an introspective self-divided character to contrast with the extravert figure of the heroic King Olaf, but he did not carry this through at psychological depth.

p. 193. *the truncheon:* broken end of a spear.

p. 199. *petraria:* rock-firing catapult; military engine for discharging stones.

p. 201. *balistæ:* crossbows.

cats: as explained here, movable pent-houses used to protect besiegers.

p. 202. *the pirates:* robbers, marauders (not necessarily connected with the sea).

p. 204. *by their fruits ye shall know them:* Matthew, VII, 16, 20.

p. 205. *tow:* textile fibre.

pitch: an inflammable substance derived from tar.

p. 206. *not armed in proof:* in 'proved', stronger armour.

pp. 208–9. The murder of Erwelt by Gherard is given an unexpected prominence in the narrative, perhaps to build up tension over the fate of the town.

p. 209. *marplot:* one who spoils a plot.

p. 215. *Domine, in manus tuas:* 'O Lord, into Thy hands', the words committing the soul of a dying man to God.

p. 217. *a mighty Church:* Morris's imagination found in such a building the proper human commemoration of courage and fidelity.

Svend and His Brethren. Appeared in the *Magazine* for August. This story of Cissela's self-sacrifice for the sake of her country is religious in feeling, at least in its early parts; there is also a possibility, as E. P. Thompson has suggested, that the opening account of King Valdemar's country may reflect Morris's feelings about contemporary England.

p. 221. *caitiffs:* wretches.

p. 223. *as I refuse not life:* as I refuse not to sacrifice life.

p. 232. *sough:* sighing.

p. 234. *Here ends what William the Englishman wrote:* i.e. William Morris; no doubt he enjoyed the mystification of this. *and I John who wrote this history saw all this with mine own eyes:* a conventional medieval apology, like that of John Mandeville in the fourteenth-century for his fabulous *Travels*.

The Hollow Land. In the *Magazine* for September and October.

p. 235. "*We find in ancient story wonders many told*": the quotation is from what Carlyle called the "brief artless proem" to the great German poem; see T. Carlyle, 'The Nibelungen Lied', *Essays*, vol. III (1891), 31; the essay was originally published in 1831.

the Hollow Land: through this mysterious country Morris is able to express his romantic longings more directly than in any other of the stories.

p. 237. *my heart was wicked:* the Christian ideal of forgiveness is felt to be better than the pagan belief in vengeance, and acting vengefully is the cause of the later disasters from which Florian is only just saved.

pp. 239–40. *"Queen Mary's crown was gold":* this carol shows Morris's skill in creating a medieval atmosphere, through his effortless identification with the period.

p. 245. *from base to cope:* from bottom to top.

p. 246. *Exsurgat Deus:* 'Let God arise'; Psalm LXVIII (Vulgate LXVII).

p. 247. *will you settle this quarrel by the judgment of God?:* by single combat.

p. 251. *left:* here, and in some other places in this story, the italics seem unnecessary.

mail-coif: a skull-cap of light mail worn under the helmet.
conies: rabbits.

p. 252. *mere glamour:* magic, enchantment.

undern: day-time; perhaps implying 'high undern' or noon.

simulacra: semblances, images without reality.

p. 253. *surcoat:* outer coat worn over armour.

hauberk: defensive armour, originally for head and shoulders; a mail-coat.

p. 254. *fealty:* loyalty.

p. 256. *Fytte:* section.

"Christ keep the Hollow land,": another of Morris's beautiful songs in the medieval manner.

p. 262. *morion:* a visorless helmet.

p. 268. *Propter amnen Babylonis:* replaced in the later editions by 'Super flumina Babylonis', 'By the waters of Babylon', the opening of Psalm CXXXVII (Vulgate CXXXVI); the source of Morris's version is obscure.

p. 270. *valves:* halves of a double door.

Golden Wings. Appeared in the *Magazine* in December; the epigraph is from 'Sir Percival', the medieval metrical romance: 'Listen, friends, to me . . .'.

p. 272. *latoun:* brass.

p. 275. *weight:* heave.

p. 282. *"He was fair and free":* the song serves to let Lionel know what has happened, as well as being attractively medieval in itself.

wight: courageous.

pleasaunce: pleasure grounds or gardens.

p. 284. *clipped:* embraced.

p. 287. *"Will not somebody weep for my darling?":* the inverted commas make this appear to be spoken by Lionel, but it is more of an inward comment.